T0304098

Port Automation and Vehicle Scheduling

Container terminals are constantly being challenged to adjust their throughput capacity to match fluctuating demand. Examining the optimization problems encountered in today's container terminals, *Port Automation and Vehicle Scheduling: Advanced Algorithms for Scheduling Problems of AGVs, Third Edition* provides advanced algorithms for handling the scheduling of Automated Guided Vehicles (AGVs) in ports.

Building on the earlier editions, previously titled *Vehicle Scheduling in Port Automation: Advanced Algorithms for Minimum Cost Flow Problems*, this book has undergone extensive revisions and includes two new chapters. New material addresses the solutions to the modeling of decisions in Chapter 3, while in Chapter 11 the authors address an emerging challenge in automated container terminals with integrated management.

Key Features:

- Classifies the optimization problems of the ports into five scheduling decisions. For each decision, it supplies an overview, formulates each of the decisions as constraint satisfaction and optimization problems, and then covers possible solutions, implementation, and performance.
- Explores in Part One of the book the various optimization problems in modern container terminals, while details in Part Two advanced algorithms for the minimum cost flow (MCF) problem and for the scheduling problem of AGVs in ports.
- Offers complete package that can help readers address the scheduling problems of AGVs in ports.

This is a valuable reference for port authorities and researchers, including specialists and graduate students in operation research. For specialists, it provides novel and efficient algorithms for network flow problems. For students, it supplies the most comprehensive survey of the field along with a rigorous formulation of the problems in port automation.

Port Automation and Vehicle Scheduling

Advanced Algorithms for Scheduling Problems of AGVs

Third Edition

Hassan Rashidi

Edward P. K. Tsang

CRC Press
Taylor & Francis Group
Boca Raton London New York

CRC Press is an imprint of the
Taylor & Francis Group, an **informa** business

Third edition published 2023
by CRC Press
6000 Broken Sound Parkway NW, Suite 300, Boca Raton, FL 33487-2742
and by CRC Press

4 Park Square, Milton Park, Abingdon, Oxon, OX14 4RN

CRC Press is an imprint of Taylor & Francis Group, LLC

© 2023 Hassan Rashidi, Edward P. K. Tsang

First edition published by VDM Verlag Dr. Müller 2010

Second edition published by CRC Press 2015

Library of Congress Cataloging-in-Publication Data
A catalog record has been requested for this book

ISBN: 978-1-032-30617-9 (hbk)
ISBN: 978-1-032-31164-7 (pbk)
ISBN: 978-1-003-30838-6 (ebk)

DOI: 10.1201/9781003308386

Typeset in Adobe Garamond Pro
by KnowledgeWorks Global Ltd.

Contents

List of Figures

List of Tables

List of Abbreviations

Abbreviation	Term / Meaning
AGV	Automated Guided Vehicle
ALV	Automated Lifting Vehicles
BDE	Borland Database Engine
CSOPs	Constraint Satisfaction Optimization Problems
DNSA	Dynamic Network Simplex Algorithm
DNSA+	Dynamic Network Simplex plus Algorithm
DSSAGV	Dynamic Scheduling Software for Automated Guided Vehicles
ERD	Entity Relationship Diagram
GVS	Greedy Vehicle Search
HOTFRAME	Heuristic OpTimization FRAMEwork
IT	Internal Trucks
MCF	Minimum Cost Flow
MCF-AGV	Minimum Cost Flow model for Scheduling problem of AGVs
NSA	Network Simplex Algorithm
NSA+	Network Simplex Plus Algorithm
OSA	Original Simplex Algorithm
PSCDS	Primary Storage Containers Discharge
PSCPI	Primary Storage Containers Pickup
PSCSS	Primary Storage Containers to Secondary Storage
QC	Quay Cranes
RTGC	Rubber Tyred Gantry Cranes
SAM	Simulated Annealing Method
SC	Straddle Carrier
SDSAGV	Static and Dynamic Scheduling of Automated Guided Vehicles
SSCGD	Secondary Storage Containers Grounding
SSCPI	Secondary Storage Containers for Pickup
SSCPS	Secondary Storage Containers to Primary Storage
TG	Terminal Gate
TSS	Taxi Service System
VRP	Vehicle Routing Problem

VRPTW	Vehicle Routing Problem with Time Window
XT	eXternal Truck
YC	Yard Cranes

Preface

This book is a scientific report of a very solid piece of research. It is useful for port authorities and researchers, including specialists and graduate students in operation research. The aim of publishing this book is to publicize our work, which advances state-of-the-art algorithms in network flow problems. For students, it provides the most comprehensive survey of the field. It also provides a rigorous formulation of the problems in port automation. For specialists, it provides novel and efficient algorithms for network flow problems.

This book is divided into two major parts: the optimization problems faced by today's modern container terminals, in general, and the advanced algorithms to tackle the scheduling of automated guided vehicles, in particular. Although we focused on the vehicle scheduling problem in ports, the techniques that we developed are very general.

We created literature over problems in container terminal. The problems are classified into five scheduling decisions. For each of the decisions an overview of the literature is presented. After that, each of the decisions is formulated as Constraint Satisfaction and Optimization Problems (CSOPs). The literature also includes solutions, implementations, and performance. The solutions are classified and summarized.

We then extend the Network Simplex Algorithm (NSA), the fastest algorithm to solve the Minimum Cost Flow problem, and found out four advanced algorithms. In order to verify and validate the algorithms, we chose one of the challenging problems in ports, the scheduling problem of Automated Guided Vehicles (AGVs) in container terminals.

Recent trends toward larger and more complex ports necessitate the use of heterogeneous AGVs. In this book, we worked on this kind of AGVs. If the capacity of the AGVs increases, the problem is an NP-hard problem. This problem has a huge search space and was tackled by the Simulated Annealing Method (SAM). Three approaches for its initial solution and a neighborhood function to the search method were implemented. A hybrid of SAM and NSA also was used. This hybrid was applied to the heterogeneous AGVs scheduling problem in container terminals. Several of the same random problems were generated, solved by SAM with the proposed approaches and the simulation results were compared. The experimental results showed that NSA provides a good initial solution for SAM when the capacity of AGVs is heterogeneous.

In recent years, integrated management of equipment in automated container terminals has become more necessary and has attracted more attention. To do this, we studied this problem with the aim of reducing the service time of berthed ships. The complexity of the proposed problem was investigated and then the problem was formulated as a linear integer-programming model. A solution based on a combination of the greedy algorithm and the genetic algorithm was proposed. This solution was named Sorting Genetic Algorithm (SGA).

This book develops a complete package for the scheduling problems of AGVs in ports. The problem divulges two types: static and dynamic. In static problems, where there is no change in situation, the challenge is to find out more efficient and faster algorithms to tackle the large-scale problems. In dynamic problems, the challenge is to respond to the changes while solving the new problem faster. The algorithms developed in this book are also two types, complete and incomplete. The complete algorithms find out the global solution for the problem, whereas the incomplete algorithms find out a local optimum solution. The experiments were performed to evaluate the performance of the developed algorithms on a large number of generated instances of the problem and the results presented were of high quality.

Hassan Rashidi
Professor in Computer Science,
Department of Statistics, Mathematics and Computer Science,
Allameh Tabataba'i University,
Tehran,
Iran

Edward P. K. Tsang
Professor in Computer Science,
School of Computer Science and Electronic Engineering, University of Essex,
Colchester,
U.K.

Acknowledgments

Many people have helped us in various ways in the preparation of this book. First of all, we are grateful to Dr. John Ford, from the School of Computer Science and Electronic Engineering at the University of Essex, for his suggestion that we should develop the Dynamic Network Simplex Algorithm and his comments on this research. We would like to thank Prof. Hu, the head of Robotics Research Group at the University of Essex, who proposed a few suggestions on our software.

We would like to thank the School of Computer Science and Electronic Engineering for the harmonious environment and the Computing Service at the University of Essex for the excellent computer facilities to perform the computational experiments reported here. We also thank the School for providing a few chances to graduate students as the students saw results of their research presented, and got the academic staff's views.

We also wish to thank Professor Sanja Petrovic, from the School of Computer Science and IT at the University of Nottingham, for giving us some valuable comments. We would like to thank Professor Klaus McDonald-Maier, from the School of Computer Science and Electronic Engineering at the University of Essex, for his feedback.

We thank Demi Stevens, from the Copywriting Company in the UK, for many helpful remarks and for proof-reading of the first edition of this book.

Above all, our greatest thanks go to our families for their patience, encouragement, and support while we were working on this book.

Authors

Hassan Rashidi earned a BSc in computer engineering in 1986 and an MSc in systems engineering and planning in 1989 with the highest honors at the Isfahan University of Technology, Isfahan, Iran. He joined the Department of Computer Science, University of Essex, United Kingdom, as a PhD student in 2002 and earned his PhD in 2006. He was a researcher in British Telecom research center in United Kingdom in 2005. He is currently a professor of computer science at Allameh Tabataba'i University, Tehran, Iran, and a visiting academic at the University of Essex. He is an international expert in the applications of the network simplex algorithm to automated vehicle scheduling and has published many conference and journal papers.

Edward P. K. Tsang has a first degree in business administration (major in finance) and an MSc and a PhD in computer science. He has broad interests in applied artificial intelligence, particularly constraint satisfaction, computational finance, heuristic search, and scheduling. He is currently a professor at the School of Computer Science and Electronic Engineering at the University of Essex, where he leads the computational finance group and the constraint satisfaction and optimization group. He is also the director of the Centre for Computational Finance and Economic Agents, an interdisciplinary center. He founded the Technical Committee for Computational Finance and Economics under the IEEE Computational Intelligence Society.

Chapter 1

Introduction

There are more than two thousand ports over the world. These ports play an important role in global manufacturing and international business, as ships come to load and/or unload their cargos. The cargo ships can be classified into two types. The first type transports huge quantities of commodities like crude oil, coal, grain, etc. The second type usually carries goods that are packed into steel containers of standard sizes. Part One of this book concentrates on the second type, which attracted more attention in both investment and automation during the last decade.

In the past few decades, much research has been devoted to the technology of Automated Guided Vehicle (AGV) systems, both in hardware and software [153]. Nowadays they have become popular over the world for automatic material handling and flexible manufacturing systems. Increasingly, these unmanned vehicles are also becoming the common mode of container transport in the seaport. Part Two of this book is therefore dedicated to the advanced algorithms tackling the scheduling problem of AGVs. Although we focused on the transport scheduling inside the port, the techniques that we developed are very general.

1.1 Objectives

There are two main objectives in this book. The first objective is to study optimization problems in container terminals. The second objective is dedicated to developing advanced algorithms for the scheduling problem of AGVs in ports.

DOI: 10.1201/9781003308386-1

1.1.1 Optimization in Ports

The first objective of publishing this book is a response to the growth of containerization and globalization. Since the 1960s, due to both increasing containerization and increasing world trade, new container terminals are being built and existing ones extended. Today over 60% of the world's deep-sea general cargo is transported in containers, whereas some routes, especially between economically strong and stable countries, are containerized up to 100% [175]. Table 1.1 presents the twenty busiest container ports in the world in terms of TEUs (Twenty-foot Equivalent Unit) handled. We note that the total volume handled in 2020 increased by 11.8% compared to 2016 and the major growth was in Ningbo-Zhoushan (China), increased by 32.96% compared to 2016. Container terminals are continuously challenged to adjust their throughput capacity to match demand. Consequently, many opportunities arise for new approaches in container terminal design, material handling equipment, and operations research applications.

Drewry is an independent maritime research consultancy offering market insights and advisory services to senior stakeholders across global shipping. The result of a study on Container Port Throughput is presented in Table 1.1. The Drewry Container Port Throughput Indices are a series of volume growth/decline indices based on monthly throughput data for a sample of over 235 ports worldwide, representing over 75% of global volumes. The base point for the indices is January 2012 = 100.

The main observations obtained from this table are as follows:

- **Observation 1-1:** The Drewry Port Throughput Index rose to 141.3 points in May 2021, an increase of 3.3 points over April, which was very nearly enough to restore it to March's reading. Annual growth of 15.8% for the month confirms that the worldwide volume recovery is showing no signs of slowing down. Container throughput is expected to increase further through the 3Q21 peak season, after which we anticipate a modest seasonal slowdown in the final quarter. Growth forecasts remain highly sensitive to COVID-19 developments.
- **Observation 1-2:** Greater China ports index recorded a 9.8% year-on-year increase in May with growth mostly concentrated at the largest Chinese gateways. The top six ports (Shanghai, Ningbo, Shenzhen, Qingdao, Tianjin, and Xiamen) accounted for close to 90% of the volume growth, representing more than 65% of the total throughput of the region. We expect China's throughput growth in full-year 2021 to be the highest in 10 years.
- **Observation 1-3:** The May throughput index for Asia (ex-China) increased by only 1.4% month-on-month to 134.6 points, but the annual comparison returned an impressive increase of 15.8% with the top three regional hubs (Singapore, Port Kelang, and Busan) witnessing double-digit annual growth. In percentage terms, Port Kelang recorded the highest growth of 33%, while in absolute terms, Singapore topped the list by handling 3.2 M-TEU, an increase of 410,183 TEU over April 2021.

Table 1.1 Business Container Terminals in the World (in Million TEU): The Top 20 Container Ports

Rank	Port	Volume 2016	Volume 2017	Volume 2018	Volume 2019	Volume 2020	Growth% During 4 Years
1	Shanghai, China	37.13	40.23	42.01	43.30	43.5	17.16
2	Singapore	30.9	33.67	36.6	37.20	36.6	18.45
3	Ningbo-Zhoushan, China	21.6	24.61	26.35	27.49	28.72	32.96
4	Shenzhen, China	23.97	25.21	27.74	25.77	26.55	10.76
5	Guangzhou Harbor, China	18.85	20.37	21.87	23.23	23.19	23.02
6	Busan, South Korea	19.85	20.49	21.66	21.99	21.59	8.77
7	Qingdao, China	18.01	18.3	18.26	21.01	22.00	22.15
8	Hong Kong, SAR, China	19.81	20.76	19.6	18.30	20.07	1.31
9	Tianjin, China	14.49	15.07	16	17.30	18.35	26.64
10	Rotterdam, The Netherlands	12.38	13.73	14.51	14.82	14.35	15.91
11	Jebel Ali, Dubai, United Arab Emirates	15.73	15.37	14.95	14.11	13.5	−14.18
12	Port Klang, Malaysia	13.2	13.73	12.32	13.58	13.24	0.30
13	Xiamen, China	9.61	10.38	10	11.12	11.41	18.73
14	Antwerp, Belgium	10.04	10.45	11.1	11.10	12.04	19.92
15	Kaohsiung, Taiwan, China	10.46	10.27	10.45	10.42	9.62	−8.03

(Continued)

Table 1.1   Business Container Terminals in the World (in Million TEU): The Top 20 Container Ports *(Continued)*

Rank	Port	Volume 2016	Volume 2017	Volume 2018	Volume 2019	Volume 2020	Growth% During 4 Years
16	Dalian, China	9.61	9.7	9.77	10.21	6.54	−31.95
17	Los Angeles, USA	8.86	9.43	9.46	9.30	9.2	3.84
18	Hamburg, Germany	8.91	8.86	8.73	9.30	8.7	−2.36
19	Tanjung Pelepas, Malaysia	8.28	8.38	8.96	9.10	9.85	18.96
20	Laem Chabang, Thailand	7.22	7.78	8.07	8.10	7.55	4.57
	Total	318.91	336.79	348.41	356.75	356.57	11.81

Source: https://www.worldshipping.org/top-50-ports

Table 1.2   The Drewry Container Port Throughput Indices in Two Years, 2020 and 2021

Index	May 2020	April 2021	May 2021*	Monthly Change (%)	Annual Change (%)
Global	122.5	138.0	141.3	2.4%▲	15.4%▲
China	137.7	147.1	151.2	2.8%▲	9.8%▲
Asia exc. China	116.3	133.2	134.6	1.0%▲	15.7%▲
Middle East & South Asia	112.8	132.7	131.8	−0.7%▼	16.9%▲
Europe	109.5	122.2	122.3	0.1%▲	11.7%▲
North America	122.0	157.0	171.0	9.0%▲	40.3%▲
Latin America	109.2	122.8	128.6	4.7%▲	17.8%▲
Africa*	82.9	112.8	107.3	−4.9%▼	29.4%▲
Oceania	120.8	134.9	141.1	4.6%▲	16.8%▲

Source: https://www.hellenicshippingnews.com/drewry-container-port-throughput-rises-during-may/

- **Observation 1-4:** The Middle East and South Asia index declined by 0.7% monthly in May, but increased by 16.9% year-on-year. More than 65% of the annual increase in throughput came from the top three ports of the region (Dubai, Mundra, and JNPT), together accounting for close to half of the total regional throughput. Mundra and JNPT registered extraordinary annual growth of 62% and 65% in May.
- **Observation 1-5:** North American ports performed strongly in May and the region index reached a record high of 171.0 points in the month. Collectively, ports in the region scored growth of more than 40% annually and 9% monthly. The top three ports—Los Angeles, Long Beach, and New York—reported 44.4%, 74.0%, and 48.2% year-on-year gains in May, respectively. Between them these three ports handled an additional 1 M-TEU compared to May 2020. Los Angeles surpassed the 1 M-TEU monthly mark for the first time in its history. However, rapid demand growth has come at a cost as the region has been struggling with severe congestion since the end of 2020, with vessel queues at almost all major gateway ports.
- **Observation 1-6:** The European Port Throughput index remained unchanged at 122.3 points. While the 16.9% year-on-year improvement indicates reasonably strong demand recovery in the market, it was still lower than the pre-pandemic high of 126.7 points recorded in May 2019.
- **Observation 1-7:** The Latin American index also performed strongly, witnessing a 4.7% monthly and 17.8% annual increase in May. The regional index reached 128.6, the highest since the inception of the Drewry Container port throughput Index. The Brazilian market is growing, with volumes at Santos up by 24% year-on-year in May. Panama hub Balboa also performed strongly, recording 32% year-on-year growth as it has been able to win back share from the neighboring Rodman port.
- **Observation 1-8:** Oceania's index returned to the March 2021 level after dipping in April and recorded a 4.6% monthly and 16.8% annual increase. Two major Australian hubs (Melbourne and Sydney) witnessed a record annual increase of 28% and 16%, respectively, in May. The Africa index was down by 4.9% in May 2021 against an increase of 29.4% over the same period in 2020. However, we advise caution when considering the Africa index as it is based on small sample size.

In global trade, the roles of containerization and container terminals are very extensive. Figure 1.1 depicts a picture of container throughput at ports worldwide from 2012 to 2020 with a forecast for 2021 until 2024 (in million TEUs). From this figure, we observe that:

- **Observation 1-9:** There is a growth rate at 18%, 23%, and 38% in 2022, 2023, and 2024, respectively, compared with 2021. These growths surprise the associated level of consumption and the physical capacity of transport

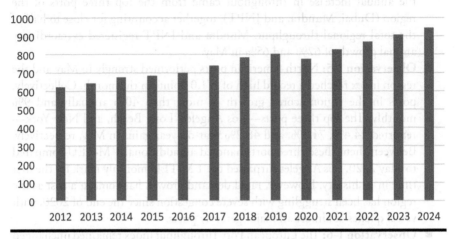

Figure 1.1 Container throughput at ports worldwide from 2012 to 2020 with a forecast for 2021 until 2024 (in million TEUs)

Figure 1.1   Container throughput at ports worldwide from 2012 to 2020 with a forecast for 2021 until 2024 (in million TEUs).

infrastructure to handle such levels of material flows. Obviously, this challenge cannot be readily responded and on several occasions in the past such points were raised and turned out to be invalid.

■ **Observation 1-10:** Figure 1.1 raises questions about the additional growth and diffusion potential of containerization in light of receding economic opportunities (production and consumption) and the expected demographic shifts, namely, the stabilization of the global population within the next decades as well as its ongoing aging. The future expectations about the growth of containerization thus need to be assessed within an economic cycle perspective instead of the rather linear perspectives in which containerization is generally considered.

However, the growth of containerization and transporting goods in containers has created many problems for the container terminals [112, 113]. They face the challenge of coping with the growing number of containers. The rapid unloading/loading and turning around of ships has been become an important problem in the container terminals. To meet these challenges, the container terminals have to innovate and optimize their logistic processes. Moreover, container terminals must use dynamic algorithms along with online optimization methods. Part One of this book classifies problems in container terminals, formulates the problems, and in general, summarizes the solutions.

Islam and Oslen (2013) reviewed a paper on using Operation Research (OR) in ports [84]. The authors provide an overview of the problems that arise in the management of a container terminal and present a comprehensive coverage and review of recent papers in the OR literature. One of the major results of the research is that OR methods and optimization processes must be used in the container terminals in order to enable them to adapt sufficiently rapidly to keep pace with environmental change and to improve their capacities in each sections.

Protectionist attempts on trade remain so far marginal [88]. Therefore, an array of growth factors is at play to explain the substantial growth of containerization and more interestingly the contribution of these factors in time varies. While additional traffic resulting from economic growth is the most salient factor, imbalanced trade flows (empty containers) and the configuration of shipping networks relying on transshipment hubs (double counting of containers) have also contributed to additional containerized flows and container handlings. As economies of scale were applied to maritime shipping, transshipment became more salient.

1.1.2 Scheduling of AGVs and Development of Advanced Algorithms

One of the main equipment in an automated container terminal is AGV. The second objective of this book is to develop efficient and effective algorithms to solve the scheduling problem of AGVs in the port. This problem is formulated as a Minimum Cost Flow (MCF) model.

This MCF model has a rich history and arises in almost all industries, including agriculture, communications, defense, education, energy, health care, manufacturing, medicine, retailing, and transportation [3]. The MCF model is generally broad and can be used as a template to model many network problems, like the classical transportation problem, the transshipment and general routing of motor vehicle transportation, the assignment problem, the maximum flow problem, production planning, scheduling, warehousing, communication networks, and the width range of hydraulic and mechanical applications.

The Network Simplex Algorithm (NSA) is the fastest solution for the MCF model. We apply it to the scheduling problem of AGVs in the port. We then extend the NSA in both static and dynamic aspects. These extensions are the Network Simplex plus Algorithm (NSA+), the Dynamic Network Simplex Algorithm (DNSA), and the Dynamic Network Simplex plus Algorithm (DNSA+). To solve the problems, NSA and NSA+ start from scratch, whereas DNSA and DNSA+ repair solutions when the changes occur.

Although NSA and its extensions are efficient, they can only work on problems with certain limits in size. When the size of the problem goes beyond the limits, incomplete search methods are used. To complement the above algorithms to tackle the MCF model, a greedy method (Greedy Vehicle Search – GVS) is designed and implemented. The GVS is an incomplete algorithm and it is used to find out a local optimum for the MCF model. This incomplete search method can be applied to both static and dynamic problems.

1.2 Structure of Subsequent Chapters

The remainder of this book is organized as follows: Chapters 2 and 3 provide a general framework and literature around the decisions in the container terminals. An outstanding matter from the literature review is that vehicle management is one of the challenging problems in the ports. Hence, the remaining chapters are dedicated to the AGVs scheduling. This book developed several algorithms for the problem in both static and dynamic aspects. In the static aspect there is no change in the situation, whereas in the dynamic one some changes could occur. The structure of each chapter is presented briefly below.

Chapter 2 describes problems and decisions to be made in container terminals. Containers are usually handled in two major compartments. These compartments and the equipment involved in them are described in this chapter. Then, the operations in container terminal are disclosed and the main decisions are classified. The decisions are subdivided into five scheduling decisions:

1. Allocation of berths to arriving vessels and Quay Cranes to docked vessels.
2. Storage space assignment.
3. Rubber tyred gantry crane deployment.
4. The scheduling and routing of vehicles.
5. Making appointment times to eXternal Trucks.

Chapter 3 reviews literature dealing with research done in container terminals and formulates the decisions (defined in Chapter 2). Our approach is to formulate the decisions as Constraint Satisfaction Optimization Problems (CSOPs). We formulate each of the decisions independently, according to the particular assumptions. After the formulation, the latest research of some of the major container terminals in the world is summarized.

Chapter 4 addresses three main issues associated with providing practical software for the decisions, defined and formulated in Chapter 3. First, we discuss the challenges related to the simulation of the operations in container terminals and then argue the design architecture toward implementation issues. After that, we classify the scheduling techniques and reviewed several frameworks. Then, we do a survey on the solution methods to scheduling problems, in general, as well as scheduling and routing vehicles, in particular. Afterwards, we suggest two approaches for simulating container terminals and propose several frameworks for implementation. Finally, several indices are suggested for evaluation and monitoring any solutions for each of the decisions.

Chapter 5 focuses on one of the most important problems in the ports and then formulates it. AGVs are part of the equipment in an automated container terminal. These robotic vehicles travel along a predefined path inside the terminal and transport containers. This chapter defines a scheduling problem for these kinds of vehicles in container terminals. The problem is to deploy several

AGVs in a port to carry many containers from the quayside to yardside or vice versa. This problem is formulated under the MCF model, which is a directed graph. There are two aspects for the problem, static and dynamic. In static problems there is no change in the situation, whereas in dynamic ones, the problem changes over time.

Chapter 6 applied the standard NSA to the scheduling problem of AGVs (defined in Chapter 5) in the static aspect. In this aspect, the number of jobs, the distance between the source and destination of the jobs, and the number of vehicles do not change. In this chapter, we collected experimental results from the efficient implementation of NSA. The NSA can find the global optimal solution for three thousand jobs and ten million arcs in the graph model within two minutes.

Chapter 7 presents a novel version of NSA, which is called the Network Simplex plus Algorithm (NSA+). In order to show that NSA+ is faster than NSA, several random problems are tackled by both algorithms and the CPU time required for solving the problems, which is tested statistically. After that, NSA+ is applied to solve the dynamic AGV scheduling problem and the results of the simulation are studied.

In Chapter 8, we extend the NSA in the dynamic aspect. In this aspect, the DNSA and the DNSA+ are presented. The objectives of the DNSA are to solve the new problem faster, to use some parts of the previous solution for the next problem, and to respond to changes in the problem. In this chapter, the NSA+ and the DNSA+ are applied to the dynamic scheduling problem of AGVs in container terminals and their results are compared.

Chapter 9 presents a greedy algorithm (GVS) to complement the above solutions for the problem defined in Chapter 5. GVS is an incomplete solution for both static and dynamic problems. In Chapters 6-8, the scheduling problem of AGVs, the problem in Chapter 5, is solved by the NSA and its extensions. Although these complete solutions are efficient, they can only work on problems with certain limits in size. When the size of the problem goes beyond these limits or the time available to solve the problem is too short, GVS is used. To evaluate the relative strengths and weaknesses of GVS and NSA+, a few comparisons are performed in this chapter.

Chapter 10 models the scheduling multi-load and heterogeneous AGVs problem in container terminals. This problem has a huge search space and must be tackled by some heuristic methods. In this chapter, we use the Simulated Annealing Method (SAM) for multi-load AGVs with three approaches for its initial solution and a neighborhood function to the search method. We also use a hybrid of SAM and NSA for the heterogeneous AGVs scheduling problem in container terminals. This hybrid is based on how an initial solution for SAM is provided. First, NSA finds the optimal solution for single-load AGVs so that each AGV has one container job. Then, SAM can continue to find a better solution for multi-load or heterogeneous AGVs. Several of the same random problems are generated, solved by SAM with the proposed approaches, and the simulation results are compared. The experimental results show that NSA provides a good initial solution for SAM when the capacity of AGVs is heterogeneous.

Chapter 11 focuses on integrated management of equipment in automated container terminals with the aim of increasing efficiency and effectiveness of the resources. Because the integrated problem in container terminals falls into NP-Hard problems, it was divided into two subproblems: allocating resources to containers and arranging the containers serviced by AGVs. Both subproblems were formulated and expressed using the linear integer-programming model. A combination of greedy algorithm and genetic algorithm was proposed to solve the problem. This solution was named Sorting Genetic Algorithm (SGA). The parameters of the proposed method are investigated using Minitab software and Taguchi method to determine the appropriate values. To show the efficiency and effectiveness of the proposed method, the results are compared with the Particle Swarm Optimization (PSO) algorithm as well as its combinations with the proposed method. Finally, execution time and objective function values of the comparison are reported.

Chapter 12 makes a summary and draws conclusions. In this chapter, we provide a comparative summary of the algorithms for the scheduling problem of AGVs (defined in Chapter 5). Since container terminals have an important role in globalization and international trade, several suggestions for further research are provided at the end of this chapter.

OPTIMIZATION PROBLEMS FACING MODERN CONTAINER TERMINALS

1

1

OPTIMIZATION PROBLEMS FACING MODERN CONTAINER TERMINALS

Chapter 2

Problems in Container Terminals

This chapter describes problems in container terminals. The main functions of these terminals are delivering containers to consignees and receiving containers from shippers, loading containers onto and unloading containers from vessels, and storing containers temporarily to account either for efficiency of the equipment or for the difference in arrival times of the sea and land carriers [215]. Containers are usually handled in two important compartments. We shall first describe what the compartments are, including the equipment involved in them. Then, the operations in the container terminal are disclosed. After that, the main decisions in the container terminal are defined. These decisions are subdivided into five scheduling problems.

2.1 Compartments

The first compartment is **Yardside,** which is sometimes referred to as the **Storage Area** or **Stacking Lane** [182]. In any container terminal, the storage yard serves as a temporary buffer for inbound and outbound containers. Inbound containers are brought into the port by vessels for importing on land, whereas outbound containers are brought in by trucks and for loading onto vessels in order to export. A large-scale yard may comprise of a number of areas called **zones** [215]. In each zone, containers are stacked side by side and on top of one another to form a rectangular shape, which is called a **block** [215]. A typical yardside with three and a half blocks in the front row is shown in Figure 2.1.

There is expensive equipment in the storage area for container handling, referred to as **Rubber Tyred Gantry Cranes (RTGCs)** [131, 182, 215]. In Figure 2.2, an RTGC can be seen across the block from the front-left to the front-right, while it is

DOI: 10.1201/9781003308386-3

Figure 2.1   The container storage area in a port. See [131].

Figure 2.2   An RTGC sits across the width of a block. See [131].

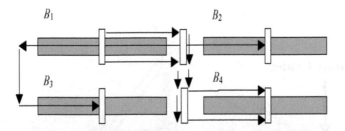

Figure 2.3   Transfer of an RTGC between two blocks. See [215].

unloading a container from a truck. The efficiency of yard operations often depends on the productivity of these RTGCs and their deployment. To balance the workload among blocks, RTGCs are sometimes moved between blocks so that they can be fully utilized.

Figure 2.3 shows a typical setup of blocks where an RTGC can move from one block to the others. For example, an RTGC can move from block B_1 to B_2 along a straight line without any rotation of its wheels because the two blocks are adjacent and align longitudinally.

To move between blocks B_1 and B_3, or between blocks B_1 and B_4, an RTGC has to make a ninety-degree rotation (of its wheels) twice to move from one block to another. Since RTGCs are big in size and slow in motion, their movements demand a large amount of road space in the terminal for a non-trivial time period. Furthermore, any RTGC movement from one block to another takes time, and will result in a loss in productivity of the RTGC.

The second compartment in the container terminal is **Quayside** [131, 182, 217]. Usually, Quayside consists of a limited number of berths, each of which is equipped by several **Quay Cranes (QCs)**. The cranes are used to unload containers from vessels of the wharf and load containers to vessels. The cranes are usually flexible to be moved from a berth to another. Figure 2.4 shows a typical QC, while it is unloading containers from a vessel to put it down on the truck in order to transport it to the storage area.

Berths are essential resources in the container terminal. Therefore, with high traffic of vessels, it would be ideal to have the optimal allocation of berths to vessels to prevent the undue delay of a vessel in the terminal. At any time, only one ship can be docked at a berth.

2.2 Operations

The main operations in the port start with a ship's arrival. After a ship is berthed, it invokes a number of delivery requests for discharging. There are some vehicles in a terminal, which are usually **Automated Guided Vehicles (AGVs)** [182, 217] (see Figure 2.5, right)**, or **Internal Trucks (ITs)** [215] (see Figure 2.4, right bottom

Figure 2.4 A typical Quay Crane. See [131].

Figure 2.5 A Straddle carrier (left) and an automated guided vehicle (right) while they are carrying a container. (SCs can load/unload and transport containers.)

corner). Idle vehicles are dispatched according to the unloading request list to deliver containers from the berth to designated places in the storage yard. The QCs first unload containers from the containership and put them onto the vehicles. After that, the vehicles carry the containers to designated storage area blocks and **RTGCs** unload the containers from the vehicles. Then the containers are put onto the yard stacks. In some terminals there are a number of **Straddle Carriers (SCs)** [182] (see Figure 2.5, left), capable of loading, transporting, and unloading containers.

After the phase of unloading the ship, the loading phase will begin. On the land side, an **eXternal Truck (XT)** [215] brings in outbound containers before the loading process of the relevant vessel, and picks up inbound containers from the storage area or from the discharged vessel by QCs. The ship issues a number of loading requests. Vehicles are dispatched corresponding to the loading request list to deliver containers to the QCs. The operation is the reverse of the unloading process.

There are two major types of waiting lists in the port. The first one relates to vehicles while the second one is dedicated to the cranes. A vehicle has to wait if it has arrived at the crane's location while the crane is busy with other vehicles. A QC has to wait for a vehicle if it is ready to put a container onto a vehicle or to pick up a container from a vehicle that has not arrived on the quayside. Usually, the cranes waiting time is more critical than the vehicle waiting time for efficiency of the terminal operations. Any delay in a QC operation will cause the same amount of time delay in all subsequent operations assigned to the same QC [217]. This delay may even affect the ship's stay at the berth. Usually every ship has a time window and any delay can lead to growing costs for the terminal. One of the most important decisions in this system is the allocation of QCs so that they satisfy the ship timing window or minimize the waiting times of the ships in the port.

2.3 Decisions to Be Made

In this section, we classify the important problems to be made in the container terminals. There are many interrelated decisions during the planning period in a port every day or week, for example. Additionally, these scheduling-resource allocation decisions involve time, space, and routes in the terminal, which increase the complexity of the system. Henry et al. (2005) are considering the interaction between QCs, AGVs, and Automated Yard Cranes (AYCs) in an integrated model [70]. They made a mixed-integer programming model and are now developing a multilayer genetic algorithm. Obviously, it is not possible to provide answers to all operations in the previous section by solving a single problem within the scope of this book. The problem is therefore divided into some subproblems.

The first classification of decisions in the container terminal has been suggested by Vis [83]. The researcher provided a webpage for the research done in container terminals. The webpage proposed four decisions (2005) for the logistics processes, i.e., arrival of the ship, unloading/loading of the ship, stacking of containers, and transportation of containers from ship to stacking area and vice versa. In the classification, each of the decisions can be studied at strategic, tactical, and operation levels, mostly based on mathematical programming approach. At the strategic level plan over future horizons, it is decided which layout, material handling equipment, and ways of operations are used. These decisions lead to the definition of a set of constraints for both the tactical and operational levels.

Another classification and literature review over operations in the container terminal has been provided by Steenken et al. (2004). They divided the decisions into ship planning processes, stowage and stacking logistics, and transportation problems [175]. In their classification, the first one consists of berth allocation, stowage planning, and crane splitting, whereas the decisions related to yard cranes and storage area allocation are in the second category.

The third category of the decisions refers to transportation problems from the quay side to the storage area or vice versa, the equipment to carry the container from their source to their destination, and traffic inside the terminal. Additionally, Murty et al. (2005) classified the daily operations of a container terminal into nine decisions [131], namely, allocation of berths to arriving vessels, allocation of QCs to docked vessels, appointment times to XTs, routing of trucks, dispatch policy at the terminal gate and the dock, storage space assignment, RTGC deployment, IT allocation to QC, and IT hiring plans. The problems were formulated as mixed-integer programming model.

Zaghdoud et al. (2016) disclosed the shape of loading and unloading containers from the ship could lead to some problems such as storage, transportation, and routing [211]. They examined the issue of allocating containers to AGVs at container terminals. They divided the problem into three subproblems: routing, container allocation to the AGVs, and scheduling problems. They presented a combined method of genetic algorithm and digest algorithm. However, some examples and numerical tests have been proposed to prove the effectiveness of the proposed method.

Table 2.1 compares the major classifications done over the decisions, along with the classification proposed in this book. In the table, the attribute/view, approach in formulation, strengths, and weaknesses of each classification are provided. With respect to scheduling, resource allocation, and transportation views, we classify important problems in the container terminals into five decisions. Our classification, as it becomes more clear in the next sections, has several main advantages over the previous ones. In the classification: (a) the whole system with more general and practical assumptions is considered; (b) full formulations are provided so that each problem can be studied independently; and (c) the decisions are usually executed in different time periods.

2.3.1 Allocation of Berths to Arriving Vessels and QCs to Docked Vessels

The first decision is to maximize utilization of the berths and QCs. Generally, a port has a limited number of berths, therefore the efficient allocation of berths to

Table 2.1 The Strengths and Weaknesses of the Major Classifications over the Decisions in Container Terminals

Classification Done by [#Problems / Decisions]	Attributes/Views	Approaches in Formulation	Strengths	Weaknesses
Vis [#4]	• Macro and micro levels • Logistics processes at strategic, tactical, and operation levels	• Mathematical programming	• Provides some lists of research done • Some qualitative and quantitative methods applied	• Not integrated approach • Partial formulation • Partial practical assumptions
Steenken et al. [#3]	• Macro and micro levels • Resource allocation and transportation	• Mathematical programming	• Current methods can solve the problems	• Partial practical assumptions • Partial formulation provided
Murty et al. [#9]	• Micro level (daily operations)	• Mathematical programming	• Current methods can solve the problems	• Partial practical assumptions • Partial formulation provided
Zaghdoud et al. [#4]	• Storage problem, transportation problem, routing problem, assigning problem	• Mathematical programming	• Current methods can solve the problems	• Not integrated approach • Partial formulation • Partial practical assumptions
This Book [#5]	• Macro and micro levels • Resource allocation, transportation, and scheduling	• Constraints satisfaction and optimization problem	• Integrated approach (considers the whole system) • Ability to solve the problems independently • Practical assumptions • Full formulation provided	• Hard to solve the problems

arriving vessels and QCs is essential to guarantee a ship's timing window, to minimize the ship's waiting time, and to maximize the port's turnaround. This decision affects the turnaround time of vessels, and the throughput rate of the terminal.

2.3.2 Storage Space Assignment

Two kinds of storage areas (**Primary** and **Secondary**) are proposed for medium and short-term storage of containers [182]. Assigning these storage spaces to arriving inbound and outbound containers is another scheduling-resource allocation problem. In this decision, it is desirable to minimize reshuffling or reorganize volume and minimize the costs of containers.

2.3.3 Rubber Tyred Gantry Crane Deployment

To maneuver the containers in the blocks, RTGCs are used (Figure 2.3). One major decision in port automation is to determine how many RTGCs work in each block, and when a RTGC needs to move from one block to another. This decision affects the port time of vessels and the waiting times of QCs and ITs or AGVs.

2.3.4 Scheduling and Routing of Vehicles

In each port, there are several vehicles to carry containers between the yardside and quayside or vice versa. The scheduling and routing of these vehicles is another important decision. The objectives of this decision are to minimize the transportation costs of the containers and the waiting times of the QCs and RTGCs.

2.3.5 Appointment Times to XTs

The fifth decision in our classification is to make appointment times for the XTs. In reality, all consignees book the time to pick up their inbound containers, by calling beforehand and taking appointments. The customers also book a time to bring in their outbound containers. This decision helps to minimize the waiting times of XTs, and congestion at the gate of the terminal.

Chapter 3

Formulations of the Problems

In the previous chapter, we defined five scheduling decisions in container terminals. To recapitulate, these decisions are:

- Allocation of berths to arriving vessels and Quay Cranes (QCs) to docked vessels.
- Storage space assignment.
- Rubber Tyred Gantry Crane (RTGC) deployment.
- Scheduling and routing of vehicles.
- Appointment times to eXternal Trucks (XTs).

The objectives of this chapter are to survey research done in these decisions and then formulate them as Constraint Satisfaction Optimization Problems (CSOPs). The five decisions are formulated separately so that they can be studied independently. After the formulation, the latest research of some of the main container terminals in the world is summarized.

According to Mark Wallace (1997), the reasons for choosing to represent and formulate the problems as CSOPs rather than mathematical programming are twofold. First, the representation as CSOP is often much closer to the original problem: the variables of the CSOP directly correspond to problem entities, and the constraints can be expressed without having to be translated into linear inequalities. This makes the formulation simpler, the solution easier to understand, and the choice of good heuristics to guide the solution strategy more straightforward. Second, although CSOP algorithms are essentially very simple, they can sometimes find a solution more quickly than if integer programming methods are used.

DOI: 10.1201/9781003308386-4

3.1 Allocation of Berths to Arriving Vessels and Quay Cranes to Docked Vessels

In container terminals, the berth is the most important resource that affects the capacity of the terminal directly. The main reason is that the construction cost of the berths is relatively very high compared with the investment on facilities in the port [141]. Thus, an effective way to increase the capacity of a terminal is to improve the efficiency of its berth. The problem here is to allocate berths to arriving vessels and to determine which cranes in the berths process the docked vessels. The operator of the terminal usually creates and maintains a berth schedule which shows the berthing position and time of each arriving vessel.

Böse et al. (2000) focused on the crane scheduling and maximizing the productivity of the cranes to reduce the time in port for the vessels [14]. The authors used an evolutionary algorithm and investigated different dispatching strategies for Straddle Carriers (SCs) to QCs in a dynamic real port. In the port, several problems for two vessels, two QCs for each vessel, and four SCs were tackled by the evolutionary algorithm, using four thousand iterations with a population size of one hundred. The experimental results showed that the productivity of the QCs and the vessel's turnaround time could be improved.

Rebollo et al. (2000) presented an architecture of the multi-agent system to minimize the ship's docking time [161]. The authors focused on the management of cranes by a "transtainer agent." This research was framed into a project to the integral management of an actual container terminal. The independence of subsystems obtained for the multi-agent approach was empathized. A prototype is still being developed.

The berth-scheduling and crane-scheduling problems have been considered to be independent of each other. Moon (2001) studied the first one over a planning horizon by a Mixed Integer Linear Program (MILP) model [126]. In the model, each vessel requires a specific amount of space on the berth during a predetermined length of time for unloading and loading containers. The author considered a penalty for the delay of the ships and tackled the model using LINDO software. The computational time of LINDO increased rapidly when the number of ships grew over seven and the length of the planning horizon exceeded seventy-two hours. Some properties of the optimal solution were investigated. Based on these properties, a heuristic algorithm for the berth scheduling was suggested. Then the performance of the heuristic algorithm was compared with the optimization technique of LINDO. The results showed that the heuristic works well on many randomly generated problems, but performs badly in several cases where the penalty for the delay is substantial.

The most important objective in berth scheduling is to reduce the amount of time required to unload and load a ship. Thurston and Hu (2002) presented distributed agent architecture to achieve the objective and increase the container throughput of a virtual port [182]. The researchers focused on QCs as being paramount to the total performance of the port. The paper assumed that the inbound containers are unloaded first and the outbound containers are loaded after unloading has been completed. However, in reality containers are loaded and unloaded simultaneously. To evaluate the solution, a simulation with randomly generated data for problems of twelve QCs was used.

The static and dynamic berth allocation problems have been studied by Hansen and Oguz (2003). In the static problem they assumed that ships arrive at the port before the berths become available. In the dynamic problem, there was no constraint on arrival time of the ships. In both problems the number of cranes has not been considered, i.e., they assumed only one crane in each berth (not a realistic assumption in modern ports). Their main focus was to make a compact model for the dynamic problem, with consideration for constraints on size and due dates of ships, and a planning horizon. In their research, the dynamic problems with up to ten berths and fifty ships have been tackled by CPLEX software [62].

Blażewics et al. (2005) modeled the berth scheduling as a moldable task scheduling problem by considering the relation between the number of QCs and the berthing time [11]. Moldable tasks form one type of parallel tasks that can be processed simultaneously on a number of parallel processors for which the processing times are a function of the number of processors assigned. The aim of the model was to minimize the idle time on processors so as to increase the utilization of the berths.

Nannan et al. (2008) present a multi-agent-based system for resource allocation and operation scheduling problems in container terminals to optimize the productivity of container terminals. In this research, a prototype of this system is built with consideration of the characteristics of container terminal production. Agent cooperation strategies, agent communication mechanism, and its implementation are partially shown with descriptions in their work [132].

Aykagan (2008) focuses on berth scheduling at dedicated terminals and its impact on vessel voyage planning [10]. At a dedicated terminal, vessels of only one carrier are serviced, and the carrier has direct control of the schedules of all vessels visiting. In this research, a mathematical model based on multi-commodity network flow is developed and solved on a series of realistic test problems. The author also shows how transshipments, terminal time windows, and service levels can be incorporated in the model.

Homayouni et al. (2011) formulated an integrated scheduling of QCs and Automated Guided Vehicles (AGVs) as a mixed-integer linear programming model [73]. In the model, the authors minimized the makespan of all the loading and unloading containers for a set of cranes in the scheduling problem. Based on the simulated annealing (SA) algorithm, a scheduling method is proposed to solve the problem. The effects of three cooling processes and two sets of control parameters on the best solution of the SA were investigated in the paper. Comparison of the respective results of the mathematical model and the SA algorithm evidently showed acceptable performance of the proposed SA algorithm in finding good solutions for the scheduling problem.

Guo et al. (2014) used the idea of Generalized Extremal Optimization (GEO) to solve the QC scheduling problem with respect to various interference constraints [58]. The resulting GEO is termed the modified GEO. A randomized searching method for neighboring task-to-QC assignments to an incumbent task-to-QC assignment was developed in executing the modified GEO. In addition, a unidirectional search decoding scheme was employed to transform a task-to-QC assignment to an active QC schedule. The effectiveness of the developed GEO was tested on a suite of benchmark problems introduced by Kim and Park (see [141]). Compared with other well-known existing approaches, the experiment results showed the modified GEO is capable of obtaining the optimal or near-optimal solution in a reasonable time, especially for large-sized problems.

Ma et al. (2014) propose a fast approach for the integrated berth allocation and QC assignment problem [114], based on genetic algorithm. The research found that holistically solving this integrated problem might not be efficient due to its complexity. Therefore, the proposed approach decomposes the integrated problem into a master problem and a sub-problem, representing the QC assignment and the corresponding vessel schedule in each berth. This decomposing approach is designed to enhance the local searching ability while maintaining the global searching ability of the genetic algorithm. To test the solution quality, the existing algorithms found in the literature, including single genetic algorithm and two-level genetic algorithm, have been used in the comparisons. Furthermore, a set of numerical experiments has been carried out to compare the proposed algorithms with the optimal solution obtained by CPLEX software. The results demonstrated the proposed algorithm outperforms the existing algorithms and can obtain near-optimal solution.

Türkogulları et al. (2016) studied optimal berth allocation, time-variant QC assignment and scheduling with crane setups in container terminals [188]. First, they formulated a mixed-integer linear program whose exact solution gives optimal berthing positions and berthing times of the vessels, along with the crane schedules when they process the vessels at the quay. Then, they proposed an efficient cutting plane algorithm based on a decomposition scheme. This approach deals with berthing positions of the vessels and their assigned number of cranes in each time period in a master problem, and seeks the corresponding optimal crane schedule by solving a sub-problem. This research proved that the crane scheduling sub-problem is NP-complete under general cost settings, but can be solved in polynomial time for certain special cases. The computational study showed that the formulation and proposed solution method yield optimal solutions for realistic-sized instances.

He (2016) studied the problem of berth allocation and QC assignment in a container terminal for the trade-off between time-saving and energy-saving [66]. This problem was formulated as a Mixed Integer Programming (MIP) model, in order to minimize the total departure delay of all vessels and the total handling energy consumption of all vessels by QCs. Furthermore, an integrated simulation and optimization method was developed, where the simulation was designed for evaluation and optimization algorithm was designed for searching solution space. This research compared two scheduling strategies: (i) the proposed method considering the energy consumption objective (namely "Energy-saving strategy") and (ii) the proposed method not considering the energy consumption objective (namely "Time-saving strategy"). Two scheduling strategies are measured in terms of departure delay costs, energy consumption costs, and total berthing costs. The experimental results illustrate "Energy-saving strategy" is more suitable for the tendency of green transportation and green port.

Huang and Li (2018) proposed a bounded two-level dynamic programming (DP) algorithm which keeps the simplicity of the bay-based approach but overcomes its shortcomings [76]. The 2-level DP algorithm first finds the optimal bay-based QC scheduling in the first level DP. Then it refines the results by allowing workload sharing between neighboring QCs in the second level DP. This research also proposed a method to estimate the lower bound to QC scheduling given the lists of unloading and loading containers and the number of QCs assigned to the vessel. This lower bound was used both to reduce the computational time of the 2-level DP algorithm and to evaluate the crane scheduling method. The experiments with real vessel unloading and loading lists for eighty vessels show that the vessel makespan is close to the lower bound. The computational times for the eighty vessels with up to 6600 container moves by cranes in loading and unloading a vessel are all under two minutes.

Malekahmadi et al. (2020) studied integrated continuous berth allocation and QC assignment and scheduling problems with time-dependent physical constraints in container terminals [119]. They proposed a model to consider the safe distance between QCs based on the fact that they cannot cross each other on the rails. Given the NP-Hard complexity of the proposed model, a Particle Swarm Optimization (PSO)-based meta-heuristic called the Random Topology Particle Swarm Optimization Algorithm (RTPSO) was developed for solving its large-size instances. To evaluate the performance of the developed RTPSO, its results were compared with the results of the exact solution and the basic PSO. The results illustrated the better performance of the proposed random topology Particle Swarm Optimization (PSO) algorithm in terms of accuracy and computational time.

Tan et al. (2021) investigated the Automated Quay Crane Scheduling Problem (AQCSP) for the automated container terminal [180]. The operation process of AQCSP was decomposed and formulated as a mixed integrated programming model. To evaluate the model, four types of instances were generated for the numerical experiments, namely, ten containers with two stacks, twenty containers with four stacks, thirty containers with six stacks, and forty containers with eight stacks. The initial numbers of containers for each stack are generated by the uniform distribution U [0, 2]. In the numerical experiments, the relation between operational efficiency and energy consumption has been quantitative analyzed by case study. Moreover, the sensitivity analysis of the ratios for all tasks in a vessel bay and the tasks in each stack were also presented. This study provided a theoretical reference for the study on the trade-off operation efficiency and energy consumption on the operational level.

Table 3.1 summarizes the major research done over this decision, the allocation of berth to arriving vessels, and QCs to dock vessels. The table shows the researchers (year), modeling approach (algorithm), experimental data size, and main results. As we can see in the table, most researches use the mathematical modeling approach for their formulations. In the experiments, the largest problem solved was a problem instance with forty ships.

However, the duration of berthing of each vessel depends on the number of cranes assigned to the corresponding vessel. When the number of cranes assigned to a vessel increases, berthing duration of the vessel can be reduced. Because of this important reason, the berth-scheduling and crane-scheduling problems must be considered simultaneously. Park and Kim (2003) made an MILP model to consider both problems [141]. They suggested two phases for solving the mathematical model: "berth scheduling phase" and "crane assignment phase" (see Figure 3.1). The first phase determined the berthing position and time of each vessel as well as the number of cranes assigned to every vessel at each time period. Assuming a convex cost function, the authors described a heuristic procedure for obtaining feasible and near-optimal solutions to the first phase. Though relevant, the heuristic was limited to the choice of the cost function.

In the second phase, a detailed schedule for each QC was constructed based on the solution found from the first phase. The dynamic programming technique was used to solve the second phase problem. The results showed that the first phase needed less computation time compared with the complete enumeration. The research was experimented in Pusan port in a static environment, where there were no changes in the port. On average, the computation time of the dynamic programming algorithm for the second phase was five seconds, which was within the range for practical use.

3.1.1 Assumptions

In container terminals, the duration of berthing of each vessel depends on the number of cranes assigned to the corresponding vessel. When the number of cranes assigned to a vessel increases, berthing duration of the vessel can be reduced. Because of this important reason, the berth-scheduling and crane-scheduling problems must be considered simultaneously. The following assumptions are considered in formulating this decision:

> **Assumption 3-1-1:** A fixed time window is considered for the QCs discharging/loading a container [14, 73, 126, 141, 182]. With this assumption, the duration of berthing or of processing a vessel is inversely proportional to the number of cranes assigned to it.

Table 3.1 The Major Research Done Around Allocation of Berths to Arriving Vessels and Quay Cranes to Docked Vessels

Researchers (Year)	Modeling (Algorithms)	Experimental Data Size	Main Results
Bose et al. (2000)	Integer Linear Programming (Evolutionary Algorithm)	#Ships: 4, #QCs: 2 for each ship, #SC: 6, #Berths: 1	Improves performance in a real port
Rebollo et al. (2000)	Multi-Agent System (Based on a Manager: called Transtainer Agent)	Not mentioned	Presents a Contract-Net Protocol, an applicable method to an actual port
Moon (2001)	Mixed Integer Linear Programming (LINDO and a Heuristic Approach)	#Ships: 7, #Berths: 1, #QCs: 1	Obtaining near optimal solution
Thurston and Hu (2002)	Multi-Agent System (Plan Merging Paradigm)	#Ships: 1, #QCs: 1, #AGVs: 12, #Berths: 1	Presents a distributed multi agent architecture
Park & Kim (2003)	• 1st phase: Integer Programming Model (sub-gradient technique) • 2nd phase: integer Programming Model (Dynamic Programming)	#Ships: 40, #QCs: 11, #Berths: 1 (Width: 1200 m)	• 1st phase: Less computation time compared with complete enumeration • 2nd phase was 5 seconds, it is within the range for practical use
Blazewics et al. (2005)	A moldable task scheduling to minimize the idle time on processors (Processor as Cranes, Task as Ships)	Randomly Generated Problems	Improvement in the idle time of processors
Hansen and Ogus (2005)	Integer Linear Programming (CPLEX)	#Berths: 10, #Ships: 50, #QC for each berth: 1	The compact model of dynamic berth allocation problem is not efficient due to the big M's in the constraints
Aykagan (2008)	Multi-Commodity Network Flow (Tabu Search Algorithm)	#Ships: 1, #QCs: 1, #Berths: 1, #Routes: 3 to 8	Proposed solution can be used in commercial MILP solvers

(Continued)

Table 3.1 The Major Research Done Around Allocation of Berths to Arriving Vessels and Quay Cranes to Docked Vessels (Continued)

Researchers (Year)	Modeling (Algorithms)	Experimental Data Size	Main Results
Homayouni et al. (2011)	Mixed Integer Linear Programming (A scheduling method based on the Simulated Annealing algorithm)	#Ships: 1, #QC: 6, #AGVs: 12, #Berths: 1	The Simulated Annealing can find the near optimal solution for medium-size cases (30 to 60 tasks)
Guo et al. (2014)	Integer Programming Model (Generalized Extremal Optimization and Searching Methods)	Benchmark problems introduced by Kim and Park	Obtaining the optimal or near-optimal solution in a reasonable time
Ma et al. (2014)	Mixed Integer Linear Programming (Genetic Algorithm)	#Ships: 11, #QC: 7, #Berths: 4	The proposed algorithm outperforms the existing algorithm and can obtain near-optimal solution
Türkogulları et al. (2016)	Mixed-Integer Linear Program (Cutting Plane Algorithm based on a Decomposition Scheme)	#Ships: 3,6,9,12,15,18,21, #QC: 12, #Berth: 24, Planning Horizon: 200 hour	The formulation and proposed solution method yielded optimal solutions for realistic-sized instances
He (2016)	Mixed Integer Programming Model (Genetic Algorithm and Simulated Annealing)	#Vessels: 1–4, #QC: 12, Time segment: 0.5, 1, 2, 4, 6 Hour	Considered total departure delay and total energy consumption of all vessels
Huand and Li (2018)	Dynamic Programming (A bounded two-level algorithm)	#Vessels: 80, #QC: 4–6, #Jobs: 6600 container	Provides a 2-level Dynamic Programming algorithm
Malekahmadi et al. (2020)	Integer Programming Model (Random Topology Particle Swarm Optimization Algorithm)	#Vessels: 20, 30, or 40, #QC: 20–40, Arrival times of the vessel: Uniform interval (1, 20)	Random Topology Particle Swarm Optimization Algorithm provided a better performance than the basic PSO
Tan et al. (2021)	Mixed Integrated Programming Model (ILOG CPLEX 12.9)	#Crane: 1, #Jobs: 10 containers with 2 stacks, 20 containers with 4 stacks, 30 containers with 6 stacks, 40 containers with 8 stacks	Absolute balance of loading and unloading tasks is not the optimal strategy for generating the vessel arrival and departure configuration

Phase I: Berth Scheduling
Determine berthing time, position of each vessel, and the number of cranes assigned to the vessels

↓

Phase II: Crane Assignment
Schedule the assignment of individual crane

Figure 3.1   Park and Kim's two phases scheduling of berths and cranes. See [143].

Assumption 3-1-2: Each vessel determines the maximum and minimum number of cranes that can be assigned to it [141]. The number of cranes can change from period to period.

Assumption 3-1-3: Each vessel has a predetermined berthing time period. A cost penalty applies if the vessel berths early or departs late.

Assumption 3-1-4: Each vessel has a preferred location of berthing [141]. This preferred location can be the location nearest to the storage area where inbound/outbound containers for the corresponding vessel are stacked. Another preference of a berthing location may also come from the depth of water or the strength and direction of currents.

Assumption 3-1-5: The container terminal has several berths for docking vessels and containers [62]. At each time period and every berth, only one container can be loaded/unloaded.

The output of one possible solution to this decision is illustrated in Figure 3.2. In the figure there are five vessels, and each rectangle represents the berthing schedule of a vessel. The berthing locations are shown on the horizontal sides, and the positions of the vertical sides correspond to the operation times of the vessels. The number on the left side of every ship shows how many cranes process the vessel at a specific time, while the crane number has been shown in the middle of the grid.

The following parameters are given at the beginning of the planning horizon:

T: The total number of time periods in the planning horizon. The time period is equal to the time window of cranes (see Assumption 3-3-1).

ETA_k: The expected time of arrival of vessel k.

a_k: The processing time of vessel k (if only one crane is assigned to vessel k).

b_k: The length of vessel k.

d_k: The due time for the departure of vessel k.

s_k: The minimum cost berthing location of the reference point of vessel k.

c_{1k}: The penalty cost of vessel k if the vessel could not dock at its preferred berth.

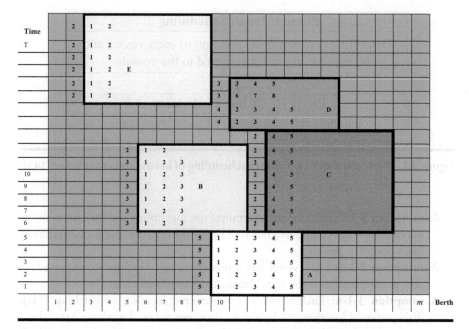

Figure 3.2 An output of the berth and crane scheduling problem.

c_{2k}: The penalty cost of vessel k per unit time of earlier arrival before ETA_k.
c_{3k}: The penalty cost of vessel k per unit time of late arrival after ETA_k.
c_{4k}: The penalty cost of vessel k per unit time delay behind the due time.
L_k: The minimum number of cranes that can be assigned to vessel k.
U_k: The maximum number of cranes that can be assigned to vessel k.
l: The number of vessels in the planning horizon.
C: The total number of cranes in the terminal ($C > Max (U_k), k = 1,2,\dots,l$).
m: The number of berths in the port.

3.1.2 Decision Variables and Domains

At_k : The arrival time of vessel k to the berth.
   Domain $(At_k) = \{1,2,3,4,\dots,T\}$
Dt_k : The departing time of vessel k.
   Domain $(Dt_k) = \{1,2,3,4,\dots,T\}$
X_{itk} : 1 if the berth i at time t is allocated to vessel k, otherwise 0.
   Domain $(X_{itk}) = \{0,1\}$
Q_{itc}: Status of crane c; it is 1 if the crane c is in the i-th berth at the time t, otherwise 0.
   Domain $(Q_{itc}) = \{0,1\}$

3.1.3 Constraints

Constraint 3-1-1: The grid squares are covered by only one vessel. In fact, each berth at time t can be assigned to only one vessel.

$$\sum_{k=1}^{l} X_{itk} \leq 1 \ for \ i = 1,2,3,\ldots,m; t = 1,2,3,..,T$$

Constraint 3-1-2: Each berth is allocated for the vessel only between its arrival and departure.

$$At_k \leq t \leq Dt_k \Leftrightarrow \sum_{i=1}^{m} X_{itk} = 1 \ for \ k = 1,2,..,l$$

$$(At_k > t) \ OR \ (t > Dt_k) \Leftrightarrow X_{itk} = 0$$

$$for \ t = 1,2,..,T; for \ i = 1,2,..,m; for \ k = 1,2,..,l$$

Constraint 3-1-3: Only one crane operates on the vessel in a certain time and berth.

$$\sum_{i=1}^{m} Q_{itc} = 1 \ for \ i = 1,2,..,m; for \ t = 1,2,..,T$$

Constraint 3-1-4: The number of QCs assigned to each vessel is limited and the vessels have to be fully processed by the QCs.

$$L_k \leq \sum_{i=1}^{m} \sum_{c=1}^{C} Q_{itc} \times X_{itk} \leq U_k, \ for \ k = 1,2,..,l; At_k \leq t \leq Dt_k$$

$$\sum_{i=1}^{m} \sum_{t=At_k}^{Dt_k} \sum_{c=1}^{C} Q_{itc} \times X_{itk} = a_k, \ for \ k = 1,2,..,l$$

Constraint 3-1-5: The crane c processes vessel k at berth i in time t, if the berth and the crane are allocated to the vessel.

$$Q_{itc} \Leftrightarrow X_{itk}, \ for \ c = 1,2,..,C; for \ i = 1,2,..,m; for \ k = 1,2,..,l; for \ t = 1,2,..,T$$

Constraint 3-1-6: Two time periods are required to set up any crane from one berth to another.

$$(Q_{itc} \ AND \ Q_{i't'c}) = 0, \ for \ c = 1,2,..,C; \ for \ k = 1,2,\ldots,l$$

$$for \ t,t' = 1,2,..,T, (|t - t'| = 1, t \neq t'); for \ i = 1,2,..,m$$

Constraint 3-1-7: If the length of a vessel is greater than the distance between two berths, other vessels are not allowed to dock at the adjacent berth.

$$\left(\left|i - i'\right| < b_k \; OR \; \left|i - i'\right| < b_{k'} \right) = True \Rightarrow \left(X_{itk} \; AND \; X_{i'tk'} \right) = 0,$$

$$for \; k, k' = 1, 2, \ldots, l; k \neq k'; for \; i, i' = 1, 2, \ldots, m; i \neq i'; for \; t = 1, 2, \ldots, T$$

In the constraint, $\left|i\text{-}i'\right|$ denotes the distance between the berths i and i'.

3.1.4 Objective Function

The objective function of this decision is to minimize the total penalty costs. In order to present the objective function, we introduce the following auxiliary variable:

Z_k: The sum of the absolute distance between the preferred location of vessel k and the berths allocated to the vessel. This variable is determined by the following function:

$$Z_k = f(X_{itk}, s_k) = \sum_{t=1}^{T} \sum_{i=1}^{m} \left\{ \left|i - s_k\right| : X_{itk} = 1 \right\}$$

Now the objective function is written as follows:

$$MinCostVessels = \sum_{k=1}^{l} \left\{ c_{1k}.Z_k + c_{2k}(ETA_k - At_k)^+ \right.$$
$$\left. + c_{3k}(At_k - ETA_k)^+ + c_{4k}(Dt_k - d_k)^+ \right\}$$

The first factor is the penalty cost incurred by the distance between the berthing locations of a vessel and the preferred location. The second and third factors are the penalty costs by the actual berthing earlier or later than the expected time of arrival. The last factor is the penalty cost caused by the delay of the departure after the promised due time. The three last terms have impacts on the objective function provided that they are only positive.

3.2 Storage Space Assignment

There is evidence that the yard plays an important role in global productivity of the terminal [56]. In fact, the efficiency and quality of management in the container yard operations affect all terminal decisions related to the allocation of available handling equipment, and the scheduling of all activities. The problem here is to determine a place in the storage area for inbound and outbound containers.

Frankel (1987) suggested three main types of storage systems: short-term, long-term, and specialized. Henesey et al. (2003) described these kinds of storage [69]. The short-term storage system is for containers that may be transshipped onto another containership. Long-term storage is for containers awaiting customs release or inspection. Specialized storage is reserved for the refrigerated (they need to be supplied with electricity) or hazardous materials. Holguin and Jara (1999) took into account the intrinsic and logistic values of containers and divided them into different priority classes [71]. For each class the optimal amount of space and the optimal price were determined under welfare and profit maximizing rules (surveyed in [29]).

Gambardella et al. (1998) developed a decision support system for the management of the La Spezia container terminal [47]. Based on the list of loading and unloading container jobs, the authors considered the allocation of QCs to loading and unloading vessels, and the allocation of Yard Cranes (YC) to stack operations. The research used techniques such as job-shop scheduling, genetic algorithms, and mixed-integer linear programming to optimize the allocation problems. During the research, a simulation along with the optimization was used. The design of the simulation model was grounded in object-oriented analysis and design paradigm. The authors modeled simulation agents and components as objects that store and exchange information on terminal inputs, states, and outputs. These objects performed actions according to their local behaviors with no supervising agents. The simulation model in its entirety would replicate the terminal activities based on the principle that external events are acted upon by agents, which in turn operate on components. The responses of agents were determined according to the policies generated by the optimization techniques. This solution was applied to the port, with five shifts and four QCs. The results showed a reduction of equipment conflicts and of waiting times for internal trucks in the port.

Winter (2000) presented an integrated just-in-time scheduling model and algorithms for combined stowage and transport planning [202]. The research considered the precedence constraints and transportation times depending on different traveling distances between the yardside and the quayside. A crane split was computed first, based on the shipping company's stowage plan, and a resulting loading sequence of container's positions and their types, respectively. The overall loading process was then optimized by assigning containers to the SCs with regard to fulfilling the stowage criteria and minimizing late arrivals. Instead of container numbers, the assignment was based on attributes of container (their positions and types). The model and the algorithms were tested with a real-world data. Ignoring special difficulties like delays of containers and incomplete information, the results showed suitability of the model and algorithm for real-time scheduling.

In the same way, Steenken et al. (2001) combined container stowage and the transport planning problem [176]. The authors presented the just-in-time container scheduling problem with one QC. Assuming an available SC and a previously unassigned container job for the crane, an MIP model was made. An exact and heuristic method to solve the model was presented in the paper. A German container terminal was selected to investigate the scheduling method in practice. The results showed a reasonable value of cumulative lateness and makespan for handling the container jobs, loading rate of about forty containers per hour.

Zhang et al. (2001) considered the storage space allocation in a rolling horizon approach [214]. For each planning horizon, the problem was decomposed into two levels. At the first level, the total number of inbound and outbound containers to be placed in every part of the storage was determined. The second level determined the number of containers in each block of the yard by solving a transportation problem. The objective of the problem was to minimize traveling times of the vehicles in the port. They applied the solution to Hong Kong Port, in which there are ten blocks with different capacities. Numerical experiments show significant reduction of workload imbalances.

Ambrosino et al. (2002) studied the impact of yard organization on the stowage of containers in terms of unproductive export container movements in a port [6]. The authors investigated two strategies: the pre-marshaling strategy and the sort-and-store strategy. In the first one the export containers were assigned to a temporary storage area in accordance to their loading ship, or more generally their shipping line, as soon as they arrived to the terminal. In the second one, the storage of the export containers were planned on the basis of all information included in their status, which is shipping line, loading containership, destination port, size, and weight. The research made a binary integer programming model and tackled the problem using a heuristic method. The results showed that the best storage strategy is strongly affected by land constraints like space available in the yard.

Chuanyu (2003) did a survey on container yard operations [29]. The author classified yard planning into three decision-making problems:

a. Stack configuration and storage allocation.
b. The number of YCs and their deployment policies.
c. Retrieval sequencing of containers.

The paper reviewed the literature around the processes and solution methods. The survey showed that most of the related studies have been found to be analytical modeling based or simulation modeling based. The survey also indicated among the various approaches proposed by the analytical modeling based studies that the most popularly used techniques are mathematical programming, branch-and-bound method, queuing theory, and network-based method.

Murty et al. (2005) studied storage space assignment and the vehicle routing problem together in the same problem [131]. For the former problem, they suggested two steps, block assignment and storage position assignment. In the first step, the research determined how many containers, inbound or outbound containers, are stored in every block at each time period. In the second step, the optimal available position in the block was determined for storing the containers. While the reshuffling of containers that may arise was minimized, the containers flow and scheduling problem had not been considered in that paper.

In another research, Murty (2007) studied some operating policies and the design of terminal layout [131]. His study posed some inherent difficulties on existing layouts based on designs prepared in the last decade. These difficulties were the cross gantry movement of YCs between zones in the yard, congestion on the road system inside the yard, YC overloading frequency, and crane clashing frequency. The author presented some newer operating policies and designs for improving performance in container terminals based on dividing the storage yard into three separate areas for: (a) import containers; (b) export containers; and (c) a special area labeled as the EMSY (EMpty container Storage Yard for temporary usage).

Delgado et al. (2009) introduced a model for stowing containers in an under deck storage area of a container vessel bay [35]. The authors have shown how to solve the model efficiently using Constraint Programming and compared their approach favorably with an Integer Programming and a Column Generation approach. The estimation algorithms introduced in their research, however, improved the performance of the branch-and-bound dramatically, good lower bounds were generated from partial solutions, and unpromising branches were pruned in early stages without discarding any optimal solution.

Güvena and Türsel (2014) work on trip allocation and stacking strategies at a container terminal [61]. This research focuses on increasing the efficiency of the yard via consideration of the container stacking optimization problem for transshipment and inbound and outbound containers at the container terminal. In the problem, transit containers require multiple sea-trips to reach their final destination. Moreover, vessels departing from the terminal and destined for the same port may provide exchangeable trips for this type of container, based on their several attributes and capacity restrictions. The objective of the problem is to minimize container storage and retrieval times through avoidance of reshuffles, resulting in more efficient loading/unloading operations, and in turn minimizing the dwell time of containers. In this study, two stacking strategies are proposed to solve the problem of allocating the transit container to outbound vessels with minimizing dwell time at the container terminal. In the first strategy, a simplistic random stacking algorithm is used in which the algorithm finds a position for an arriving container by randomly selecting a new lane, bay and stack. If the stack is not full, and the containers in the stack are of the same type as the arriving container, then an acceptable position has been found and the container can be placed in this stack. Otherwise, a new random stack is considered. In the second strategy, the research considers several attributes of the containers while determining a stacking position. The first attribute is the expected departure time, which is defined as the time when a container will be removed from the stack to leave the terminal by a vessel, truck, or train. Moreover, the category of each container is considered. The solution of this problem also has implications for the storage space management.

Yu et al. (2021) studied flexible yard management in container terminals for uncertain retrieving sequence [208]. They considered several clusters in the yard to store export containers for different loading liners and discussed the application of flexible loading clusters, where the number of bays, rows, and tiers can be changed based on service requirement. This study wanted to find out the optimal choice of flexible loading clusters and better solutions for export container allocation. A bi-objectives model which considers both the transportation distance and the handling congestions was built. A heuristic approach is developed to solve the real-life cases. The authors emphasized the possible rehandles during loading process and concluded that the application of flexible loading clusters is efficient for uncertain retrieving sequence.

Hu et al. (2021) studied the container storage space assignment problem in two terminals with the consideration of yard sharing [75]. The problem was studied based on the storage yard of the combined container terminal and dry port. First, a multiple-objective mixed-integer programming model that considers yard sharing strategy with the objectives of minimizing total travel distance, minimizing imbalance in number of containers, and maximizing shared storage space of the dry port was formulated to obtain optimal solutions. After that, a non-dominated sorting genetic algorithm II (NSGA-II) was proposed. Next, the performance of the algorithm was verified by a set of instances. Numerical experiments were conducted to elucidate the problem with the yard sharing strategy intuitively. Furthermore, the performance of the model in four aspects proclaims the advantages of yard sharing strategy and certifies comprehensiveness. Finally, sensitivity analysis is conducted by two aspects which are weight coefficient and feasible distance to verify the efficiency of the proposed method.

Table 3.2 summarizes the major research done over this decision, the storage space assignment in container terminals. The table shows the researchers (year), modeling approach (algorithm), experimental data size, and main results. As we can see in the table, most researchers collected data from the main real ports in the world (in Italy, Hong Kong, Germany, and Turkey).

3.2.1 Assumptions

We assume that the storage area is divided into the short-term and medium-term storage types. These two storage types are usually referred to as the primary and secondary [182]. Figure 3.3 shows a layout of the port with these types of storage. The purposes of the primary storage are to store transit containers [69] (from one ship to another), to minimize waiting times of QCs and ships [182], and to be used in emergency situations such as deadlock of the vehicles. The secondary storage is where the inbound containers are picked up by their consignees, and the outbound ones are brought in by customers. The QCs and RTGCs handle containers in the primary and secondary area, respectively. The size of the secondary storage is usually greater than the primary.

Table 3.2 The Major Research Done Around the Storage Space Assignment in Container Terminals

Researchers (Year)	Modeling (Algorithm)	Experimental Data Size	Main Results
Gambardella et al. (1998)	Integer Programming and Simulation (ILP for optimization and discrete event simulation)	Data from La Spezia Port, 5 Shifts, 4 QCs	Reduction of equipment conflicts and of waiting times for internal trucks
Steenken et al. (2001)	Mixed Integer Linear Programming (an exact and heuristically methods)	Data from German container terminal for just-in-time container scheduling with one quay crane	Loading rate of about 40 containers per hour results in a reasonable value of cumulative lateness and makespan
Zhang et al. (2001)	Mixed Integer Linear Programming — a Rolling Horizon Approach with Two levels (CPLEX)	Data from Hong Kong Port (10 blocks with different capacities)	Reduces the workload imbalance in the yard, avoiding possible bottlenecks in terminal operations
Ambrosino et al. (2002)	Binary Linear Programming (Pre-marshaling and Sort-and-store strategy)	Data from Genoa port (Italy)	The best storage strategy is strongly affected by land constraints like space available for the yard
Henesey et al. (2003) followed Frankel (1987)	Multi-Agent System (searching, coordinating, communicating, and negotiating with other agents via a market-based mechanism)	Not mentioned	Provide a simulator to run scenarios (dynamic yard and dynamic berth allocation)
Murty et al. (2005)	A Multi-Commodity Network Flow and Integer Programming (CPLEX)	Data from Hong Kong Port	A Decision Support System

(Continued)

Table 3.2 The Major Research Done Around the Storage Space Assignment in Container Terminals *(Continued)*

Researchers (Year)	Modeling (Algorithm)	Experimental Data Size	Main Results
Delgado et al. (2009)	Constraint Programming (Branch-and-Bound and a Column Generation approach)	Not mentioned	Improved the performance of the Branch-and-Bound
Güvena and Türsel (2014)	Mathematical Programming Model (two dynamic strategies for stacking containers)	Data from Port of Izmir in Turkey	Strategy 2 outperforms random stacking in terms of the number of reshuffles performed
Yu et al. (2021)	A bi-objectives model, both the transportation distance and the handling congestions (a heuristic approach)	26 export blocks; several fixed clusters (2 bays, 4 bays, and 5 bays) for uncertain retrieving sequence	Improved the yard management for boosting container capacities.
Hu et al. (2021)	Mixed Integer Programming (Non-Dominated Sorting Genetic Algorithm II)	3 sets with 50 blocks in container terminals and 20 blocks in dry port, #Block Size: 1200 TEU	The proposed optimization model considered yard sharing strategy and imbalance of containers outperforms traditional storage mode to achieve better solution quality

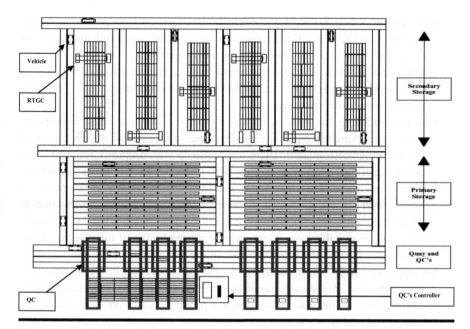

Figure 3.3 Port's layout with the primary and secondary storage types. See [184].

Our approach is to consider the interaction of containers between the primary and secondary storage types. Based on the layout of storage, containers are classified into the six following types according to their status at different stages:

a. Primary Storage Containers to Secondary Storage (PSCSS): Containers in the primary storage waiting to be moved to the secondary storage.

b. Secondary Storage Containers to Primary Storage (SSCPS): Containers in the secondary storage waiting to be moved to the primary storage.

c. Secondary Storage Container Pickup (SSCPI): Inbound containers in the secondary storage waiting for pickup by consignees.

d. Secondary Storage Container Grounding (SSCGD): Outbound containers before being allocated to the secondary storage.

e. Primary Storage Container Pickup (PSCPI): Outbound containers in the primary storage waiting to be loaded on the arriving vessels.

f. Primary Storage Container Discharging (PSCDS): Inbound containers being discharged from the arriving vessels to be allocated to the primary storage.

The following assumptions are considered to formulate this decision:

Assumption 3-2-1: As stated in Chapter 2, the storage areas are divided into different blocks. In this decision, it is necessary to determine which blocks and how many spaces in them are to be allocated to the six types of container.

Assumption 3-2-2: Several QCs might be busy with other operations. So we assume that there is a tight constraint on the minimum and maximum of QCs in the primary storage during each time period.

Assumption 3-2-3: Our objectives are to balance the workload of RTGCs in the secondary storage [214] and to minimize the handling costs of containers in those two kinds of storage.

Assumption 3-2-4: The maximum dwell times of the inbound and outbound containers approximately equal the maximal free storage period, which is beyond the planning horizon [214]. There are containers with unknown removal times at the planning period or containers with known departure times beyond the planning horizon. Their associated workload does not occur in the planning horizon and consequently such containers cannot be considered in this storage allocation model. Instead, these containers are distributed to blocks in proportion to their available storage capacities at the beginning of the planning horizon so as to balance the block densities in the secondary storage.

Assumption 3-2-5: Within each block, the exact location of a container can be assigned to shorten the handling time by minimizing reshuffling [214]. This decision about storage location is a problem at a lower level, and is not considered in this formulation.

Assumption 3-2-6: The secondary storage is where the customers bring in their outbound containers and the consignees pick up their inbound containers. The outbound containers are then transported to the primary storage. Also it is assumed the inbound containers are first stored in the primary storage and then transported to the secondary storage. We assume that the primary and secondary storage types have enough space to store all the containers over the planning horizon.

In order to make the model, the following parameters are known at the beginning of a planning horizon:

$\mathbf{TP}_{ij}$: The traveling time between block i of the primary storage to block j of the secondary.

$\mathbf{TS}_{ij}$: The traveling time between block i of the secondary storage to block j of the primary.

T: The total number of time periods in the planning horizon. The time period has to be greater than the maximum traveling time between the primary storage and the secondary storage or vice versa.

B: The total number of blocks in the secondary storage.

$\mathbf{C}_i$: The storage capacity of block i of the secondary storage.

P: The total number of blocks in the primary storage.

$\mathbf{F}_i$: The capacity of block i of the primary storage.

$\mathbf{H}_{i0}$: The initial inventory of block i of the primary storage, i.e., the number of containers in primary storage at the beginning of the planning horizon.

S_{i0}: The initial inventory of block i in the secondary storage, i.e., the number of containers in block i at the beginning of the planning horizon.

PEO_{it}: The expected number of initial SSCPI containers stored in block i of the secondary storage to be picked up during period t.

LO_{it}: The expected number of initial PSCPI containers stored in block i of the primary storage to be moved to the arriving vessels during period t.

GE_{tk}: The expected total number of SSCPS containers that are to be allocated in the secondary storage during period t and to be moved to primary storage in period $t + k$.

DE_{tk}: The expected total number of PSCSS containers, allocated in the primary storage during period t, and to be picked up from the secondary storage in period $t + k$.

G_t: The expected total number of SSCGD containers that arrive at the terminal during period t and to be stored in the secondary storage.

D_t: The expected total number of PSCDS containers that arrive to the terminal during period t by vessels and to be stored in the primary storage.

α_t: The expected number of SSCGD containers storing in secondary storage during period t, and to be moved to the primary storage in periods beyond the current planning horizon.

β_t: The expected number of PSCDS containers arriving at the terminal during period t, and to be moved to the secondary storage, with an unknown pickup time or pickup time beyond the planning horizon.

Q_t, R_t: The maximum and minimum number of available QCs, respectively, to handle PSCSS, SSCPS, PSCPI, and PSCDS containers in the primary storage during period t.

3.2.2 Decision Variables and Domains

The following decision variables are defined:

X_{ijt}: The total number of PSCSS containers in block i of the primary storage to be moved to block j in the secondary storage during the time period t.
  Domain $X_{ijt} = \{0,1,2,\ldots, \text{Max}\ (F_i, C_j)\ |\ i = 1,2,\ldots P, j = 1,2,\ldots B\}$

Y_{ijt}: The total number of SSCPS containers in block i of the secondary storage to be moved to block j in the primary storage during the time period t.
  Domain $Y_{ijt} = \{0,1,2,\ldots, \text{Max}\ (C_i, F_j)\ |\ i = 1,2,\ldots B, j = 1,2,\ldots P\}$

GS_{it}: The total number of SSCGD containers that arrive at the terminal during the time period t and to be stored in block i of the secondary storage.
  Domain $GS_{it} = \{0,1,2,\ldots, \text{Max}\ (C_i)\ |\ i = 1,2,\ldots B\}$

DP_{it}: The total number of PSCDS containers that arrive to the terminal during period t by vessels and to be stored in block i of the primary storage.
  Domain $DP_{it} = \{0,1,2,\ldots, \text{Max}\ (F_i)\ |\ i = 1,2,\ldots P\}$

3.2.3 Constraints

In order to present the constraints of this decision, we introduce the following auxiliary variables:

PE_{it}: The total number of SSCPI containers stored in block i of the secondary storage that is picked up by consignees during period t. This variable is determined by the following expression:

$$PE_{it} = \sum_{t'=1}^{t-1}\sum_{j=1}^{P} X_{jit'} + PE0_{it}, \, for\, i = 1,2,...B; \, for\, t = 1,2,..,T$$

L_{it}: The total number of PSCPI containers stored in block i of the primary storage that are to be moved to the arriving vessels during period t. This variable is determined by the following expression:

$$L_{it} = \sum_{t'=1}^{t-1}\sum_{j=1}^{B} Y_{jit'} + L0_{it}, \, for\, i = 1,2,...P; \, for\, t = 1,2,..,T$$

H_{it}: The inventory of block i of the primary storage at the beginning of period t. This variable is determined by the following expression:

$$H_{it} = H_{i(t-1)} + DP_{it} + \sum_{j=1}^{B} Y_{jit} - \sum_{j=1}^{B} X_{jit} - L_{it}, \, for\, t = 1,2,..,T; \, for\, i = 1,2,.., P$$

The expression represents the updating of the inventory in the primary storage from a period to the next period. The first term is the initial inventory of block i. The second term is the number of PSCDS containers being allocated in block i. The third and fourth terms state the inventory of block i is increased and decreased by the number of SSCPS and PSCSS containers, respectively. The last term is the number of PSSPI containers being moved from block i to the arriving vessels.

S_{it}: The inventory of block i of the secondary storage at the beginning of period t. This variable is determined by the following expression:

$$S_{it} = S_{i(t-1)} + GS_{it} - \sum_{j=1}^{P} Y_{jit} + \sum_{j=1}^{P} X_{jit} - PE_{it}, \, for\, t = 1,2,..,T; \, for\, i = 1,2,.., B$$

The expression represents updating of the inventory in the secondary storage from a period to the next period. The first term is the initial inventory of block i. The second term is the number of SSCGD containers being allocated in block i. The third and fourth terms state that the inventory of block i is decreased and increased by the number of SSCPS and PSCSS containers, respectively. The last term is the number of SSCPI containers being picked-up from block i.

QC_t: The number of QCs required to handle the four different types of container (PSCPI, SSCPI, PSCSS and PSCDS) in the primary storage during period t. This variable is determined by the following expression:

$$QC_t = \sum_{i=1}^{P} L_{it} + \sum_{i=1}^{B}\sum_{j=1}^{P} Y_{ijt} + \sum_{i=1}^{P}\sum_{j=1}^{B} X_{ijt} + \sum_{i=1}^{P} DP_{it}$$

Now we present the constraints for this decision:

Constraint 3-2-1: Constraints on inventory of each block in the primary and secondary storage and their densities.

$$S_{it} \leq \lambda C_i, \, for \, t = 1,2,..,T; \, for \, i = 1,2,..,B$$
$$H_{it} \leq \gamma F_i, \, for \, t = 1,2,..,T; \, for \, i = 1,2,..,P$$

The first constraint ensures that the inventory in each block of the secondary storage in each time period will not exceed the threshold level (which is being controlled by λ; $\lambda < 1$). The latter ensures that the inventory of each block of the primary storage in each planning period will not exceed the allowable block density (which is being controlled by γ; $\gamma < 1$).

Constraint 3-2-2: Constraints on flow of the containers.

$$\sum_{i=1}^{P}\sum_{j=1}^{B} X_{ijt} = \sum_{k=t+1}^{T} DE_{tk} + \beta_t; \, for \, t = 1,2,..,T$$

$$\sum_{i=1}^{B}\sum_{j=1}^{P} Y_{ijt} = \sum_{k=t+1}^{T} GE_{tk} + \alpha_t; \, for \, t = 1,2,..,T$$

$$D_t = \sum_{i=1}^{P} DP_{it}; \, for \, t = 1,2,..,T$$

$$G_t = \sum_{i=1}^{B} GS_{it}; \, for \, t = 1,2,..,T$$

The first constraint ensures that the expected total number of PSCSS containers to be moved to the secondary storage, DE_{tk}, and the number of containers with known departure, β_t, is the sum of PSCSS containers moved from each block of the primary storage to all blocks in the secondary storage during period t. The second constraint has a similar meaning except for the SSCPS containers. The third constraint ensures that the expected total number of PSCDS containers allocated to all blocks in the primary storage is the sum of the total number of containers arriving to the terminal by the vessels during period t. The fourth constraint has a similar meaning except for the SSCGD containers.

Constraint 3-2-3: Constraints on the number of available QCs in the primary storage.

$$R_t \leq QC_t \leq Q_t, \ for \ t = 1,2,..,T$$

3.2.4 Objective Function

The objective function is to minimize distribution of the total number of containers among blocks in the secondary storage and the sum of the transportation costs between both storage types. In order to present the objective function in the simpler form, we define the following auxiliary variables:

RTGC$_{it}$: The number of RTGCs required to handle the four different types of container (SSCGD, SSCPS, PSCSS, and SSCPI) in block i of the secondary storage during period t. This variable is determined by the following expression:

$$RTGC_{it} = GS_{it} + \sum_{j=1}^{P} Y_{ijt} + \sum_{j=1}^{P} X_{jit} + PE_{it}$$

M$_t$, N$_t$: The maximum and minimum number of RTGC$_{it}$ during period t, respectively. These variables are determined by the following constraints:

$$M_t = \underset{i=1,2,..B}{Max} (RTGC_{it}), \ for \ t = 1,2,..,T$$

$$N_t = \underset{i=1,2,..B}{Min} (RTGC_{it}), \ for \ t = 1,2,..,T$$

Now the objective function is written as follows:

$$MinCostStorages = \sum_{t=1}^{T} \left\{ W_1(M_t - N_t) + W_2 \left(\sum_{i=1}^{P}\sum_{j=1}^{B} X_{ijt} \cdot TP_{ij} + \sum_{i=1}^{B}\sum_{j=1}^{P} Y_{ijt} \cdot TS_{ij} \right) \right\}$$

Note that W_1 is the weight of the distribution of containers among blocks in the secondary storage, and W_2 is the weight of transportation cost inside the terminal.

3.3 Rubber Tyred Gantry Crane Deployment

The RTGC is a critical resource, whose performance in the storage yard affects the waiting times of XTs, ITs or AGVs, and QCs [131]. The waiting time of vessels is also indirectly affected by the productivity of RTGCs. As the workload in the different storage blocks changes over time, deployment of RTGCs among storage blocks in order to provide more RTGCs to blocks with heavier workloads is an extremely important problem in the terminal. The problem here is to determine how many RTGCs work in each block, and when an RTGC needs to be moved from one block to another.

Lin (2000) studied the movement problem of YCs in the container terminal so as to minimize workloads at the end of each time period [108]. The author made an MILP model, and tackled it by Lagrangian decomposition. In the research, the complexity of the MILP was analyzed. Besides the Lagrangian decomposition solution, a new approach with so-called "successive piecewise-linear approximation" was discussed. This approach was used on large size problem instances and the computational experiments showed efficiency and effectiveness in the method.

Lim et al. (2002) studied a set of spatial constraints in a YC scheduling problem [107]. The most interesting one was the non-crossing constraint, i.e., the crane arms could not be crossed over each other simultaneously. It was a structural constraint on cranes and crane tracks. The problem was modeled as bipartite graph matching. The authors suggested the Squeaky Wheel Optimization (SWO) with local search technique. The SWO is based on a cycle, into which three steps (constructer, analyzer, and prioritizer) find solutions. The cycle repeats until a termination condition is satisfied. Using randomly generated problems, the results showed that SWO with local search is better compared with Hill Climbing and probabilistic Tabu Search.

Zhang et al. (2002) described the dynamic RTGC deployment problem with forecasted workload per block in the storage area [215]. Over the planning horizon of a day, the research minimized the total delayed workload in the yard by an MIP model. The objective was to find routes of RTGC movements among blocks within a period of four hours. During the period, only one movement of an RTGC in and out of a block could happen. The authors tackled the model by a modified Lagrangian relaxation and obtained excellent results.

Narasimhan and Palekar (2002) considered the minimization of a YC's handling time for executing a given load plan with a given yard plan for export containers [133]. The authors developed an exact branch-and-bound based algorithm and a heuristic method. Besides the algorithmic approaches, the authors provided a mathematical programming formulation and also considered some complexity issues. The research tested the methods by computational experiments on randomly generated problems.

Linn et al. (2003) solved the RTGC deployment problem in a different way [108]. The authors reduced the size of the problem by sorting blocks of the yard into three categories: (a) the "sink block," which needs and can take additional help; (b) the "source block," which has extra capacity of RTGCs and can send its RTGCs to others; and (c) the "neither block," which needs help but cannot take help, because the RTGCs are currently at work in the block that does not need help. The research excluded the "neither blocks" and formulated the problem as MILP. The approach was tested with a set of real data in Hong Kong. The results demonstrate "an excellent capability and the potential of the model in minimizing the yard-crane workload overflow."

Murty et al. (2005) used the previous approach in a decision support system [131]. The author classified all RTGCs into two types based on their current positions at the beginning of each time period: eligible RTGCs (those that can be moved from their current blocks in the period), and ineligible RTGCs (those that will be kept in their current blocks in the period). The research made an integer programming model by defining a Sink block in which the expected workload exceeds the capacity of its RTGCs. The model was tackled by the Vogel solution and used in practice in the terminals of Hong Kong. Based on the results, the authors proposed a planning period of four hours (i.e., half of an eight-hour shift) for the terminals.

Narasimhan and Palekar (2002) considered the minimization of a yard-crane's handling time for executing a given load plan with a given yard plan for export containers [133]. The authors developed an exact branch-and-bound based algorithm and a heuristic method. Besides the algorithmic approaches, the authors provided a mathematical programming formulation and also considered some complexity issues. The research tested the methods by computational experiments on randomly generated problems.

Guo et al. (2008) studied the problem of real-time YC dispatching in container terminals [59]. Many technologies, including Transponders, Radio-Frequency IDentification (RFID), and Global Positioning System (GPS), have been used for real-time tracking of terminal equipment. The researchers proposed a YC dispatching algorithm based on real-time data-driven simulation to solve the problem of YC job sequencing to minimize the average vehicle waiting time. The algorithm produced an optimal operation sequence for each planning window. Several policies to select jobs to form the planning window were also proposed. The simulation results showed that dispatching YC based on real-time data-driven simulation is of great value in improving YC performance in three scenarios with different vehicle arriving patterns. Additionally the results were 10% worse off a loosely estimated overall optimal performance result.

Guo et al. (2012) also investigated the problem of scheduling gantry cranes, the main handling equipment in railway container terminals [57]. The scheduling problem was formulated as an integer programming model. In this paper, a PSO algorithm was proposed to tackle the model. The effectiveness of the PSO algorithm was evaluated by comparing its results to traditional genetic algorithm and CPLEX on some random instances. Experimental results showed that the PSO algorithm performs better quality solution in a short time on larger problem instances.

Sha et al. (2017) studied scheduling optimization of YCs with minimal energy consumption at container terminals [170]. This study proposed an integer programming model to solve the optimal problem of YC scheduling with minimal energy consumption at container terminals from the low carbon perspective. In this research, an optimal model was built with consideration of such key factors as the crane moving distance, turning distance, and the practical operation rules. In accordance with the general kind of handling system at container terminals in China, an integer programming model was proposed to optimize the scheduling of YCs at container terminals with the purpose of minimizing the total energy consumption of the RTGC. Then, on the basis of the actual operational data of the Shanghai Yangshan Deep Water Port (SYDWP), the container volume of each block was calculated and used to solve the model. The computational experiments are proposed to illustrate and validate the solutions for YC scheduling.

He et al. (2019) addressed YC scheduling problem in a container terminal considering risk caused by uncertainty [87]. It did not only optimize the efficiency of YC operations but also optimize the extra loss caused by uncertainty for reducing risk of adjusting schedule as the result of the task groups' arriving times and handling volumes deviating from their plan. A mathematical model was proposed for optimizing the total delay to the estimated ending time of all task groups without uncertainty and the extra loss under all uncertain scenarios. Furthermore, a GA-based framework combined with three-stage algorithm was proposed to solve the problem. The numerical experiments showed that the model and solution is convenient for the situation with uncertainly.

Rizald et al. (2015) studied the YCs coordination schemes for automated container terminals, using an agent-based approach [162]. The schemes were used to increase the efficiency and the service level of the landside containers' pick-up operation, improving the YCs. This study proposed three schemes (i.e., the market-based scheme, the zonal 1-1 scheme, and the zonal scheme 1-2 scheme) for coordinating multiple RTG YCs. Using agent-based simulation, this research evaluated the performance of the proposed coordination alternatives by assessing the trucks' waiting time, the RTGs' utilization, and the RTGs' fuel consumption values.

Table 3.3 summarizes the major research done over the decision, and the deployment of RTGC in container terminals. The table shows the researchers (year), modeling approach (algorithm), experimental data size, and main results. As we can see in the table, the largest and second largest problems that have been solved so far are the instances in the experiments in [65] and [217], respectively. The assumptions of those researches are more convenient for practical situations in modern ports.

3.3.1 Assumptions

Here, we present a combination of the assumptions in Zhang's model [215] and Lim's formulation [107] for this decision. These assumptions are:

Assumption 3-3-1: The capacity of RTGCs is measured in time-unit (minutes, for example) [215]. Similarly, the workload of each block is converted to time-unit. It is also assumed the nominal numbers of container moves are given in each time period. These containers are handled by the RTGCs in the yard. Since containers are stacked on each other and may be stored in a predefined

Table 3.3   The Major Research Done Around the RTGC Deployment in Container Terminals

Researchers (Year)	Modeling (Algorithm)	Experimental Data Size	Main Results
Lin (2000)	Mixed Integer Linear Programming (Lagrangian decomposition and successive piecewise-linear approximation)	#Blocks: 6 and 24, Workload Arrival in Poison Distribution with average rate 0.4 and 0.8	Successive piecewise-linear approximation method is better than Lagrangian decomposition
Lim et al. (2002)	Bipartite Graph Matching (Squeaky Wheel Optimization with local search technique)	110 instances: (10 × 10 to 100 × 2000)	Squeaky Wheel Optimization with local search is better than Applied Hill Climbing, Probabilistic Tabu Search
Zhang et al. (2002)	Mixed Integer Linear Programming (Lagrangian relaxation)	#Blocks: 20 #RTGCs: 30	Lagrangian relaxation method generates near optimal solutions in a reasonably short time
Murty et al. (2005)	Integer Linear Programming (Vogel solution)	Samples collected from Hong Kong Port	A Decision Support System
Guo et al. (2008)	Three Dispatching Strategy (First Come First Serve, Nearest Job First, and Fixed Window Size with 1, 3, 6, 9 jobs)	#Vehicles: 6 #Yard Cranes: 2	Great value in improving Yard Crane performance in three strategy
Guo et al. (2012)	Integer Programming (Particle Swarm Optimization algorithm)	Tasks × Cranes: 8 × 2 to 18 × 3	Effectiveness of the Particle Swarm Optimization algorithm is evaluated by comparing its results to traditional genetic algorithm

(Continued)

Table 3.3 The Major Research Done Around the RTGC Deployment in Container Terminals *(Continued)*

Researchers (Year)	Modeling (Algorithm)	Experimental Data Size	Main Results
Rizald et al. (2015)	Coordination Schemes (Market-Based Scheme, Zonal 1-1 Scheme, and Zonal Scheme 1-2 Scheme)	4 blocks, 40 column – 6 rows, one crane to one yard block	Zonal 1 in 1 coordination scheme provided the best overall performance
Sha et al. (2017)	Integer Programming (Simulation)	Container yard has 16 rows, each row has 11 columns	the actual operational data of the Shanghai Yangshan Deep Water Port
He et al. (2019)	A mathematical model (genetic algorithm combined with a three-stage algorithm)	48 blocks in the yard and 15 available Yard Cranes	The model and solution is suitable for a situation with uncertainty

pattern, each nominal container retrieval or storage may take more than one real RTGC move. So the total number of container moves is converted into the workload-times by multiplying the average number of real moves per nominal move with the average time needed per move.

Assumption 3-3-2: Because of the limitation of blocks size and the potential danger of RTGC collision, there is a limited number of RTGCs in each block at any time. There are situations where up to two RTGCs can be worked in each block [215]. But we do not allow more than K RTGCs to be moved from one block to another in a time period.

Assumption 3-3-3: Every RTGC movement starts and finishes within the same time period [215]. This assumption entails that the time period has to be greater than the maximum traveling times of RTGCs among blocks.

Assumption 3-3-4: It is assumed that unfinished work in a block at the end of a time period will be carried over to the next period [215]. As a result, the workload of a block in a time period is the sum of the workload in the current period and the workload carried over from the previous time period. The workload carried over from the previous period will be finished during the early part in the current period.

Assumption 3-3-5: The maximum number of RTGCs or YCs moved in the yard is known and fixed during each time period.

Assumption 3-3-6: The RTGCs cannot cross over each other in the same period [107]. Figure 3.4 shows a part of the storage yard. Moving an RTGC from block 1 to block 4 and another one from block 3 to block 2 at the same period produces a dangerous situation in the yard.

The following parameters are known at the beginning of the planning horizon:

TT_{ij}: The traveling time of an RTGC from block i to block j.

T: The total number of time periods in the planning horizon. The time period has to be greater than the maximum traveling time of RTGCs between the blocks.

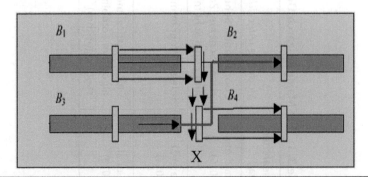

Figure 3.4   Cross over problem for two RTGCs in the storage area.

X$_{ii0}$: The numbers of RTGCs in block i at the beginning of the planning horizon.

C: The capacity of an RTGC within a time period.

K: The total permitted number of RTGCs in each block.

N: The total number of blocks in the yard.

B$_{it}$: The workloads of block i within the time period t. Average time to handle a container are used to determine the workload of each block in time-unit.

M$_t$: The maximum number of RTGCs or YCs moved in the yard during the time period t.

L$_{ij,\,kl}$: 1 if the movement of RTGC from block i to block j and from block k to block l creates a cross over problem. Otherwise it is zero. These parameters are determined according to the layout of the storage area.

W$_{i0}$: The workload of block i at the beginning of the planning horizon.

3.3.2 Decision Variables and Domains

The decision variables are defined as follows:

X$_{ijt}$: The number of RTGC moving from block i to block j during the time period t.

    Domain $(X_{ijt}) = \{0,1,2,\ldots,K\}$, for $i, j = 1,2,\ldots,N$; $t = 1,2,3,\ldots,T$, $i \neq j$.

    Note that when $i = j$, X_{ijt} indicates the RTGCs stay in the same block during the time period t.

Z$_{ijt}$: The workload fulfilled in block i by RTGCs that move from block i to block j during the time period t. Domain $(Z_{ijt}) = \{0,1,2,\ldots,B_{it}\}$.

3.3.3 Constraints

Constraint 3-3-1: Maintaining the RTGC flow or movement conservation in each block when RTGCs are deployed from one period to the next period [215].

$$\sum_{j=1}^{N} X_{ijt} = \sum_{j=1}^{N} X_{ji(t-1)}, \text{ for } i = 1,2,\ldots,N; \ t = 1,2,\ldots,T.$$

Constraint 3-3-2: Only K RTGCs can serve a block in a time period.

$$\sum_{j=1}^{N} X_{ijt} + \sum_{j=1,\,j\neq i}^{N} X_{jit} \leq K, \text{ for } i = 1,2,\ldots,N; \ t = 1,2,\ldots,T.$$

Constraint 3-3-3: The total maximum and minimum available numbers of RTGCs or YCs in the yard are limited.

$$0 \leq \sum_{i=1}^{N} \sum_{j=1}^{N} X_{ijt} \leq M_t; \text{ for } t = 1,2,\ldots,T$$

Constraint 3-3-4: Two RTGCs cannot cross over each other in the same time period.

$$L_{ij,kl} = 1 \Rightarrow [(X_{ijt} > 0)\, XOR\,(X_{klt} > 0)\, XOR\,(X_{ijt} + X_{klt} = 0)]$$
$$for\ i,j,k,l = 1,2,3,..,N;\ i \neq j,\ k \neq l,\ k \neq i,\ l \neq j, for\ t = 1,2,...,T$$

3.3.4 Objective Function

The objective function of this decision is to minimize the remaining workload at each block [215] and the traveling time of the RTGCs among blocks during the planning horizon. In order to formulate the objective function, we introduce the following auxiliary variables:

Y_{ijt}: The workload fulfilled in block j by the RTGCs that move from block i to block j during the time period t. This variable is determined by the following expression:

$$Y_{ijt} = (C - TT_{ij})X_{ijt} - Z_{ijt}, for\ i,j = 1,2,...,N; t = 1,2,3,..,T$$

The first term represents the total net capacity of RTGCs that move from block i to block j (a part of their capacity is missed due to the traveling time from block i to block j). The second term is the workload fulfilled in block i by the RTGC.

W_{it}: The workload left in block i at the end of the time period t. This variable is determined by the following expression:

$$W_{it} = W_{i(t-1)} + B_{it} - \sum_{j=1}^{N} Z_{ijt} - \sum_{j=1}^{N} Y_{jit}; for\ i = 1,2,...,N; t = 1,2,3,..,T$$

The first term is the workload in block i from the previous period. The second term is the workload of block i within the time period t. The third term states the workload fulfilled in block i by RTGCs that move from this block to others. The last term represents the workload fulfilled in block i by RTGCs that move from the other blocks to this block.

Now the objective function is written as follows:

$$MinCostRTGCs = \left[w1\left(\sum_{i=1}^{N}\sum_{t=1}^{T} W_{it}\right) + w2\sum_{t=1}^{T}\sum_{i=1}^{N}\sum_{j=1}^{N} TT_{ij} \cdot X_{ijt} \right]$$

The first term is the sum of workload left in all blocks and the second term is traveling times of RTGCs between the blocks. Note that w_1 and w_2 are the weights of those two terms in the objective function.

3.4 Scheduling and Routing of Vehicles

The Vehicle Routing Problem (VRP) is a well-known integer programming problem which falls into the category of NP-Hard problems. This means that the computational effort required solving this problem increases exponentially with the problem size. The VRP is being studied in a broad class of routing problems [197]. Some of these variants are Capacitated Vehicle Routing Problem (CVRP), Vehicle Routing Problem with Time Windows (VRPTW), Capacitated Vehicle Routing Problem with Time Windows (CVRPTW), Multiple Depot Vehicle Routing Problem (MDVRP), Periodic Vehicle Routing Problem (PVRP), Split Delivery Vehicle Routing Problem (SDVRP), Stochastic Vehicle Routing Problem (SVRP), Vehicle Routing Problem with Backhauls (VRPB), Vehicle Routing Problem with Satellite Facilities (VRPSF), and Time Dependent Vehicle Routing Problem (TDVRP).

In each port, there are several vehicles to carry containers in the port. The scheduling and routing of these vehicles is an extremely important decision. In this section, we review the latest research around dispatching and scheduling of AGVs. After that, scheduling and routing problems of vehicles in the container terminal is formulated as a VRPTW.

Böse et al. (2000) focused on the process of container transport by QCs and SCs between the container vessel and the container yard [14]. The objective was a reduction of the time in port for the vessels by maximizing the productivity of the QCs. The authors investigated dispatching approaches for SCs to QCs in order to minimize a vessel's turnaround time. The first approach was the SC pooling, which used a dynamic strategy where a predetermined number of carriers perform container transports for several QCs. Depending on the number of loading and discharging containers, the carriers could be used in a double-cycle mode, in which empty traveling is replaced by jobs for other QCs. The author considered two different cases of the SC pooling: semi-dynamic assignment (a fixed number of SCs to the QCs of one vessel) and dynamic assignment (a fixed number of SCs for all QCs). The authors presented an evolutionary algorithm to solve the problems and did a simulation for real data. The results showed that the influence of the number of sequenced containers is not a major concern in the dynamic assignment when the carriers operate in the double-cycle mode.

Wook and Hwan (2000) applied two different dispatching strategies for AGVs in container terminals [203]: "dedicated dispatching" and "pooled dispatching." In the dedicated dispatching, every AGV is assigned to a single QC. In pooled dispatching, an AGV performs delivery tasks for more than one QC. Their primary goal of dispatching AGVs was to complete all the loading and discharging operations as early as possible and their secondary goal was to minimize the total travel distance of AGVs. The author made integer programming models and tackled them by LINDO software. The research was used in Pusan in a case study and showed that the "pooled dispatching" is preferred over the "dedicated dispatching."

Meersmans (2001) considered the problem of integrated scheduling of AGVs, QCs, and RTGCs at automated terminals [122]. The author presented a branch-and-bound algorithm and a heuristic beam search algorithm in order to minimize the makespan of the schedule. A beam search algorithm and several dispatching rules were compared in a computational study under different scenarios with similar results. In the results, near optimal solutions were obtained in a reasonable time. The study also indicated "that it is more important to base a planning on a long horizon with inaccurate data, than to update the planning often in order to take newly available information into account."

Qiu and Hsu (2000–2001) addressed scheduling and routing problems for AGVs. The authors developed conflict-free routing algorithms for two different path topologies and two scheduling strategies. The methods were applied together in a case study [148, 150, 152]. To route the vehicles without conflicts and to minimize the space requirement of the layouts, critical conditions for certain key parameters of the path and vehicle were derived. The routing efficiency was analyzed in terms of the distance traveled and the time requirement for AGVs to complete all pickup and drop-off jobs. The research also showed theoretically that a high degree of concurrency of AGV moves could be achieved, although the routing decision took only a constant amount of time for each vehicle.

Leong (2001) developed an efficient dynamic deployment algorithm scheme for AGVs. The objective was to dispatch AGVs to containers in order to minimize loading and unloading time for a vessel [104]. Following the work, Moorthy et al. (2003) studied deadlock of AGVs in a container terminal while the AGVs are moving inside the port and carrying the jobs. The authors developed a deadlock prediction and avoidance algorithm [127] for a zone-controlled AGV system. The algorithm is based on wait-and-proceeds strategy. The algorithm was compared with the current scheme at a terminal in Singapore in a simulation experiment. Analysis of the results showed that the algorithm makes improvements in throughput of the terminal.

Zhang et al. (2002) presented two integer programming models for dispatching vehicles to accomplish a sequence of container jobs from quayside to yardside [217]. In the models, the order of vehicles for carrying out the jobs needed to be determined. Two heuristic algorithms were constructed based on the two integer programming models respectively. Using a formulation as the Lagrangian relaxation dual problem, the authors provided a lower bound for the objective function of the second model. Numerical results of the two heuristic algorithms applied to a real size virtual terminal were reported. Based on the second model, the author derived a formula to determine the optimum number of vehicles to handle a sequence of container jobs.

Cheng et al. (2003) studied dispatching AGVs in a container terminal [25]. The authors presented a network flow formulation to minimize the waiting time of the AGVs on the berth side. In a similar paper concerning the same project, Chan [23] models a network flow in order to develop an efficient dispatching strategy for

AGVs. In the model, the constraints described disparate instances of AGVs carrying one container or two containers. The author proposed a heuristic algorithm and tested it in the case of a single load AGV, compared with the current deployment strategy in a port. The results showed some improvements by the model and algorithm in a case study of a Singapore port.

Grunow et al. (2004) studied dispatching multi-load AGVs in highly automated seaport container terminals [53]. They made a Mixed Integer Linear Program (MILP) model and presented some priority rules to handle container jobs in the container terminals. The performance of the priority rule-based approach and the MILP model has been analyzed for different scenarios with respect to total lateness of the AGVs. The main focus of their numerical investigation was on evaluating the priority rule-based approach for single and dual-load vehicles as well as comparing its performance against the MILP modeling approach.

Murty et al. (2005) presented an integrated approach and proposed a decision support system [131] for operations in a container terminal, focusing on a system that reacts adequately to changes in the workloads over time and to uncertainty in working conditions. One of the functions in the decision support system was an estimation of the number of vehicles required each half-hour and to hire the minimum number of vehicles over a planning horizon of each day. At the end of each planning period, the system used the latest information for the next period. Following the practice of the terminals in Hong Kong, the authors proposed a planning period of four hours (i.e., half of an eight-hour shift) since the workloads could be estimated with reasonable accuracy over the period.

Rashidi and Tsang (2005) also studied the dynamic scheduling of AGVs in container terminals [155]. The problem was formulated as a minimum cost flow model. The authors considered three terms in the objective function: (a) traveling time of the AGVs in the route of terminal; (b) waiting time of the AGVs on the berth-side; and (c) the lateness of serving the container jobs. To solve the problem, the authors extended the standard network Simplex Algorithm (NSA) and obtained a novel algorithm, NSA+. Using randomly generated problems, NSA+ could find the global optimal solutions for three thousand jobs and ten million arcs in the graph model within two minutes on a 2.4 GHz Pentium PC. To complement NSA+, the authors presented an incomplete algorithm, Greedy Heuristic Search (GHS). To evaluate the relative strength and weakness of NSA+ and GHS, the two algorithms were compared for the dynamic automated vehicle scheduling problem.

Corréa et al. (2007) proposed a hybrid method designed to solve a problem of dispatching and conflict-free routing of AGVs in a flexible manufacturing system [31]. The problem considered simultaneous assignment, scheduling, and conflict-free routing of the vehicles. The hybrid method consists of a decomposition method where the master problem (scheduling) is modeled with constraint programming and the subproblem (conflict-free routing) with MIP. Some logic cuts are generated by the subproblems and used in the master problem to prune optimal scheduling solutions whose routing plan exhibits conflicts. The method presented is capable to solve instances of problems with up to six AGVs.

Nguyen et al. (2009) considered buffer spaces in the berth side and yard-side and present a dispatching method for Automated Lifting Vehicles (ALV) in automated port container terminals [135]. An ALV is capable of lifting a container from the ground by itself. The authors discussed how to dispatch ALVs by utilizing information about pickup and delivery locations, and time in future delivery tasks. A mixed-integer programming model is provided for assigning optimal delivery tasks to ALVs and it is tackled by ILOG CPLEX. In this paper, a procedure for converting buffer constraints into time window constraints and a heuristic algorithm for overcoming the excessive computational time required for solving the mathematical model were suggested. Numerical experiments were reported to compare the objective values and computational times by a heuristic algorithm with those by an optimizing method, and to analyze the effects of dual cycle operation, number of ALVs, and buffer capacity on the performance of ALVs.

Rashidi (2010) proposed three solutions for scheduling problem of the Single-Load and Multi-Load AGVs in Container Terminals [157]. The problem is formulated as CSOP. When the capacity of the vehicles is one container, the problem is a minimum cost flow model. This model is solved by the highest performance algorithm, i.e., NSA. If the capacity of the AGVs increases, this problem has a huge search space and is tackled by the Simulated Annealing Method (SAM). Three approaches for its initial solution and a neighborhood function to the search method are implemented. The third solution is a hybrid of SAM and NSA. This hybrid is applied to the heterogeneous AGVs scheduling problem in container terminals. Several same random problems are generated, solved by SAM with the proposed approaches, and the simulation results are compared. The experimental results show that NSA provides a good initial solution for SAM when the capacity of AGVs is heterogeneous.

Cai et al. (2012) present a multi-objective optimization model for the Autonomous Straddle Carriers Scheduling (ASCS) problem in automated container terminals [17], which is more practical than the single objective model. The model considers three objectives in the objective function, i.e., SC traveling time, SC waiting time, and finishing time of high-priority container-transferring jobs. The presented model is formulated as a pickup and delivery problem with time windows in the form of binary integer programming. In the model the weighted sum of each term in the objective function is investigated as the representative example. An exact algorithm based on Branch-and-Bound with Column Generation (BBCG) is employed for solving the multi-objective ASCS problem. Based on the map of an actual fully-automated container terminal, simulation results are compared with the single-objective scheduling to demonstrate the effectiveness and flexibility of the presented multi-objective model, as well as the efficiency of the BBCG algorithm for autonomous SC scheduling.

Héctor et al. (2014) present an in-depth overview of transport operations and the material handling equipment used, highlight current industry trends and developments, and propose a new classification scheme for transport operations and scientific journal papers published up to 2012 [66]. The paper also discusses and challenges current operational paradigms of transport operations. Lastly, the paper identifies new avenues for academic research based on current trends and developments in the container terminal industry.

Wang et al. (2014) propose a model that determines the strategy of owning and renting trucks in combinations with internal truck scheduling and storage allocation problems in container terminals [198]. In this research, the combined problem is decomposed into two levels and a two-level heuristic approach is developed. The first level of the problem determines the daily operations of the internal trucks, while the second level determines the truck employment strategy based on the calculation at the first level. The results show that even if the cost of owned yard trucks is much lower than the cost of rented yard tucks, the terminal companies should not purchase too many trucks when the purchasing price is high. In addition, the empirical truck employment strategies and purchasing all the trucks or renting all the trucks are not cost-effective when compared with the proposed yard truck employment strategy.

Yang et al. (2018) studied an integrated scheduling method for AGV routing in automated container terminals [205]. This paper proposes an integrated scheduling for handling equipment coordination and AGV routing. With the goal of minimizing makespan, we set up a bi-level programming model. To solve the model, we investigate and compare the Rolling Horizon Procedure (RHP) and Congestion Prevention Rule-based Bi-level Genetic Algorithm (CPR-BGA). It is shown that the CPR-BGA algorithm is highly effective for the integrated scheduling in automated container terminals.

Stojaković and Twrdy (2021) determined the optimal number of yard trucks in smaller container terminals [177]. This research is based on the allocation of the right number of yard trucks to QCs in order to assure better productivity levels in the berth and yard subsystems. For this purpose, a discrete-event simulation modeling approach is used. The approach is applied to a hypothetical small container terminal, which includes operations on the berth-yard-berth relation.

Table 3.4 summarizes the major research done over the decision, scheduling, and/or routing vehicles in container terminals. The table shows the researchers (year), modeling approach (algorithm), experimental data size, and main results. As we can see in the table, most researchers model the problem as MIP. The largest and second largest problems in the experiments that have been solved so far are the instances in [157] and [217], respectively.

3.4.1 Assumptions

It is assumed that there are several vehicles in the port in order to transport the inbound and outbound containers from a pickup location to a delivery location

Table 3.4 The Major Research Done Around the Scheduling and Routing Vehicles in Ports

Researchers (Year)	Modeling (Algorithm)	Experimental Data Size	Main Results
Bose et al. (2000)	Integer Programming Model (Evolutionary Algorithm)	#Ships: 4 #QCs: 2 for each ship # SC: 6	Applied to a real port Performance could be improved
Cheng et al. (2003)	Minimum Cost Flow (Network Simplex Algorithm)	#AGVs: 20 #QCs: 16	Minimum cost flow is better than First-Input-First-Output rule
Grunow et al. (2004)	Mixed Integer Linear Programming (CPLEX 7.0. and priority rules)	S-Layout, #QCs: 3, #AGVs: 3; L-Layout #QCs: 6, #AGVs: 6	Performance of Mixed Integer Linear Programming is almost the same as priority rule for small layout
Thurston and Hu (2002)	Multi Agent System (Plan Merging Paradigm)	#Ships: 1 #AGVs: 12	Presents a distributed multi-agent architecture and provides a feasible optimization solution
Wook and Hwan (2000)	Mixed Integer Linear Programming (LINDO)	#QCs: 2 #AGVs: 1–5 #Jobs: 15–30	Pooled Dispatching is preferred over Dedicated Dispatching
Zhange et al. (2002)	Mixed Integer Linear Programming (Two heuristic algorithms: Forward Search and Backward Search)	#IT: 30–100	Lagrangian relaxation has provided a better solution for the second model
Corréa et al. (2007)	Constraint Programming and Mixed Integer Programming (ILog Solver 5.2 and CPLEX 8.0)	#AGVs: 6	Present a decomposition method to solve a difficult combinatorial integrated scheduling and conflict-free routing problem

(Continued)

Table 3.4 The Major Research Done Around the Scheduling and Routing Vehicles in Ports *(Continued)*

Researchers *(Year)*	Modeling *(Algorithm)*	Experimental Data Size	Main Results
Nguyen et al. (2009)	A Mixed Integer Programming (ILOG CPLEX)	#ALVs Per QC: 1–4, # Operations for each QC: 1–2, 4–12, Buffer Capacities: from 1 to 2	Improvements in the total travel time of ALVs, delay time of QCs, and completion time in ship operations
Rashidi (2010)	Constraint Satisfaction Optimization Problem (Network Simplex Algorithm and Simulated Annealing Method)	#QCs : 7 #AGVs: 50	Network Simplex Algorithm provides a good initial solution for Simulated Annealing Method
Cai et al. (2012)	Multi-objective optimization model in the form of binary integer programming (Branch-and-Bound with Column Generation)	# SC: 9	Effectiveness and flexibility of the presented multi-objective model compared with the single-objective scheduling
Wang et al. (2014)	Mathematical Programming (Two-Level Heuristic Approach)	#Trucks (Owning and Renting): 15–54	Better solution than empirical method for employing different types of yard truck
Yang et al. (2018)	Bi-level programming model (rolling horizon procedure and Congestion Prevention Rule-based Bi-level Genetic Algorithm- CPR-BGA)	#Container jobs: 1–2000 #QC: 2–8 #AGV: 8–20	CPR-BGA algorithm is highly effective for the integrated scheduling in automated container terminals
Stojaković and Twrdy (2021)	Scenario based with "what-if" analysis (Discrete-Event Simulation)	Seven different scenarios #YC: 5–16	Good guidelines for efficient optimization of operation in small container ports

inside the terminal. The inbound containers in the berth are transported to the storage area, whereas the outbound containers in the storage area are moved to the berth. The following assumptions and notations are used to formulate this decision:

Assumption 3-4-1: The problem is serving a number of transportation requests. Each request involves moving a number of container jobs. A directed graph or network is considered for this transportation system. Given n request in the problem, let the node i and node $n + i$ represent the pickup and delivery location of the i-th job, respectively. In this network, different nodes obviously may represent the same physical location in the yard to berth. By adding the node 0 and node $2n + 1$, as the depot, to the network, it has the node set $N = \{0, 1, 2,...,n, n + 1, n + 2,..., 2n, 2n + 1\}$. The pickup and delivery points are respectively included into two sets $P^+ = \{1, 2,..., n\}$ and $P^- = \{n + 1, n + 2,...2n\}$. Therefore, $P = P^+ \cup P^-$ is the set of nodes other than the depot nodes.

Assumption 3-4-2: We are given a fleet of $V = \{1,2,..., |V|\}$ vehicles. The vehicles are heterogeneous and every vehicle transports a few containers from a given node, i, to a destination node, j $(j \neq i)$, which is more generally applicable to modern ports. At the start of the process, the vehicles are assumed to be empty.

Assumption 3-4-3: It is assumed the vehicles move with an average speed so that there are no Collisions, Congestion, Livelocks, Deadlocks [153] or breakdown problems while they are carrying the containers. These traffic problems are at a lower level, and are not considered in this model.

Assumption 3-4-4: To load/unload the containers from the vessel or in the yard, a QC or RTGC is used. Every pickup/delivery node has a certain time window. Each node should be served within its time window.

Assumption 3-4-5: We assumed the container jobs are distributed in the terminal so that each node is visited once only by a vehicle. In other word, a QC or RTGC is not busy in each node with a different container job at the same time.

Assumption 3-4-6: Each job has a time window to be served. In practice it is not possible to serve every job. Hence, the objective function of this decision is to minimize the transportation costs, to serve each job within its time window as much as possible, and to minimize the total number of jobs left at the end of the process.

The following parameters are known at the beginning of the process:

TS_{vo}: The times at which the vehicle v leaves the depot.
S: The processing time of a container job to be picked up or dropped off.
q_v: The capacity of vehicle v.

TT$_{Li, Lj}$: The travel time from the physical location of the node i, Li, to the physical location of the node j, Lj (for each pair of i, j in N).

C$_{Li, Lj}$: The cost of traveling from the physical location of the node i, Li, to the physical location of the node j, Lj (for each pair of i, j in N).

d_j: The number of container jobs to be moved from the node j to the node $n+j$.

$[a_i, b_i]$: The time window to pick up the container jobs at the node i.

$[a_{n+i}, b_{n+i}]$: The time window to deliver the container jobs at the node $n+i$.

$[a_0, b_0]$: The time window of the vehicles to departure the depot.

$[a_{2n+1}, b_{2n+1}]$: The time window of the vehicles to go back to the depot.

3.4.2 Decision Variables and Domains

X$_{ijv}$: 1 if the vehicle v moves from the node i to the node j. Otherwise it is 0.
Domain (X_{ijv}) = {0,1}, $\forall i, j \in P$ ($i \neq j$), $\forall v \in V$.

F$_j$: The number of jobs that are fulfilled at the node j.
Domain (F_j) = {0,1,...,d_j}, $\forall i \in P^+$.

3.4.3 Constraints

In order to present the constraints and to formulate the objective function, we need the following auxiliary variables:

Z$_j$: The number of jobs left at the node i at the end of the process. At the start of the process **Z$_j$ = 0**.

Y$_{vi}$: The load of vehicle v when it leaves the node i. At the start of the process **Y$_{v0}$ = 0**.

Q$_j$: The number of jobs to be lifted or dropped off at the node j.

These variables are determined by the following conditional statements:

$$(1)\begin{cases} (X_{0jv} = 1)\,AND\,(d_j = F_j) \Rightarrow Z_j = 0, Q_j = Q_{j+n} = d_j, Y_{vj} = Q_j \\ (X_{0jv} = 1)\,AND\,(d_j \succ F_j) \Rightarrow Z_j = d_j - F_j, Q_j = Q_{j+n} = d_j - Z_j, Y_{vj} = Q_j \\ \forall v \in V, \exists j \in P^+ \end{cases}$$

$$(2)\begin{cases} (X_{ijv} = 1)\,AND\,(d_j = F_j) \Rightarrow Z_j = 0, Q_j = Q_{n+j} = d_j, Y_{vj} = Y_{vi} + Q_j \\ (X_{ijv} = 1)\,AND\,(d_j \succ F_j) \Rightarrow Z_j = d_j - F_j, Q_j = Q_{n+j} = d_j - Z_j, Y_{vj} = Y_{vi} + Q_j \\ \forall v \in V, \exists j \in P^+, \forall i \in P, i \neq j \end{cases}$$

$$(3)\begin{cases} X_{ijv} = 1 \Rightarrow Y_{vj} = Y_{vi} - Q_j \\ \forall v \in V, \forall i \in P, \exists j \in P^-, i \neq j \end{cases}$$

The first set of the statements represents the number of jobs left and lifted at the node j as well as the load of the vehicle when it leaves the first pickup point after the depot. The number of jobs left at the node j is the difference between the number of jobs requested and the number of jobs fulfilled. The number of jobs to be picked up at the node j and the number of deliveries at the destination node are updated. Additionally, the load of vehicle v when it leaves the node j is equal to the number of jobs picked up at the node. The second set of the statements has a similar meaning but is for when the vehicle goes to any pickup or drop-off point after the first pickup. The last set of the statements mean that if the vehicle goes to a certain delivery point, its load is decreased by the number of deliveries.

TS_{vi}: The time at which the vehicle v starts service at the node i ($TS_{v0} = 0$). This variable is determined by the following conditional statements:

$$X_{0jv} = 1 \Rightarrow TS_{vj} = TS_{v0} + TT_{L0,Lj}; \exists j \in P^+, \forall v \in V$$

$$X_{ijv} = 1 \Rightarrow TS_{vj} = TS_{vi} + S \times Q_j + TT_{Li,Lj}; \forall v \in V, \forall i \in P, \exists j \in P, (i \neq j)$$

$$X_{i(2n+1)v} = 1 \Rightarrow TS_{v(2n+1)} = TS_{vi} + S \times Q_j + TT_{Li,L(2n+1)}; \exists i \in P^-, \forall v \in V$$

The first statement represents leaving the depot where the vehicles follow by a pickup point. The second statement shows that the vehicles can go to any pickup or delivery point after the first pickup. The last statement represents going to the depot where the vehicles have a delivery before that. To calculate the starting service time at each node, the service time of the current node and the traveling time between the previous and current nodes have to be considered.

Now we present the constraints as follows:

Constraint 3-4-1: Constraints on pickup and delivery points.

$$\sum_{v \in V} \sum_{j \in N} X_{ijv} = 1, \forall i \in P^+$$

$$\sum_{j \in N} X_{ijv} - \sum_{j \in N} X_{jiv} = 0, \forall i \in P, \forall v \in V$$

$$\sum_{j \in N} X_{ijv} - \sum_{j \in N} X_{j(n+i)v} = 0, \forall i \in P^+, \forall v \in V$$

The first constraint ensures that each pickup point is visited once by one of the vehicles. The second constraint indicates that if a vehicle enters a node it exits it. The third constraint ensures that if a vehicle visits a pickup node, then it has to visit the associated delivery node.

Constraint 3-4-2: Constraints on the first and last visit points.

$$\sum_{j\in P^+} X_{0jv} = 1, \forall v \in V$$

$$\sum_{i\in P^-} X_{i(2n+1)v} = 1, \forall v \in V$$

The first constraint ensures that the first visit of every vehicle is a pickup node. The second constraint ensures that the last visit of the vehicles is a delivery node.

Constraint 3-4-3: Constraints on the capacity of the vehicles.

$$Y_{vi} \le q_v, \forall v \in V, \forall i \in P$$

The load of vehicle v when it leaves the node i must not exceed the capacity of the vehicle.

3.4.4 Objective Function

According to Assumption 3-4-6, this function is as follows:

$$MinJobsCost = \left\{ \sum_{v\in V} w_1 \left[\sum_{i\in P} \sum_{j\in P, j\neq i} X_{ijv} \cdot C_{Li,Lj} + w_2 \sum_{i\in P} |a_i - TS_{vi}|^+ \right. \right.$$

$$\left. \left. + w_3 \sum_{i\in P} |TS_{vi} - b_i|^+ \right] + w_4 \sum_{i\in P+} Z_i \right\}$$

The first term is the sum of transportation costs. The second and third terms are the penalty costs by the actual arriving of vehicle v to the node i earlier than the expected time and the penalty by the delay of the arriving time after the promised due time. These two last terms have impacts on the objective function provided that they are only positive. The last term is the jobs left at the end of the process. Note that w_1, w_2, w_3, and w_4 are the weights of those four terms in the objective function.

3.5 Appointment Times to eXternal Trucks

A port usually serves as an interface and temporary storage of containers between ocean and land. In this way the main functions are to receive outbound containers from customers for loading into vessels, and unload inbound containers from

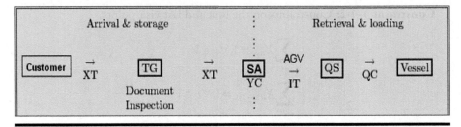

Figure 3.5   Flow of outbound containers (SA = storage area, QS = quayside).

vessels for picking up by consignees. The outbound containers are brought in by XTs. The inbound containers are also received by XTs. The problem here is to make appointment times for these XTs.

The flow of outbound containers is represented in Figure 3.5 [131]. These containers are brought in by customer's XTs into the terminal through the Terminal Gate **(TG)** where the containers and their documentations are checked. The TG then instructs the XT to go to the storage block where the container will be stored until the vessel arrives. The YC or RTGC working at that block removes the container from the XT and puts it in its storage position. When the time to load comes true, the YC removes the container from the stored position, puts it on an IT or AGV. Then, the IT or AGV carries the container to a QC for loading into the vessel. The flow of inbound containers is the reverse as depicted in Figure 3.6.

Murty et al. (2005) described a dispatching policy at the terminal gate [131]. According to their policy, the consecutive trucks are dispatched to different blocks in the storage yard, so that each block has adequate time to process the truck reaching it before the next truck is sent to this block. Also, the dispatching policy should distribute these trucks in all directions to ensure that the truck traffic on the roads is evenly distributed in all directions.

Froyland et al. (2008) considered the problem of operating a landside container exchange area. The problem is serviced by multiple semi-automated Rail Mounted Gantry Cranes (RMGs) that are moving on a single bi-directional traveling lane [45].

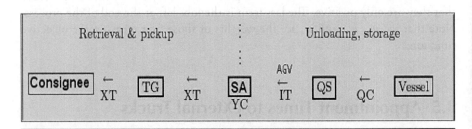

Figure 3.6   Flow of inbound containers (SA = storage area, QS = quayside).

The researchers proposed an integer programming-based heuristic consisting of three stages: (a) the scheduling of cranes; (b) the control of associated short-term container stacking; and (c) the allocation of delivery locations for trucks and other container transporters. The key components of the heuristic were a time scale decomposition, whereby an integer program controls decisions across a long time horizon to produce a balanced plan that is fed to a series of short time scale online subproblems, and a highly efficient space-time division of short-term storage areas. A computational evaluation showed that the heuristic can find effective solutions for the planning problem.

Asperen et al. (2011) use a discrete-event simulation model to evaluate the impact of an external truck announcement system on the performance of online container stacking rules [9]. The information contained in the announcement (the expected departure time for an import container) is used to schedule preemptive re-marshal moves. These moves can then be performed when the workload is low in order to decrease the export time and the crane workload at peak times. The researchers first test the impact of truck announcement with the reference algorithms (random stacking and leveling). To test the potential benefit of having more accurate information on the container departure time, they have run both algorithms without the truck announcement and with announcement a number of hours before the departure time. The actual announcement times are not fixed constants but drawn from a uniform distribution around the stated mean value (for the four hour announcements, the interval is between three and five hour). The results show that the departure announcement for containers that will be picked up by truck provides several benefits.

Phan and Kim (2016) study collaborative truck scheduling and appointments times for a couple of trucking companies and container terminals [118]. This study suggested a new appointment process by which trucking companies and terminals collaboratively determine truck operation schedules and truck arrival appointments. This study formulated a mathematical model involving a subproblem for each trucking company to determine the optimal dispatching schedules for trucks and the other subproblem for the terminal to estimate the expected truck system time in each time interval. An iterative collaboration process was proposed based on a decomposed mathematical formulation. The numerical experiments were conducted to investigate the performance of the decision process and the robustness of the process in practical operation conditions. The results conducted to evaluate the procedure's performance showed that the average computational time needed for each truck to construct an operational schedule was around 2.62 s per iteration, and the number of iterations (communications) between the terminal and each trucking company was 9.2 on average.

Table 3.5 summarizes the major research done over this decision, determining appointment times for external trucks. The table shows the researchers (year), modeling approach (algorithm), experimental data, and main results. As we can see in

Table 3.5   The Major Research Dedicated to the Decision of Appointment Times for External Trucks

Researchers (Year)	Modeling (Algorithm)	Experimental Data	Main Results
Murty et al. (2005)	A dispatching policy at the terminal gate (uniform probability among all those in the storage yard)	• One Gate • Samples collected from the Hong Kong Port	The dispatching policy should distribute the trucks in all directions to avoid traffic
Froyland et al. (2008)	Integer Programming Based heuristic consisting of three stages (CPLEX 10)	• One Gate • Truck arrivals for import containers are booked 24 hours in advance • For export containers, the time window starts with the arrival of the truck, and ends 12 hour before the ship arrives	The heuristic can find effective solutions for the planning problem
Asperen et al. (2011)	Discrete-Event Simulation Model (Java Programming language)	• One Gate • Arriving 139 and 736 containers during the 12 weeks of simulation	An average announcement time of 0.5–24 hours significantly improves the efficiency
Phan and Kim (2016)	Integer Programming (Iterative Procedure, Implemented in Java and CPLEX 12.6)	• Two companies with nine task groups from/to two yard blocks to/from customers during 16 time intervals of 15 min each	The average computational time needed for each truck to construct an operational schedule was around 2.62 s per iteration, and the number of iterations (communications) between the terminal and each trucking company was 9.2 on average

Table 3.5, only one gate is considered for the studies. In order to avoid congestion, we must consider several gates in our assumptions.

3.5.1 Assumptions

In order to make appointments for the XTs, we consider the following assumptions:

Assumption 3-5-1: According to Assumption 3-2-6, the inbound containers are stored in the storage area (secondary storage) before they are picked up by their consignees. Also it is assumed the outbound containers are stored in the storage area before they are loaded to the corresponding vessels.

Assumption 3-5-2: According to the definition of SSCPI and SSCGD in Section 3.2.1, they are inbound containers in the storage area waiting for pickup by consignees and outbound containers before being allocated to the storage area, respectively.

Assumption 3-5-3: The storage area has enough space to store all outbound containers in the planning horizon. Note the Storage Space Assignment (see Section 3.2.1) has considered this problem for the outbound containers.

Assumption 3-5-4: It is assumed that the container terminal has several gates for picking up the inbound containers and delivering the outbound containers. At each time period, only one pickup or one delivery is performed on a certain gate.

Assumption 3-5-5: We assume that the objective is to minimize interval time between picking up the inbound containers and delivering the bound containers.

Assumption 3-5-6: We assume that the containers are distributed among blocks in the storage area so that there are no Collision, Livelock, or Deadlock [153] problems while the XTs are carrying the containers. Note that to guarantee this assumption, we considered the dispatching policy presented at gates presented by Murty et al. [131] (see Assumption 3-2-3).

The following parameters are known at the beginning of the planning horizon:

N: The total number of SSCPI containers over the planning horizon.

M: The total number of SSCGD containers over the planning horizon.

$TSSCPI_i$: The time at which the SSCPI container i is placed into the secondary storage area after discharging from the ships.

TPG_i: The processing time of a container i, either the SSCPI or the SSCGD, to be picked up or delivered. It consists of unloading/loading time and gating time.

T: The number of time periods in the planning horizon. The time period has to be greater than the maximum of TPG_i, $i=1,2,...,M+N$.

G: The number of gates in the container terminal.

3.5.2 Decision Variables and Domains

The following decision variables are defined:

DT$_i$: Delivery time of the SSCGD container i to the port.
Domain (DT$_i$) = {1,2,...,T}
GD$_i$: The gate number to deliver the SSCGD container i to the port.
Domain (GD$_i$) = {1,2,...,G}
PT$_j$: Pickup time of the SSCPI container j from the port.
Domain (PT$_j$) = {1,2,...,T}
GP$_j$: The gate number to pick up the SSCPI container j from the port.
Domain (GP$_j$) = {1,2,...,G}

3.5.3 Constraints

Constraint 3-5-1: There is no conflict on a certain gate between the delivery time of the SSCGD containers and the pickup time of the SSCPI containers.

$$GD_i = GP_j \Leftrightarrow (DT_i + TPG_i \geq PT_j)\, OR\, (PT_j + TPG_j \geq DT_i);$$
$$for\ j = 1,2,...N;\ i = 1,2,..,M$$

Constraint 3-5-2: Any SSCPI container can be picked up after it is moved to the storage area.

$$PT_j \geq TSSCPI_j, for\ j = 1,2,...,N$$

Constraint 3-5-3: There is no conflict on a specific gate for a pickup or delivery, i.e., delivery time of any two SSCGD containers and pick up time of any two SSCPI containers on a certain gate are performed in a different time period.

$$GD_i = GD_{i'} \Leftrightarrow (DT_i + TPG_i \geq DT_{i'})\, OR\, (DT_{i'} + TPG_{i'} \geq DT_i);$$
$$for\ i,i' = 1,2,..,M, i \neq i'$$
$$GP_j = GP_{j'} \Leftrightarrow (PT_j + TPG_j \geq PT_{j'})\, OR\, (PT_{j'} + TPG_{j'} \geq PT_j);$$
$$for\ j,j' = 1,2,..,M, j \neq j'$$

3.5.4 Objective Function

The objective function of this decision is to minimize the terminal gate's cost. In fact, delivery of the outbound containers and pickup of the inbound containers should be carried out as soon as possible in the planning horizon. This function is written as follows:

$$MinCostGate = w_1 \sum_{i=1}^{N} DT_i + w_2 \sum_{i=1}^{M} PT_i$$

The first term is the sum of time periods spent on the delivery time of the outbound containers. The second term is the sum of time periods that is spend on pickup time of the inbound containers. Note that w_1 and w_2 are the weights of those two terms in the objective function.

3.6 Container Terminals over the World: A Survey

In this section, we summarized the latest research in some of the major container terminals in the world. Table 3.6 shows this summary. In the table, the first and second columns show the country and the port name. The third column shows decisions and solutions for the problem. The fourth column shows the researchers, year, and reference, respectively. From the table, we can observe that:

- **Observation 3-1:** Most of the container terminals considered their vehicle problems in the research. If the management can use the vehicles with full efficiency at minimum waiting and travelling times, the performance of the port is increased.
- **Observation 3-2:** There is a limited research with focus on the whole system. This observation shows that the decisions in container terminals are very complicated.

3.7 Summary and Conclusion

In this chapter, we systematically surveyed the literature over the problems and solutions in container terminals. After reviewing the literature for the five decisions, defined in Chapter 2, each decision was formulated as CSOPs. The latest researches around the decisions in some of the major container terminals have been summarized. From the summarized table (see Table 3.6), we observe that most container terminals have considered their vehicles in the research.

It is clear that any implementation of these decisions studied in this chapter requires additional studies where the assumptions should be refined and adapted with a particular container terminal.

Table 3.6   Container Terminals Around the World and Their Decisions

Country	Ports	Decisions (Solution Method)	Authors (year) [Ref. No]
Germany	(a) Port of Hamburg; (b) Port of Bremen	• Storage Space Allocation (MILP) • Generating Scenarios (Simulation) • Vehicle Scheduling (Evolutionary/Genetic Algorithms) • Whole System (Simulation)	Steenken et al. (2001) [176] Saanen et al. (2003) [165, 166] Hartman (2002) [63] Bose et al. (2000) [14] Liu et al. (2002) [109]
Italy	(a) Contship La Spezia; (b)Terminal in Genoa; (c) Port of Salerno	• Storage Space Allocation (Simulation) • Yard Storage Management (Integer Programming) • Whole System (Simulation)	Gambardella et al. (1998) [47] Amberosino et al. (2002) [6] Luca et al. (2013) [111]
Korea	Port of Pusan	• Berth Allocation (MILP) • Berth Allocation and Quay Crane Assigning (Lagrangian Relaxation, Dynamic Programming) • Dispatching of Automated Guided Vehicles (Linear Programming Relaxation)	Moon (2001) [126] Park and Kim (2003) [141] Wook and Hwan (2000) [203]
Netherlands	(a) Port of Rotterdam; (b) Port of Amsterdam	• Vehicle and Crane Scheduling, but its data has been collected by simulation (Branch-and-Bound/Beam Search Heuristic Method) • Deadlock prediction and avoidance (Wait and Proceed strategy) • Whole System (Simulation)	Meersman et al. (2001) [122] Saanen et al. (2003) [165, 166] Meersman et al. (2001) [123] Moorthy et al. (2003) [127] Liu et al. (2002) [109]
Singapore	Port of Singapore	• Routing AGVs (Sorting Techniques) • Whole System (Simulation) • Dispatching of Automated Guided Vehicles (Network Flow Model)	Qiu and Hsu(2000) [149] Liu et al. (2002) [109] Cheng et al. (2003) [25]

(Continued)

Table 3.6 Container Terminals Around the World and Their Decisions *(Continued)*

Country	Ports	Decisions (Solution Method)	Authors (year) [Ref. No]
USA	Port of Los Angeles	• Vehicle Scheduling and Routing (Dynamic Programming and Genetic Algorithms)	Ioannou et al. (2002) [80]
Hong Kong	Hong Kong Container Terminal No 9 (New)	• RTGC Deployment in the yard (Vogel Solution) • Storage Space Assignment and Vehicle Routing (Linear Programming) • Storage Space Allocation (Integer Programming) • Crane/RTGC Deployment in the yard (MILP and Lagrangian relaxation) • Whole System (Simulation)	Murthy et al. (2005) [127] Zhang et al. (2001) [214] Zhang et al. (2002) [215] Liu et al. (2002) [109]
China	Port of Dalian	• Integrated QCs, YCs, and AGVs (Simulation Optimization)	Zeng and Yang (2009) [213]
	Shanghai Yangshan Deep Water Port	• Optimization of Yard Cranes (Integer Programming)	Sha et al. (2017) [170]
	Qingdao Port	• Collaborative scheduling model for automated quayside cranes and AGVs (Two-Stage Tabu Search Algorithm)	Zhao et al. (2019) [219]
Turkey	Port of Izmir	• Container stacking optimization problem (Two dynamic strategies for stacking containers)	Güvena and Türsel (2014) [61]
Not Mentioned	Real Port	• Whole System (Multi-Agent System, Not Implemented)	Rebollo (2000) [161]
	Real Size Terminal	• Vehicle Scheduling (Heuristic Algorithm/ Lagrangian Relaxation) • Scheduling of Quay Cranes and Vehicles (Distributed-Agent System)	Zhang et al. (2002) [217] Thurston and Hu (2002) [182] Carrascosa et al. (2001) [18]

Table 5.6 Container Terminals Around the World and Their Decisions Confirmed

Chapter 4

Solutions to the Decisions: Review and Suggestions

In the previous chapter, we formulated the decisions in container terminals as Constraint Satisfaction Optimization Problems (CSOPs). To recapitulate, these decisions are:

- Allocation of berths to arriving vessels and Quay Cranes (QC) to docked vessels.
- Storage space assignment.
- Rubber Tyred Gantry Crane deployment.
- Scheduling and routing of vehicles.
- Appointment times to eXternal Trucks.

This chapter aims to discuss solution methods to the decisions. There are three main challenges associated with providing practical software for the decision-making: (a) simulating a container terminal, (b) selecting a design architecture, and (c) choosing appropriate solution methods. In this chapter, we address the first and second challenges and then classified the scheduling techniques. To address the third challenge, we do a survey on the solution methods to scheduling problems, in general. Then, we suggest two approaches for simulating container terminals and propose several frameworks for implementation. Finally, several indices are suggested for evaluation and monitoring any solutions for each of the decisions.

DOI: 10.1201/9781003308386-5

4.1 Simulation of Container Terminals

To study container terminals and their decisions, we propose to design a program to animate or simulate some operations in the terminal. The program will be very useful to evaluate different values for the parameters and to generate some input data for the next steps. In the problem specification, some operations or decisions should be synchronized to each other, if two or more decisions are likely to be studied together. For example, scheduling and routing of vehicles (the problem in Section 3.4) can be combined with the storage space assignment (the problem in Section 3.2). In the complex system, a few parameters should be considered in the integrated model to synchronize the decisions. Tsang (1998) suggested some methods to represent time and space [184].

Gambardella et al. (1998) [47], Hartman (2002) [63], as well as Thurston and Hu (2002) [182] applied some scenarios for simulation of terminal systems with several restrictions. Additionally, Kim et al. (2000) introduced a simulation-based test-bed to test various control rules. They suggested a control system consists of ship operation managers, system controllers for Automated Guided Vehicles (AGVs), automated Yard Crane, and QC [92]. Three control strategies, synchronization, postponement, and re-sequencing, were introduced in the paper as promising alternatives for controlling the traffic of vehicles.

Rizzoli et al. (1999) presented a simulation model for terminal resource allocation policies and ship loading/unloading policies that are obtained by means of Operations Research techniques [163]. During the research, the simulation model for a case study of La Spezia container terminal was designed, implemented, and validated. The results showed that the application of computer generated management policies could improve the performance of the terminal, making possible the allocation of fewer resources, and to better usage of the Yard Cranes.

Duinkerken and Ottjes (2000) implemented a simulation model for automated container terminals and applied their model to Delta Sealand container terminal of ECT Rotterdam [36]. Their objectives were to determine the sensitivity concerning a number of parameters like the number of AGVs, maximum AGV speed, crane capacity, and stack capacity. The authors concluded that the most critical performance indicators were the average number of moves per hour per QC, QC-utilization (percentage of time that the QCs are not waiting for AGVs), and the average trip duration ratio (the ratio between the actual duration of a trip divided by the technical trip time-Distance/Speed) and averaged over all connections between the stack and quay. Some experimental results were presented.

Another research group, Ioannou et al. (2001) proposed a microscopic simulation model [81]. In their paper an ACT (Automated Container Terminal) system was proposed. They collected data from a conventional terminal and simulated the ACT system for the same operational scenario in order to evaluate and compare their performances. A cost model was also developed to calculate the average cost per container. They assessed the performance of the model by throughput (moves per hour per QC), throughput per acre, annual throughput per acre (number of processed TEUs per acre per year), ship turnaround time, truck turnaround time, gate utilization, container dwell time, and the idle rate of equipment.

Carrascosa et al. (2001) designed an architecture of a distributed multi-agent system [18] for a real port. In the architecture, the research considered five agent classes: (a) ship agents: they control the ships loading and unloading sequence scheduling process; (b) stevedore agents: they manage the loading and unloading of all the ships docking in the port; (c) the service agents: they distribute the containers in the port; (d) the transtainer agents: they optimize the use of the vehicles in the port; and (e) gate agents: they handle the inbound and outbound containers to the land. To solve the configuration problem, the goal of the service agents is to maximize the stacking density in the yard, based on criteria such as, time, stack allocation conflicts, low stacking density, and so on. A preliminary version of the system is currently being developed and implemented, which models the functions of the port.

Ioannou et al. (2001) presented and simulated an Automated Container Terminal (ACT) [80, 82]. The ACT system is based on Automated Guided Vehicles (AGVs), Grid RAIL (GRAIL), and Automated Storage/Retrieval System (AS/RS). The main objective of the research was automation in improving terminal capacity and efficiency in the context of the agile port concept, in general, and to use of GRAIL, in particular. Based on future projections made by several ports, regarding container volume and the use of larger ships to be served at terminals as fast as possible, the research came up with design characteristics needs to meet the projected demand. During the research, a general layout of the ACT was designed with considering the interfaces of the storage yard with the ship, internal trucks, and trains as well as the desired storage capacity of the yard to meet the projected demand. The layout was such that different concepts regarding the storage yard and the container movements between the storage yard and the ship/truck/train buffers could be considered without major changes to the configuration of the ACT. During the research, a cost model was developed, and then the simulation was performed to compare several competitive concepts that include the GRAIL, AS/RS, and AGVs. The authors assessed the performance of the model by throughput (moves per hour per QC), throughput per acre, annual throughput per acre (number of processed TEUs per acre per year), ship turnaround time, truck turnaround time, gate utilization, container dwell time, and the idle rate of the equipment. The results indicated that the proposed GR-ACT system is an attractive solution for places where land is limited and expensive and high terminal productivity is required. Based on cost data found in the open literature and a base scenario considered for a conventional terminal, the average cost per container is about 60% less for the proposed GR-ACT system.

During the MARTHA project [182], Thurston and Hu (2002) implemented a multi- and distributed agent simulator for a virtual container terminal. The layout of the terminal (space, roads, and junctions) was modeled in grids, comprising cells.

The researchers proposed four different types of agents in the system: (a) the Quay Crane Agents (QCAs); (b) Straddle Carrier Agents (SCAs); (c) the Traffic Agents (TAs); and (d) the Area Manager Agent (AMA). Each QC is controlled by a QCA, each straddle carrier is controlled by an SCA, and each cell of the yard highway that contains more than one entry point, such as a crossing, is governed by a TA. The AMA agents represent the physical resources of the system and oversee the initial assignment of container jobs for any SCAs in the area it is in charge of. The current standard for fine-grained route-scheduling was developed. In this approach, which is known as the Plan Merging Paradigm (PMP), each straddle carrier is allowed to reserve resources. Each straddle carrier may reserve up to 'n' cells ahead of its route. In the project, the researchers adopt a strategy akin to the PMP. The research found that if 'n' is too small, a straddle carrier cannot reach its top speed, since it can only travel as fast as it can safely break in time before a crossing which it does not own (hence not necessarily clear). Conversely, if 'n' is too large, then the straddle carrier prohibits others from using the resource unnecessarily. However, even if 'n' is set to an optimum setting for the straddle carrier's capabilities, there is no notion of priority and thus a straddle carrier with a heavily constrained deadline might have to wait for a straddle carrier with ample time to reach its destination.

Liu et al. (2002) studied four automated container terminals, Port of Rotterdam, Port of Hamburg, Port of Hong Kong, and Port of Singapore, and then evaluated their operations by a simulation [109]. The simulation used future demand scenarios to design the characteristics of the terminals in terms of configuration, equipment, and operations. The authors developed a microscopic simulation model and used it to investigate several different terminal systems for the same operational scenario and evaluate their performance. During the research, the authors evaluated ship turnaround time, the throughput of terminals, gate utilization, idled time of Yard Crane and buffer cranes, dwelling times of containers, and the average cost of a container during the simulation time. The research found AGVs to be the most effective in terms of performance and cost. Additionally, the results indicated that automation could substantially improve the performance of terminals.

Hartmann (2002) developed an approach for generating realistic scenario data of port container terminals as input for simulation models, and testing optimization algorithms [63]. In the scenario, the research considered data concerning arrivals of ships, trains, and trucks within a time horizon and information about containers being delivered or picked up. In the developed software, the user can control various typical parameters. On the basis of statistics from a container terminal in the port of Hamburg, the simulation helped to improve the use of the block capacities in the yard.

Saanen et al. (2003) presented a simulation model to account for cost values of different types of equipment to be installed at a terminal [165, 166]. The simulation was performed in a case study for the layout of terminals in Hamburg and Rotterdam. The authors compared the productivity of equipment to handle container jobs when straddle carriers could be used instead of automated guided vehicles. One of the major results was that at a certain point adding further equipment could no longer increase productivity. The simulation also showed that if too many vehicles are blocking each other, productivity would have to decrease.

Valkengoed (2004) did a simulation to study how passing cranes influence yard operations in a container terminal [165]. The authors assumed that in a high-density storage yard, each block is served by two rail mounted gantry cranes. Using two cranes has the advantage that both sides of a block can be served at the same time with higher performance. But because they share the rails they hinder each other and each crane can only serve one particular side of the yard. During the research, two different configurations (the yard operations with and without passing cranes), were compared. The results found very little difference in performance for the two different configurations. The research also obtained results for an entire terminal where passing cranes were implemented, with AGVs transporting the containers between the quay-side and yard-side. Compared to the no passing cranes the research found the passing cranes, when the gain in flexibility is used, able to give a higher quay-side performance.

Zeng and Yang (2009) developed a simulation-optimization method for scheduling loading operations in container terminals [212]. The method integrates the intelligent decision mechanism of optimization algorithm and evaluation function of the simulation model. Its procedures are to initialize container sequence according to certain dispatching rules and then to improve the sequence through genetic algorithm, using the simulation model to evaluate the objective function of a given scheduling scheme. Meanwhile, a surrogate model based on a neural network is designed to predict objective function and filter out potentially bad solutions, thus decreasing the times of the running simulation model. The numerical tests show that the simulation-optimization method can solve the scheduling problem of container terminals efficiently and the surrogate model can improve the computation efficiency.

Luca et al. (2013) investigated the prediction reliability of two different approaches to container terminal simulation: microscopic and macroscopic [111]. The former simulating single container movement, the latter simulating container flow movement. The microscopic model was a discrete event simulation model; the macroscopic model was a dynamic discrete time-based (space-time) network assignment model. Both modeling approaches were implemented and compared taking advantage of some significant investment made by the Salerno Container Terminal (Italy) between 2005 and 2011. In particular, disaggregate (microscopic) and an aggregate (macroscopic) simulation models implemented in 2005 were validated with a large set of data acquired in 2011 after some structural and functional terminal modifications. Through this analysis it was possible to analyze the prediction reliability of both simulation approaches and to draw some operational guidelines.

In order to ameliorate the productivity in a confined space of container terminals, it is important to optimize the assignment of the existing distributed resources, such as the cranes, storage, vehicles, and routs inside terminals. Zhang et al. (2013) study how to run container terminals in the maximum productivity with minimum cost [216]. In this paper, given a P-time Petri Net model of a small or middle size port with repetitive and periodic operation process, the authors propose a method to adjust the initial setting of system's parameters to keep itself run with maximum productivity and minimum cost. Moreover, the necessities for changing the parameters of the resources are studied and a simple mathematical model to evaluate the cost of change is also proposed at the end of this paper.

Bohács et al. (2014) make an overview of container terminal processes and related optimization models [12]. In the overview, a simulation-based model for intermodal systems is presented. Upon the drawn conclusions from the surveyed papers, a novel simulation model is described. The model enables applicability of adaptive and intelligent methods and enables optimization of the certain modules and the whole model as well. Within the model, the authors propose implementation of behavior-based control with several modules. The modules continuously observe behavioral-states of the other modules and change their own behavioral-state if necessary. These methods are widely used at other areas of intelligent computing and each module may work in various operational modes. The proposed simulation model was implemented in Simul8 logistic simulation software environment.

4.2 Selecting an Architecture

To study the decisions in Chapter 3, the second challenge is related to design architecture for the system. Two distinct systems architectures including **Centralized system** and **Distributed system** have been suggested by Thurston and Hu (2002) [182]; the latter was implemented by agents. For the first architecture, Tsang (1993) provided different solutions to satisfy the constraints of every Constraint Satisfaction Problem (CSP) [185]. The solutions are divided into four groups, including problem reduction, complete search methods, stochastic method, and synthesis of the solutions. For the distributed system, Yokoo et al. (1998) formalized the Distributed Constraint Satisfaction Problem [206]. They also developed asynchronous backtracking, asynchronous weak-commitment search solutions, distribution breakout, and distributed consistency algorithms for these kinds of problem [207].

Bontempi et al. (1997) presented a modular architecture for a decision support system to improve the management of intermodal container terminals [13]. The researchers developed the architecture for La Spezia container terminal and implemented it as an integrated system, comprising of a forecasting model, a planner, and a simulation module. While the forecasting module estimated container traffic, the planner module used this information to generate efficient policies for storage, resource allocation, and scheduling. The design had two hierarchies of classes: (a) terminal components and (b) management policies. The terminal components were objects such as vehicles, cranes, and yard areas. The management policies were classified into resource allocation, container storage in the yard, and ship loading/unloading scheduling. The performance of management policies was assessed via computer simulation. Genetic algorithms, Taboo search, and dynamic programming techniques were used to implement management policies. Moreover, some experimental results were provided.

Moreover, multi-agent architecture has been used to solve scheduling problems. Cowling et al. (2004) presented a multi-agent system and used it as a case study for integrated dynamic scheduling of steel milling and casting [32]. In the system, a set of heterogeneous agents was used to integrate and optimize a range of scheduling objectives related to different processes of steel production and could adapt to changes in the environment while still achieving overall system goals. In other papers [138, 139], Quelhadj et al. (2003, 2005) described a negotiation protocol in the multi-agent system. The purpose of that protocol was to allow the agents to cooperate and coordinate their actions in order to find globally near-optimal robust schedules, while minimizing the disruption caused by the occurrence of unexpected real-time events.

In another research, Kocifaj (2014) worked on modeling container terminals using two-layer agent architecture [97]. This is based on utilization of agent-based architecture ABAsim for the creation of two-layer agent model of container terminal operation that reflects the hierarchical structure of the modeled system. ABAsim is mainly developed for simulation of large service systems [96]. The approach presented is different particularly in utilization of two-layer agent-based architecture with hierarchical structure of managing agents, exclusive message communication between agents, and support for microscopic modeling. A brief description of all employed model agents and their mutual cooperation and communication is provided. The presented model has been successfully implemented and integrated into Villon, which is an existing transportation terminal simulation tool.

4.3 Classification of Scheduling Methods

In this section, we classify scheduling methods. Generally, scheduling is a type of resource and task allocation problem that is performed over time. In scheduling decisions in container terminals, the sources include berths, QCs, Yard Cranes, vehicles, storage space, and so on that must be allocated to the container jobs. Different scheduling techniques are employed for both centralized and distributed systems that are used for proper utilization of these resources and for improving system performance. In this section, we classified the solution methods for scheduling decisions. Few research were focused on classification of scheduling methods [98, 186, 189]. In this section, based on the research by Tyagi and Gupta (2018) [189], we classified the scheduling methods as follows:

■ **Local versus Global:** Local scheduling decides the appropriate set of container jobs to be handled next by a resource. Global scheduling is done before local scheduling and is used to allocate the resources within the system to the container jobs. A new concurrency control criterion is proposed for local and flexible transactions execution through global scheduling in heterogeneous distributed environment. Local scheduler requires global information for maximizing the performance of system.

■ **Static versus Dynamic:** Static algorithms are used for scheduling when information available at the beginning time and the problem doesn't change during the process. On the other hand, dynamic algorithm takes all factors and changes of problems into account during execution time.

■ **Optimal versus Suboptimal:** Optimal techniques provide a global solution for the problems. Suboptimal techniques provide a local optimum solution for the problems.

■ **Distributed versus Centralized:** In centralized algorithms, one unit handles the problem of resource allocation. In the distributed algorithm, on the other hand, all subsystems decide how resources are allocated.

■ **Approximate versus Heuristic:** Heuristic algorithms use various guidelines for scheduling such as allocate jobs to a resource with heavy inter-task communication, while approximate algorithms use the same method that is used by optimal solutions but within an accepted range.

■ **Cooperative versus Non-cooperative:** In non-cooperative algorithms, each resource is independent of making choices from other resources for scheduling, while in the cooperative, all resources coordinate with each other to achieve a goal.

This classification can be used for categorizing different types of solutions that are employed for allocating different resources to jobs and also they are useful for consideration in choosing between major scheduling techniques.

4.4 Frameworks for Optimization and Scheduling Problems

Several frameworks can be used to tackle optimization and scheduling problems. Some well-known software such as GAMS (Generalized Algebraic Modeling System), LINDO (Linear INteger and Discrete Optimizer), and others can be used to solve the problems. Another framework is ILOG Solver since a lot of the classical, heuristic and meta-heuristic approaches have been used in their components library [78]. The components of ILOG Optimization Suite rely on mathematical programming and constraint-based optimization. A core of a large number of successfully deployed applications was provided in ILOG. In addition, it is the most comprehensive portfolio of optimization components for efficient resource allocation, involved in scheduling and planning of resource utilization.

Moreover, Voβ (2000) provided high-quality solutions to important applications in business, engineering, economics, and science in reasonable time-horizons [196]. A family of meta-heuristic search methods including simple Local Search,

Adaptive Memory Procedures, Tabu Search, Ant System, Greedy Randomized Adaptive Search, Variable Neighborhood Search, Evolutionary Methods, Genetic Algorithms, Scatter Search, Neural Network, Simulated Annealing, and their hybrid have been presented briefly in the study. Also, important references for solving combinatorial optimization problems have been provided in this research.

Fink and Voβ (2002) surveyed, designed, and implemented HOTFRAME [42], a Heuristic OpTimization FRAMEwork that provides reusable software components in the meta-heuristics domain. The framework architecture, which has been implemented by C++, defined the collaborations among software components, in particular with respect to the interface between meta-heuristic components and problem-specific components. Also in this framework, different applications have been considered. The scope of HOTFRAME comprises meta-heuristic solutions such as iterated Local Search, Simulated Annealing method and its variations, different kinds of Tabu Search (e.g. static, strict, and reactive), Evolutionary Algorithms, Candidate Lists, Neighborhood Depth variations, and Pilot Method [42, 196]. The primary design objectives of HOTFRAME have provided run-time efficiency and a high degree of flexibility with respect to adaptations and extensions. Then, their developers built generic meta-heuristic components, which are parameterized by some concepts such as the solution space, the neighborhood structure, or Tabu-criteria. Note that in C++, generic components can be implemented as template classes or a function, which enables achieving abstraction without loss of efficiency.

Furthermore, hyper-heuristic framework emerged to solve scheduling problems. Burke et al. (2003) defined hyper-heuristic ideas based on the heuristic approach [16]. The main motivations behind the development of the hyper-heuristic were to automate scheduling methods and to raise the level of generality. They suggested a framework for the hyper-heuristic and investigated it on various instances of two distinct timetabling and rostering problems. In the framework, heuristics compete using rules based on the principles of reinforcement learning. A Tabu list of heuristics was also maintained which prevented certain heuristics from being chosen at certain times during the search. In another paper [90], Kendall and Hussin (2005) investigated a Tabu search-based hyper-heuristic for solving examination timetabling problems. They claimed that their approach can produce good quality solutions.

In some situations when a scheduling problem is dealing with imprecision and uncertainty, frameworks of fuzzy sets are employed. Petrovic and Fayad (2004) described a fuzzy Shifting Bottleneck Procedure (SBP) hybridized with a genetic algorithm for a real-world job-shop scheduling problem [145]. In each iteration, the SBP selects a machine and the genetic algorithm proposed a sequence of job operations to be processed on that machine. In another paper, Petrovic et al. (2005) proposed an algorithm for a real-world job shop-scheduling problem, where both lot-sizing and batching processes were considered [146]. A fuzzy rule-based system was developed for determining lot sizes, where the input variables were workload on the shop floor, size of the job, and urgency. A fuzzy multi-objective genetic algorithm was developed to generate schedules of jobs whose processing times and due dates were imprecise and modeled by using fuzzy sets. A genetic algorithm took into consideration the determined size of lots for jobs and considered batching together jobs of similar characteristics in order to reduce the required setup time. The objectives considered were to minimize average tardiness, number of tardy jobs, setup times, idle times of machines, and throughput times of jobs.

Another framework is based on Radio Frequency Identification (RFID) that has a widespread application, in reality, involved in scheduling problems. Ma et al. (2014) present a novel optimization algorithm, namely, Hierarchical Artificial Bee Colony optimization (HABC), to tackle the RFID Network Planning (RFINP) problem [114]. The authors proposed a multilevel model, in which the higher-level species can be aggregated by the subpopulations from a lower level. In the lower level, each subpopulation employing the canonical ABC method searches the part-dimensional optimum in parallel. A complete solution is constructed for the upper level. In this paper, the comprehensive learning method with crossover and mutation operators is applied to enhance the global search ability between species. The experiments are conducted on a set of ten benchmark optimization problems. The results demonstrate that the proposed HABC obtains remarkable performance on most chosen benchmark functions. Then HABC is employed for solving the real-world RFINP problem on a couple of instances with different scales. The simulation results show that the proposed algorithm is superior for solving RFINP, in terms of optimization accuracy and computation robustness.

To sum up the major solution methods in the frameworks, for solving scheduling problems, we provided a comparative, as shown in Table 4.1. The methods have been divided into three groups, including considerations in choosing between the major scheduling techniques. The first group consists of the methods for Simplex Method, Dijkstra, Branch-and-Bound, and Branch-and-Cut. They are being studied extensively in Operation Research and find global or optimal solutions for the problems. The second group consists of Hill Climbing, Tabu Search, Simulated Annealing and Genetic Algorithm, and some other techniques. They have been studied in Artificial Intelligence and can find local or suboptimal solutions for the problems, i.e., they do not guarantee that a globally optimal solution can be found. In fact, they provide a sufficiently good solution to an optimization problem, especially with incomplete or imperfect information or limited computation capacity. In the third group, we consider neural networks, GEneral NEural SImulation System (GENESIS), connectionism, expert systems, fuzzy systems, agent systems, and micro-application layer traffic optimization (ALTO) method. Most of these techniques work on some decision rules to find a better solution or improve the current solution for the problems. They are approximate techniques and can work in cooperative or non-cooperative fashion.

Table 4.1 Major Solutions in the Frameworks with Considerations for Choosing

Category	Major Solution Methods	General Considerations	Major Technique-Specific Considerations
Global / Optimal Techniques	Simplex	• Find the optimal solutions • Intractable	• Problem must be specified in the standard forms, by a set of inequalities and objective function
	Dijkstra, Network Simplex	• Find the optimal solutions • Intractable	• Problem must be presented by a graph
	Branch-and-Bound, Branch-and-Cut	• Used for optimization • Intractable	• Requires heuristic for pruning • Ordering of branches is important
Heuristic / Local / Suboptimal Techniques	Hill Climbing, Gradient Descent, Sweep, Matching-Based Savings, Chain-Exchange, Local Search, Adaptive Memory Procedures, Greedy Randomized Adaptive Search, Scatter Search, Variable Neighborhood Search	• Search attempt to escape from local optimal • Useful for both constraint satisfaction and optimization when near-optimal solutions are acceptable • Flexible in computation time, this makes them widely useful	• Requires a neighborhood function which is crucial to its effectiveness • Effectiveness mainly depends on strategy on Tabu-list manipulation • Representation is crucial • Effectiveness could be sensitive to choice of parameters values and operators
	Genetic Algorithms, Simulated Annealing, Tabu Search, Artificial Bee Colony, Ant Colony	• Useful for finding near-optimal solutions • Requires non-trivial time, but hopefully will search a wider part of the solution space	• Representation is crucial. • Effectiveness could be sensitive to choice of parameter values and operators • Cooling schedule could be important

(Continued)

Table 4.1 Major Solutions in the Frameworks with Considerations for Choosing *(Continued)*

Category	Major Solution Methods	General Considerations	Major Technique-Specific Considerations
Approximate/ Cooperative/ Non-Cooperative Techniques	Neural Networks, Connectionisms, GENESIS	• Useful for satisfiability problems or for finding near optimal solutions • Good potential for parallel implementation which may suit real time application	• Setup and network updating mechanism are crucial to its effectiveness • Specialized network may be expensive to build
	Expert Systems, Agent Systems, Fuzzy Systems, ALTO	• Wide range of applicability can be tailor-made to meet the requirements (including time and optimality requirement) • Power comes from domain-specific knowledge	• Expert knowledge elicitation is important and may be difficult • Conflict resolution may be non-trivial

4.5 Solution Methods for Vehicle Problems, Developed before 2000

In this section, we provided a survey on solution methods, associated to scheduling and routing vehicles, developed before 2000. To review these solution methods, Gunadi et al. (2002) studied different types of problems and solutions to the vehicle routing problem [56]. They classified the solutions into three groups: Operations Research algorithms, Artificial Intelligence techniques, and Decision Support System solutions. Table 4.2 summarized their studies.

In another research, Qiu et al. (2002) provided a survey of scheduling and routing algorithms for AGVs that developed before 2000 [153]. They showed similarities and differences between scheduling and routing AGVs and related problems like the vehicle routing problem, the shortest-path problem, and the scheduling problem. They classified algorithms in groups for general path topologies, path optimization, specific path topologies, and dedicated scheduling algorithms.

In the general path topologies, the methods adopted have been classified into three categories:

1. Static methods, where an entire path remains occupied until a vehicle completes the tour.
2. Time-window-based methods, where a path segment may be used by different vehicles during different time-windows.
3. Dynamic methods, where the utilization of any segment of path is dynamically determined during routing rather than before routing as in cases (a) and (b).

In the path optimization, the methods have been classified into three categories:

4. Zero/one integer programming model, where the path layout problem is as a binary integer programming model with considerations of the given facility layout and Pickup/Delivery stations.
5. Intersection graph method, where only a reduced subset of nodes in path network is considered and only intersection nodes are used to find the optimal for solving AGV.
6. Integer LP model, where the problem is modeled as an Integer linear programming of selecting the path and location of Pickup/Delivery stations.

In the specific path topologies, the three different layouts could be considered as Linear, Circle, Mesh topology, S-Layout, and L-Layout.

Tables 4.3–4.5 summarize the most important research done before the twenty-first century. These tables show that the routing algorithms for specific path topologies usually have relatively lower computational complexity compared with those for general path topology. Moreover, routing algorithms for specific path topologies are relatively more feasible than those for general path topology. Additionally, the routing algorithms for dynamic routing problems cannot guarantee optimality.

Table 4.2 Summary of Vehicle Routing Problems and Solutions, before 2000. See [156].

Classifications	Solutions & Authors (Year)	Application	Characteristics
Operation Research Algorithms	Sweep Algorithm: Gillet & Miller (1971)	• Goods delivery vehicle • Public bus with capacity constraint	• Minimum total length of route is a major concern • Additional distance may occur • Demand is uncertain
	Matching Based Savings Algorithm: Desrochers & Verhoog (1990)	• Goods delivery vehicle	• Solving fleet size and mix vehicle • Short distance is a major concern
	Chain Exchange Principle: Fahrion & Wrede (1990)	• Goods delivery vehicle • Vehicle routing problem with time windows	• Number of customers is known • Time constraint is a major concern
	Branch-and-Bound Algorithm: Laporte et al. (1992)	• Shortest-Path Problem and goods delivery	• Short distance is a major concern • Focuses on the minimum number of visits
	New Crossover: Uchimura & Sakaguchi (1995)	• Shortest round trip tour	• Short distance and time constraint
	Parallel Branch-and-Bound Algorithm: Lau & Kumar (1997)	• Vehicle routing problem on Networks of Workstation	• Minimum total distance for goods delivery
	Dijkstra Method: Ikeda et al. (1994)	• Shortest-Path Problem	• Short distance is a major concern • All-directional approach
	Modified Dijkstra Method: Eklund et al. (1996)	• Emergency service vehicles routing	• Shortest path is the main concern
	Tabu Search : Taillard et al. (1996)	• Shortest-Path Problem • One depot VRP	• Short distance is a major concern • Number of customers is known

(Continued)

Table 4.2 Summary of Vehicle Routing Problems and Solutions, before 2000. See [156]. (Continued)

Classifications	Solutions & Authors (Year)	Application	Characteristics
	Tabu Search : Garcia et al. (1993)	• VRP with time windows constraint	• Solving VRP with time windows constraint • Demand is known.
	A* Algorithm	• Shortest-Path Problem	• Shortest distance is a major concern
	2-opt* Exchange: Potvin & Rousseau (1995)	• VRP with time windows • Best implemented for travelling salesman problem	• Time constraint is a major concern
	Or-opt-1 & Or-opt exchange	• Goods delivery vehicle	• Focus on node exchange • Number of customer is known
Artificial Intelligence Techniques	GENESIS: Thangiah & Gubbi (1993)	• Goods delivery vehicle	• Demand is known
	Niche Search: Pedroso et al. (1998)	• Goods delivery vehicle	• Route is selected based on time average
	Bimodal Dial-A-Ride: Liaw et al. (1996)	• Paratransit vehicle routing	• Involves transit between a paratransit vehicle and a fixed bus route
Decision Support System Solutions	Micro-ALTO: Potvin et al. (1994)	• Goods delivery vehicle	• Concerns on minimum operational cost, service quality, and service time
	Fuzzy-neural approach: Takahashi et al. (1995);	• In-vehicle route guidance system	• Route selection based on driver's preference
	Fuzzy Route Choice: Shaout et al. (1993), Pang et al. (1995)	• Automotive Navigation System, Dynamic Route Guidance	• Route selection based on driver behavior

Table 4.3   Summary of Algorithms for AGVs in General Path Topologies, before 2000. See [153].

Authors (Year)	Problems Solved	Basic Algorithms	Path Topologies	Path Direction	Advantages	Disadvantages
Gaskins & Tanchoco (1987)	Path optimization to minimize total distance traveled by loaded vehicles	Zero-one integer programming	General	Uni-directional	Very easy to implement for a fleet of AGVs with the same origins and destinations	Conflicts may occur when there are AGVs with different origins and destinations; heavy computation; low system throughput
Kaspi & Tanchoco (1990)	Path optimization to minimize total distance traveled by loaded vehicles	Zero-one integer programming; branch-and-bound	General	Uni-directional	An improvement of the approach in Gaskins & Tanchoco (1987); reduced computation; optimality guaranteed	Distance traveled by unloaded AGVs is not considered; low system throughput; still heavy computation
Goetz & Egbelu (1990)	Path optimization to minimize total distance traveled by loaded and unloaded vehicles	Integer linear programming	General	Uni-directional	Problem size is reduced; distance traveled by unloaded vehicles is considered together; optimality is hence better ensured	Routing control and vehicle number are not considered in the study which are important for AGV systems
Sinriech & Tanchoco (1991)	Path optimization to minimize total distance traveled by loaded and unloaded vehicles	Intersection Graph Method; Branch-and-bound	General	Uni-directional	An improved model of that proposed in Kaspi & Tanchoco (1990); reduced number of problem branches; optimality guaranteed	Only intersection nodes of the path network are considered; optimal solutions may be missed

Table 4.4 Summary of Algorithms for AGVs in Specific Path Topologies, before 2000. See [153].

Authors (Year)	Problems Solved	Basic Algorithms	Path Topologies	Path Direction	Advantages	Disadvantages
Tanchoco & Sinriech (1992)	Optimizing the path layout configuration in a closed single circle	Integer programming	Closed single-circle	Uni-directional	Routing control is very easy; no conflicts or deadlocks will occur; easy for implementation	Low system throughput; only suitable for small system
Lin & Dgen (1994)	Routing AGVs among several non-overlapping closed circles; finding shortest travel time path	The task-list time-window algorithm	Multi-circle	Bi-directional or Uni-directional	Easy for routing control since every circle is served by a single vehicle	Low system throughput; additional cost needed for transit device between two adjacent circles; indirect transportation may cause delay
Sinriech & Tanchoco (1994)	Routing AGVs among several non-overlapping path segments; finding shortest travel time path	Integer programming	Segmented path topology	Bi-directional or Uni-directional	An alternative design of that in Lin & Dgen (1994); relatively low value of flow's distance	Low system throughput with one vehicle serving in a segment; additional cost for transit device; indirect transportation may cause delay
Hsu & Huang (1994)	Route planning for basic routing functions on several specific basic path topologies	Not Mentioned	Linear array, ring, H-tree, star, 2D-mesh, n-cube, cube-connected cycles, complete graph	Bi-directional	Gives the time and space complexities for basic routing functions which are upper-bounded by $O(n^2)$ and $O(n^3)$ respectively	Routing control not given in detail; the assumption of arbitration capability for every buffer is too idealized

Table 4.5   Summary of Static and Dynamic Routing Algorithms for AGVs in General Path Topology, before 2000. See [153].

Category	Authors (Year)	Problems	Path Direction	Basic Algorithms	Advantages	Computational Complexity
Static Routing Problem	Broadbent et al. (1985)	Finding conflict-free shortest time routes for AGVs	Bi-directional	Dijkstra's Shortest Path Algorithm	Easy to execute	$O(N^2)$ (Average Case)
	Daniels (1988)	Finding conflict-free shortest time routes for AGVs	Bi-directional	Partitioning Shortest Path Algorithm	Easy to execute and faster than Broadbent's	$O(N \times A)$ (Average Case)
	Huang et al. (1989)	Finding conflict-free shortest time routes for AGVs	Bi-directional	Labeling Algorithm	Time windows are used for every node; the utilization of path segments is increased	$O((N + A)^2 \text{Log} (N + A))$ (Average Case)
	Kim & Tanchoco (1991, 1993)	Finding conflict-free shortest time routes for AGVs	Bi-directional	Dijkstra's Shortest Path Algorithm; Conservative Myopic Strategy	Easy to execute and control; fast	$O(V^4 \times N^2)$ (Worst Case)
Dynamic Routing Problem	Taghaboni & Tanchoco (1995)	Finding a conflict-free route for AGVs	Bi-directional & Uni-directional	Incremental Route Planning	Relatively fast in routing decision	Not Available; No Guaranteed Optimality
	Langevin et al. (1996)	Integrated solution for AGV dispatching, conflict-free routing and scheduling	Bi-directional	Dynamic Programming	Easy to execute and control	Not Available; Not Guaranteed Optimality

N—The number of nodes in the path network; A—The number of arcs in the path network; V—The number of AGVs

From Tables 4.3 to 4.5, we can observe that:

- **Observation 4-1:** All of the algorithms for both static and dynamic scheduling of AGVs are developed for moving the vehicles in bi-directional path.
- **Observation 4-2:** The solutions for dynamic routing algorithms don't guarantee Optimality.
- **Observation 4-3:** The main advantages of most algorithms are easy to execute and control the AGVs.
- **Observation 4-4:** In static scheduling of AGVs, the problem is to finding conflict-free shortest time routes for AGVs.

4.6 Solution Methods for Vehicle Problems, Developed in the Twenty-First Century

As one of the enabling technologies, scheduling and routing of AGVs have attracted considerable attentions in the twenty-first century. Rashidi and Tsang (2005) used a simple network algorithm as a solution to the problem of scheduling AGVs [154]. They formulated the problem as a model of minimum flow cost, and to solve the problem, the simple network algorithm and its extensions as a complete algorithm that finds the overall optimal solution, and the greedy search algorithm as an incomplete algorithm that finds the optimal local solution. Produces presented. In this research, the results of a complete algorithm for large size problems and an incomplete algorithm for small size problems are reported. Rashidi and Tsang also studied the issue of dynamic AGVs in 2011 [158].

Lau and Zhao (2008) introduced an integrated schedule for managing the equipment of automated container terminals [103]. They formulated the problem with a mixed planning model. In this model, various constraints related to integrated operations between different types of transport equipment are considered. To solve the problem, he has presented a multi-layered genetic algorithm to create an almost optimal solution and an improved innovative algorithm to reduce the complexity of the calculations.

Zeng and Yang (2009) examined the issue of planning loading operations at expanded container terminals [213]. They proposed a neural network-based model for the problem and reduced the model run time by filtering out bad solutions. In this way, they combined an intelligent decision mechanism with an optimization algorithm. Numerical experiments show that the hybrid optimization method can effectively solve the problem of scheduling container terminals. In addition, the alternative model can improve the performance of simulation optimization calculations.

Rashidi (2010) proposed a schedule for single-capacity and multi-capacity AGVs at container terminals [157]. This problem is formulated as an optimization problem and satisfying the limitations. To solve the problem, a combined method of simple network algorithm and simulated refrigeration algorithm is used. In this algorithm, first, the problem for the monovalent AGV is solved with a simple network algorithm and the answer is considered as a suitable initial solution for the simulated refrigeration algorithm.

Gudelj et al. (2012) modeled the problem of optimizing and routing AGVs using the Petri net and solved the problem by combining the genetic algorithm with an MRF1 class of the Petri net [54]. The purpose of this is to specify a set of machines to improve the efficiency of a system and reduce the latency of loading and unloading of containers under restrictions such as priority and congestion. In addition, the ultimate goal is to optimize process time and minimize the number of AGVs to increase system power.

Fazlollahtabar et al. (2012) studied Tandem Automated Guided Vehicle (TAGV) configurations as material handling devices and optimizing the production time [40]. The authors consider effective time parameters in a flexible automated manufacturing system (FAMS) using Monte Carlo simulation. Due to different configurations of TAGVs in a FAMS, the material handling activities are performed. With respect to various stochastic time parameters and the TAGV defects during material handling processes, sample data are collected and their corresponding probability distributions are fitted. Using the probability distributions, a model of the TAGV material handling problem is made and solved via Monte Carlo simulation. The effectiveness of the proposed model is illustrated in a case study.

Fazlollahtabar and Saidi (2013) discussed literature related to different methodologies to optimize AGV systems for the two significant problems of scheduling and routing at manufacturing, distribution, transhipment, and transportation systems [41]. The authors categorize the methodologies into mathematical methods (exact and heuristics), simulation studies, meta-heuristic techniques, and artificial intelligence-based approaches.

Kim et al. (2013) presented a multi-objective strategy to improve the performance of AGVs in automated container terminals [93]. A criteria employed by the strategy were carefully devised so that the enforcement of the strategy can lead to achieving two objectives, minimization of the delay of QCs and minimization of empty travel by AGVs. Optimization of the strategy was done by using a multi-objective evolutionary algorithm (MOEA) to obtain a set of Pareto optimal strategies. When dispatching AGVs, the research can apply any strategy from this set depending on which objective is more important than the other at that moment. Since the evaluation of a strategy during the search requires a computationally expensive simulation, it becomes inaccurate unless done thoroughly.

Zhicheng et al. (2014) studied allocation container transporting works among Automated Lifting Vehicles (ALV) in container terminals [221]. The author presented a real-time dispatching method, consisting of an allocation model for instantaneous ALV dispatching. In the model, a set of events trigger a new instantaneous dispatching. A modified Hungarian Algorithm is applied to solve the instantaneous dispatching model. It is verified that the modified algorithm outperforms the original one, even CPLEX, in solving these allocation problems.

Umar et al. (2015) investigated the issue of dynamic scheduling and routing of work and AGVs in a flexible production system [190]. They proposed a hybrid genetic algorithm to solve the problem. This algorithm produced an integrated schedule and route details. They also used a fuzzy expert system to control genetic operators by improving the overall performance of the two-generation population. Computational experiments on algorithms developed in MATLAB environment confirmed the feasibility and effectiveness of all solutions.

Li et al. (2018) examined the issue of route planning for AGVs [105]. To solve the issue, they proposed an ant colony algorithm based on the pheromone blunt coordinates. To evaluate the accuracy and efficiency of the proposed method, it was compared with three other methods. The numerical simulation results showed the superiority of the proposed algorithm

Murakami (2020) studied a time-space network model for conflict-free routing problem of a capacitated AGV system [128]. This research formulated the problem as mixed integer linear programming (MILP) and proposed a new approach known as dispatch and conflict-free routing problem of a capacitated AGV system (DCFRPC). This research also considered the splitting and merging of some materials (tasks) in the DCFRPC. A valid inequality was added into the MILP formulation to shorten the computation time. The model and formulation can obtain optimal solutions to most of the instances in a previous study.

Zhong et al. (2020) combined the two issues of integrated scheduling of container terminal equipment and multivariate AGV interference without interference [222]. They formulated the problem by mixed integer programing model with the aim of minimizing the latency of AGVs based on integrated scheduling, optimal route, and elimination of interference and congestion. To solve the problem, they proposed a hybrid genetic-particle swarm algorithm with fuzzy logic. Dynamic simulation of path nodes showed that the proposed model could solve the problem of interference and congestion of AGVs and is applicable to existing container terminals.

Tables 4.6 and 4.7 summarize the major research that has been done on the static and dynamic routing of AGVs in container terminals during the twenty-first century, respectively.

From the tables, we can observe that:

- **Observation 4-5:** Most of the algorithms for static scheduling of AGVs are uni-directional.
- **Observation 4-6:** Almost all solutions for dynamic routing algorithms don't guarantee Optimality.
- **Observation 4-7:** The major research, done in recent years, considered conflict-free routing problem for the AGVs in container terminals.

Table 4.6 Summary of Algorithms for Static Scheduling of AGVs, since 2000

Authors (Year)	Problems Solved	Basic Algorithms	Path Topologies	Path Direction	Advantages	Disadvantages
Grunow et al. (2004)	Optimizing Path Layout Configuration	Mixed Integer Linear Programming (MILP)	Closed Single Circle	Uni-directional	Performance of MILP is almost the same as priority rule for small layout	Low system throughput; only suitable for small system
Zeng and Yang (2009)	Minimize the makespan	Combination of Rules with Genetic Algorithm	Mesh-Like Path Topology	Uni-directional	Involves various kinds of equipment (QCs, YCs, YTs) simultaneously	Deal with complex constraints in scheduling model
Rashidi and Tsang (2011)	Minimize Total Distance Traveled and Total Waiting Time of AGVs	Network Simplex And Network Simplex Plus	General, Point to Point	Uni-directional	Produce optimal solution; optimality guaranteed	Time-consuming to rebuild the graph in dynamic problem
Fazlollahtabar et al. (2012)	Scheduling problem of tandem automated guided vehicle (TAGV) configurations	Monte Carlo Simulation	Closed Circle	Uni-directional	Considers effective time parameters in a flexible automated manufacturing system	Deals with probability distributions

(Continued)

Table 4.6 Summary of Algorithms for Static Scheduling of AGVs, since 2000 (Continued)

Authors (Year)	Problems Solved	Basic Algorithms	Path Topologies	Path Direction	Advantages	Disadvantages
Gudelj et al. (2012)	Optimize process time and minimize the number of AGVs	Combination genetic algorithm with an MRF1 class of the Petri net	Closed Circle	Uni-directional	Modularity and simplicity of the proposed approach	Solutions Are Local; Only Suitable for Small System
Kim et al. (2013)	Minimization of QC Delay and Minimization of Empty Travel By AGVs	Multi-Objective Evolutionary Algorithm (MOEA)	Linear	Uni-directional	A Strategy to Make a Dispatching Decision Based on a Set of Criteria	Solutions Are Local; Only Suitable for Small System
Rashidi (2014)	Minimize Total Distance Traveled and Total Waiting Time of AGVs	Dynamic Network Simplex and Dynamic Network Simplex Plus	General, Point to Point	Uni-directional	Produce optimal solution; optimality guaranteed	Needs memory management; adding, removing, and updating nodes and arcs
Li et al. (2018)	AGVs Path Planning Based on Bloch Coordinates of Pheromones	Ant Colony Algorithm	Linear and Mesh-Like Path Topology	Uni-directional	Balance the Search Accuracy and Speed, and Obtain the Shortest Paths With Safe Space–Time Distances Among AGVs	Low System Throughput; Only Suitable for Small System

Table 4.7 Summary of Dynamic Routing Algorithms for AGVs, since 2000

Authors (Year)	Problems	Path Direction	Basic Algorithms	Advantages	Disadvantages
Qiau and Hsu (2001)	Routing AGVs concurrently without congestion and conflicts	Linear and mesh-like path topology	Grouping AGVs, Routing Rules	Continuously schedule AGVs for achieving a batch of containers	Not Guaranteed Optimality
Thurston and Hu (2002)	Routing AGVs among several non-overlapping path segments; finding Shortest travel time path	Layout includes Space, roads, and junctions	Plan Merging Paradigm	Presents a distributed multi agent architecture	No priority for any AGVs, so an AGV must waits to free the rail and then moves
Corréa et al. (2007)	Finding conflict-free shortest time routes for AGVs	Bi-directional	Constraint Programming and Mixed Integer Programming	A decomposition method to solve a difficult combinatorial integrated scheduling and conflict free routing problem	Not Guaranteed Optimality
Zhicheng et al. (2014)	Allocate ALV to Handle Container Jobs	Mesh-Like Traffic Topology	Modified Hungarian Algorithm	A Real-Time Dispatching for ALV Problem	Not Guaranteed Optimality

(Continued)

Table 4.7 Summary of Dynamic Routing Algorithms for AGVs, since 2000 (Continued)

Authors (Year)	Problems	Path Direction	Basic Algorithms	Advantages	Disadvantages
Umar et al. (2015)	Optimizing Makespan, AGV travel time, and penalty cost due to jobs tardiness	bidirectional graph network	Hybrid genetic algorithm	Ensures the feasibility and effectiveness of all the solutions	Not Guaranteed Optimality
Yang et al. (2018)	Minimizing Makespan with Congestion Prevention in routes for AGVs	Clockwise Motion	Congestion Rule-based Bi-level Genetic Algorithm (CPR-BGA)	CPR-BGA is highly effective for the integrated scheduling in automated ports	Not Guaranteed Optimality
Murakami (2020)	Conflict-free routing problem of a capacitated AGV System (DCFRPC)	Network with Small Nodes and Junctions	Mixed-Integer Linear Programming	Optimal Solutions to the Majority of Instances Examined	Needs Computation Time to Solve Larger-Scale Problems
Zhong et al. (2020)	Conflict-free AGV path planning and integrated scheduling with QCs and RMGs	Clockwise conformable path Uni-directional	Hybrid GA-PSO Algorithm with fuzzy logic controller	Easy to execute and control	Not Guaranteed Optimality

4.7 Suggestions for How to Do the Simulation

We reviewed the research devoted on simulations of container terminals in Section 4.1. Generally, simulation allows the port manager to pose what-if questions. The managers can use a trial-and-error approach to problem solving and can do so faster, at less expense, more accurately, and with less risk. Moreover, the manager can experiment to determine which decision variables and which parts of the container terminal are really important, and with different alternatives. For example, we can assess the performance of a simulation model by throughput (moves per hour per QC), throughput per acre, annual throughput per acre (number of processed TEUs per acre per year), ship turnaround time, truck turnaround time, gate utilization, container dwell time, and the idle rate of equipment. For evaluating and monitoring any solution for each of the decisions in Chapter 3, several indices are suggested in Section 4.9.

In this section, we suggest two different approaches to container terminal simulation: microscopic and macroscopic. The benefits of these two approaches are described in several research (see [20, 80, 109, 111]). These approaches are described briefly in the following sections with some examples. Basically, refining and consolidating the solutions to simulate and decisions will be beyond the scope of research reported in this chapter.

4.7.1 Microscopic Simulation

The microscopic model describes both the entities and their interactions at a high level of detail. This type of simulation model includes elements of entities, resources, control elements, and operations.

4.7.1.1 Entities

Entity is a generic element in a microscopic simulation. In the container terminals, entities can be ships in a container terminal, container jobs in process of loading/unloading, and so on. As the time is going on, entities take actions that change the state of a system. Modeling languages provide tools used to create and destroy entities in the simulation model. Entities come into the model from time to time, just as ships come to a container terminal from time to time. Similarly, entities leave the model from time to time, just as served ships leave the container terminal. Entities can have attributes. Attributes of a ship include arrival time, ship type, the number of container jobs for loading/unloading, a distribution of loading times, and so on. The number of entities in a model usually varies at random during a simulation.

In the simulation model, it is useful to distinguish between two types of entities, here referred to as external entities and internal entities. External entities are those whose creation and actions are explicitly visualized and arranged for by the modeler. Entities of the types mentioned above (e.g., ships, container jobs in process) are examples of external entities.

In contrast to external entities, which are highly visible conceptually, internal entities are "behind the scenes" entities that some modeling languages use to support various needs in discrete-event modeling. Internal entities are created and manipulated implicitly by the simulation software itself and, in this sense, are invisible to the modeler. The model designer might not even be aware that internal entities are at work in a model.

For example, internal entities are used in some modeling languages to trigger AGV breakdowns and the later return of the broken-down AGV to a working-order state. The specifications for breakdowns and repair have to be supplied by the model designer, of course, but the designer does not have to provide the logic for implementing the breakdowns if internal entities are used for this purpose. In contrast, some modeling languages do not use internal entities to model AGV breakdowns. In such languages, the model designer works with external entities and explicitly provides the logic needed to implement such breakdowns. As another example, an internal entity is used in some languages to stop a simulation. A model designer might state that a simulation is to stop at the end of the eighth simulated hour, for example, and the modeling software provides an internal entity to make this happen. If internal entities are not provided for this purpose, the modeler works with external entities to achieve the effect desired.

4.7.1.2 Resources

In the simulation model, a resource is an element that provides service. For example, resources in a container terminal include QCs, automated guided vehicles, and berths. Some resources can only serve one user at a time. For example, a berth can hold only one ship at a time, and a QC can handle only one container job at a time in the terminal, as shown in Figure 3.2 in Chapter 3. In some cases, however, a resource can serve two or more users at a time. An automated guided vehicle, for instance, might be able to move two container jobs from point A to point B at the same time.

Resources are limited in number. For example, in a container terminal there might be three QCs, two berths of type A, and three berths of type B. There might be fifty automated guided vehicles in the container terminal.

The users of resources are usually entities. For example, a ship-entity captures a berth and then several QCs so it can be processed in the berth. A container job entity captures QCs, and then captures an AGV so that it can be moved from its current position on the ship to the internal truck in the container terminal. The fact that resources are limited means that entities must sometimes wait their turn to use resources. When a container job asks for an AGV, it might have to wait for its request to be loaded/unloaded.

Modeling languages have constructs that are used to control direct access to resources by entities. Such constructs provide for the automatic recording of the resource's capture status ("idle" or "captured") and operating condition ("in working order" or "broken down"). When an entity tries to capture a resource, its capture status and operating condition can be tested by the software to determine if the attempted capture can take place.

4.7.1.3 Control Elements

In addition to resource constructs, modeling languages provide other constructs to support various control-related aspects of a system's state. The term control element is used here for such constructs. In the microscopic simulation, the control elements can be switch, counter, arithmetic expression, and Boolean expression.

- **Switch**: A switch is an example of a control element that can be a two-state variable (on or off). A switch might be used in a model if a berth is engaging by a ship in a container terminal, for example, to signal another ship so it cannot be docked.
- **Counters**: Counters are another type of control element. A counter might be used to count the number of container jobs that are being transported by an automated guided vehicle (AGV) from quay-side to yard-side or vice versa, during a period of time. The policy might be to recharge an AGV after 200 uses. Implementing this policy requires that a count be kept. The counter is used to help control this aspect of simulation model.
- **Arithmetic expressions**: Arithmetic expressions can be the basis for control elements. Consider a container terminal that uses a multiple-berth, multiple-cranes such as Figure 3.2 in Chapter 3. There might be fifty automated guided vehicles (AGVs), but only several might be available at a given time. Suppose when the average number of AGVs waiting is five or more, another AGV must be come into the process. The modeler can introduce an arithmetic expression to compute the average number of AGVs. An entity used to simulate the "AGV manager" can monitor the value of this expression to determine if conditions require another AGV. Here an arithmetic expression is used to control the behavior of the AGV manager.
- **Boolean expressions**: Boolean expressions are truth-valued expressions composed with logical operators such as 'and', 'or', and 'not'. A ship is not able to leave the container terminal, for example, until it can be fully processed, and there are no container jobs for loading/unloading. Like resources, control elements can force entities to wait, delaying their movement through a model.

4.7.1.4 Operations

In the simulation model, an operation is a step or action carried out by or on an entity during its movement through a system. Examples of operations include the arrival of an order of container jobs and the capturing of an AGV by the container jobs. An ordered set of operations is a sequence of steps or actions taken or experienced by an entity while it moves from point to point in a system. An integrated sequence of operations is sometimes called operation logic. For example, this might be the operation logic for movement of a ship through a container port: (a) arrive outside the port; (b) capture a berth; (c) capture two QCs in the berth; (d) use the QCs to be processed in the berth; and (e) depart the container port.

4.7.2 Macroscopic Simulation

The macroscopic model is based on dynamic discrete time and takes place on a section-by-section. If there is a higher level of autonomy in behaviors and interactions between sections of simulation models, we have agent-based simulation (ABS), which is contributed to Macal and North [116], Siebers et al. [173], and Macal and North [117]. If we consider a lower level of autonomy in making simulation model, entities (objects) are elements of models, known as object-based simulation (OBS). In this section, we briefly describe ABS and OBS. More details on ABS and OBS are provided by Rashidi (2017) [154].

4.7.2.1 Agent-Based Simulation (ABS)

This type of simulation is a relatively new approach to modeling systems into which agents interact. Agents are individual, autonomous, and their behaviors affect others. A typical agent-based model has three elements: (a) Agents, their attributes and behaviors; (b) Agent relationships and methods of interaction; and (c) Agents' environment. For making a model for container terminal, we have four different types of agents in the system: (a) the Quay Crane Agents (QCAs); (b) Straddle Carrier Agents (SCAs); (c) the Traffic Agents (TAs), and (d) the Area Manager Agent (AMA). Each QC is controlled by a QCA, each straddle carrier is controlled by an SCA, and each cell of the yard highway that contains more than one entry point, such as a crossing, is governed by a TA. Desktop computing for ABS application development are Spreadsheets, Dedicated Agent-based Prototyping Environments, and General Computational Mathematics Systems such as MATLAB and Mathematica. For ABS, large-scale agent development environments are Repast, Swarm, MASON, and AnyLogic.

4.7.2.2 Object-Based Simulation (OBS)

This type of simulation is like traditional simulation models in which objects have attributes, methods, and states. For example, attributes of a ship at a port include arrival time, ship type, the number of QCs needed for loading/unloading, a distribution of loading times, and so on. Most modeling languages provide tools used to create and destroy entities during execution of a simulation model.

Objects come into a model from time to time; few ships come to a container terminal, for example. Similarly, objects leave a model from time to time, just as served ships leave a port. The objects in the simulation models must be supervised and managed by the kernel of software. The Kernel manages objects by organizing them in linear lists and controls the state transitions. PORTSIM, Minion, and AnyLogic are general purpose for OBS. If we use general Object-oriented programming languages for OBS, most important languages are Java, C++, and Python.

4.8 Proposed Frameworks for Implementation

We reviewed the research devoted on selection of an architecture for implementation of software in Section 4.2 and the classification of scheduling decisions, in general, in Section 4.3. After that, we reviewed the frameworks and solutions in Sections 4.4 and 4.5, respectively. In this section, we propose several frameworks for implementation of decisions container terminals as shown in Table 4.8. These frameworks are general for implementation of models in Constraint Satisfaction Optimization Problems (CSOPs), on the basis of which the five scheduling decisions in Chapter 3 were formulated. In these frameworks, most algorithms in Table 4.1 are available for finding single or all solution satisfying constraints. Moreover, a large number of algorithms are available in both complete and incomplete classes. These algorithms are particularly useful when a problem involves non-trivial amounts of constraints.

4.9 Evaluation and Monitoring

To evaluate the decisions, different indices may be considered to measure efficiency of the terminal. Liu et al. (2002) designed, analyzed, and evaluated four different automated container terminal (ACT) concepts [109]. These concepts are based on the use of automated guidance vehicles (AGVs), a linear motor conveyance system (LMCS), an overhead grid rail system (GR), and a high-rise automated storage and retrieval structure (AS/RS). This research studied four automated container terminals, Port of Rotterdam, Port of Hamburg, Port of Hong Kong, and Port of Singapore, and then evaluated their operations by simulation. This research evaluated ship turnaround time, throughput of terminals, gate utilization, idled time of Yard Crane and buffer cranes, dwelling times of containers, and the average cost of a container during the simulation time.

Luca et al. (2013) investigated the prediction reliability of two different approaches to container terminal simulation: microscopic and macroscopic [111]. The former simulating single container movement, the latter simulating container flow movement. The microscopic model was a discrete event simulation model;

Table 4.8 General Framework for Implementation of the Five Scheduling Decisions in Container Terminals

Frameworks	Description	Link
Cassowary Constraint Solver	It is an open source project for constraint satisfaction (accessible from C, Java, Python, and other languages).	https://constraints.cs.washington.edu/cassowary/
Comet	It is a commercial programming language and toolkit. Comet is a domain-specific language for hybrid optimization, featuring solvers for constraint programming, mixed integer programming, and constraint-based local search	https://www.csplib.org/Languages/Comet/
Gecode	It is an open source portable toolkit written in C++ developed as a production-quality and highly efficient implementation of a complete theoretical background.	https://www.gecode.org/
Gelisp	It is an open source portable wrapper of Gecode to Lisp.	http://gelisp.sourceforge.net/
HotFrame	A heuristic optimization framework that has been implemented by C++ defined the collaborations among software components, in particular with respect to the interface between meta-heuristic components and problem-specific components.	https://www.swmath.org/software/13457
IBM ILOG CP Optimizer	C++, Python, Java, .NET libraries (proprietary, free for academic use). It is successor of ILOG Solver/Scheduler, which was considered the market leader in commercial constraint programming software as of 2006.	https://www.ibm.com/analytics/cplex-cp-optimizer
JaCoP	It is an open source Java constraint solver. The major focus of JaCoP is its constraints. These constraints include rich set of primitive, logical, and conditional constraints as well as many global constraints.	https://github.com/radsz/jacop

(Continued)

Table 4.8 General Framework for Implementation of the Five Scheduling Decisions in Container Terminals *(Continued)*

Frameworks	*Description*	*Link*
Koalog	It is a commercial Java-based constraint solver. It provides cutting-edge technology for solving satisfaction and optimization problems, including scheduling, time-tabling, resource-allocation, and puzzles.	https://www.swmath.org/software/5449
Logilab-Constraint	An open source constraint solver written in pure Python with constraint propagation algorithms.	https://pypi.org/project/logilab-constraint/
Minion	An open-source constraint solver written in C++, with a small language for the purpose of specifying models/problems.	https://swmath.org/software/10176
OptaPlanner	It is another open source Java constraint solver. OptaPlanner combines sophisticated Artificial Intelligence optimization algorithms such as Tabu Search, Simulated Annealing, Late Acceptance, and other meta-heuristics.	https://www.optaplanner.org/
ZDC	An open source program developed in the Computer-Aided Constraint Satisfaction Project for modeling and solving constraint satisfaction problems.	https://www.swmath.org/software/10499

the macroscopic model was a dynamic discrete time-based (space-time) network assignment model. Both modeling approaches were implemented and compared taking advantage of some significant investment made by the Salerno Container Terminal (Italy) between 2005 and 2011. In particular, disaggregate (microscopic) and an aggregate (macroscopic) simulation models implemented in 2005 were validated with a large set of data acquired in 2011 after some structural and functional terminal modifications. This research evaluated the container terminal turnaround time, including the time to bring terminal macro-operations (e.g., import, export) to a close with respect to a pre-fixed time interval (days, months). It also evaluated handling equipment activity's duration (vessel loading and/or unloading time; Quay/Yard crane idle time; shuttle waiting time; shuttle transfer time; reach stacker stacking time; reach stacker idle time; gate in/out waiting time). Moreover, it evaluated containers operation time (time required to move a container with a handling equipment—e.g., time spent moving a container from quay to vessel or from shuttle to stack). Through this analysis it was possible to analyze the prediction reliability of both simulation approaches and to draw some operational guidelines. Obviously, not all the performance indicators could be estimated for all the approaches implemented; for the macroscopic approaches the local indicators related to the single container cannot be estimated due to the aggregate nature of the model

Schwientek et al. (2020) studied effects of terminal size, yard block assignment, and dispatching methods on container terminal performance [168]. This study did a discrete-event simulation model and examined the influence of various terminal parameters on dispatching strategies. The two most influencing terminal parameters, including terminal size and yard block assignment to containers, were analyzed with detail. This research evaluated the number of vehicles, speed of vehicle, yard block assignment to container, utilization of seaside capacity, vessel size, terminal size, equipment types, rate of handling times, storage strategy handling rate, quay layout and share of landside traffic. The results showed that the best choice of yard block assignment and dispatching method for a given terminal size depends on the combination of both parameters and the aspired targets.

Here, we provide some indices to evaluate the decisions as Table 4.9. The right column of the table lists corresponding indices to evaluate each of the five defined decisions.

4.10 Summary and Conclusion

In this chapter, we addressed three main challenges associated with providing practical software for decision-making. First, we discussed the challenge related to the simulation of the operations in container terminals and then argued the design architecture toward implementation issues. After that, we classified the scheduling techniques and reviewed several frameworks. Then, we did a survey on the

Table 4.9 Some Important Indices to Evaluate the Decisions in the Container Terminals

Decisions	Indices
Allocation of berths to arriving vessels and QCs to docked vessels	• Ship around time • Throughput of Terminal (container/ ship) • Idle Time of QCs • Total Waiting Time of QCs • Berths and QCs Utilization • Average cost per ship
Storage Space Allocation	• Average size of the block in the yard • Largest and Smallest Block in the yard • Average Cost of containers in the yard • Container dwell time
RTGC deployment in the yard	• Idle rate of Yard Cranes or RTGCs • Maximum, minimum, and average workload in the yard • Average movement of RTGCs in the yard
Scheduling and Routing of Vehicles	• IT or AGV turnaround time • Average transportation cost per container • Number of AGVs used • Number/Percentage of idle AGVs • Total Waiting Time of AGVs • Total Delay Times of AGVs • Route Utilization • Average trip duration ratio • Longest and Shortest trip • Number of trips for each vehicle • Percentage of Moving vehicles with/ without a container
Appointment times to XTs	• Gate utilization • Container dwell time

solution methods to scheduling problems, in general, as well as scheduling and routing vehicles, in particular. Afterwards, we suggested two approaches for simulating container terminals and proposed several frameworks for implementation. Finally, several indices were suggested for evaluation and monitoring any solutions for each of the decisions.

ADVANCED ALGORITHMS FOR THE SCHEDULING PROBLEM OF AUTOMATED GUIDED VEHICLES

2

Chapter 5

Vehicle Scheduling: A Minimum Cost Flow Problem

This chapter focuses on scheduling problem of Automated Guided Vehicles (AGVs) in the container terminals. The problem is to deploy several AGVs in a port to carry many containers from the quayside to yardside or vice versa. This problem is defined in Section 5.2 and is formulated as a Minimum Cost Flow (MCF) model in Section 5.5 of this chapter.

5.1 Reasons to Choose This Problem

In the past few decades, much research has been devoted to the technology of AGV systems, both in hardware and software [153]. Nowadays they have become popular over the world for automatic material-handling and flexible manufacturing systems. Qiu et al. (2002) surveyed the scheduling and routing algorithms for AGVs. One of their suggestions for future research is to develop more efficient algorithms for different path topologies where AGVs are employed [153]. These unmanned vehicles are increasingly becoming the common mode of container transport in the seaport.

Moreover, there are some other reasons for concentrating on this decision. The efficiency of a port is directly related to the amount of time that each vessel spends in the port. A major challenge in port management is to reduce the turnaround time of the container ships. If the management can use the AGVs with full efficiency at

DOI: 10.1201/9781003308386-7

minimum waiting and traveling times, the performance of the port is increased. However, most existing scheduling and routing solutions are applicable to a small number of AGVs [153]. Although the majority of references in the paper were over-use of AGVs in material handling systems, we investigated the latest research in container terminals. The number of AGV in the problems, which have been experienced by Wook and Hwan (2000) [203], Böse et al. (2000) [14], Grunow et al. (2004) [53], Thurston and Hu (2002) [182], and Cheng et al. (2003) [25], were five, five, six, twelve, and eighty, respectively. The largest problem in the recent research experienced was a problem with a hundred vehicles. This experiment has been done by Zhang et al. (2002) [217], but the problems were static. When the number of container jobs and AGVs increase, we need to find some efficient solutions to tackle over the huge search space of this problem.

We believe that some of its solutions and algorithms can be applied to other transportation systems such as Pickup/Delivery system in real-time. From Table 3.6, it can be seen that most container terminals have considered this problem in their research. Decreasing costs of the terminal, speeding up the transportation system inside the port, rising customer demand, and globalization of trade outside the terminal are all affected by making a good operational plan for the AGVs.

5.2 Assumptions

The problem is to transport many containers in the port from the storage areas to the berth or vice versa by AGVs in their appointment times. Each container job involves the loading of the container onto the AGV, the movement of the vehicle to the destination, and the unloading of the container by the QCs or RTGCs.

In order to define and formulate the decision, the following assumptions are considered:

Assumption 5-1: The layout of a port container terminal can be visualized in Figure 5.1 [203]. In this example, there are five working positions of QCs in the berth (Seaside workplace) and five yard blocks in the storage area for containers (blocks A to E). In the figure, the locations of RTGCs or Yard Cranes for unloading or picking up the containers are in front of each block. The path between two points is not necessarily unique and the system controller may change the route of AGVs to designated points due to congestion in the next lane or junction.

Assumption 5-2: We assume that the problem involves only one ship and therefore the number of QCs and their location do not change until all container jobs under consideration for the docked ship are completed.

Assumption 5-3: Generally the following listed phenomena occur when scheduling and routing AGVs are being studied [153]:

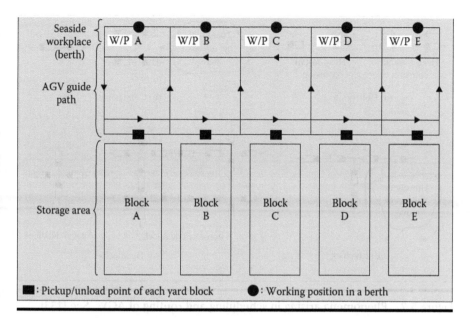

Figure 5.1   Layout of the container terminal.

- **Collisions:** When more than one AGV attempts to occupy the same segment of the path at the same time, there is potentially a collision. Figure 5.2(a) shows two examples.
- **Congestion:** Congestion arises at a location where there is insufficient resource so for a period of time there are too many vehicles in a path. Figure 5.2(b) depicts such a case. Congestion must be reduced or eliminated because it will produce a lower throughput of the system or even lead to deadlock.
- **Livelocks:** As shown in Figure 5.2(c), a livelock may arise at the junction where the horizontal stream of traffic is given higher priority over the vertical one. In this case, the queue in the vertical line never moves.
- **Deadlocks:** A deadlock will arise when multiple AGVs mutually wait for the release (which will never occur) of the resource held by the others. Figure 5.2(d) shows two cases, local deadlock and non-local deadlock.

We assume that the AGVs are reliable and travel at a certain predetermined average speed so that Collisions, Breakdowns, and Livelocks as well as Deadlocks can be eliminated in our model.

Assumption 5-4: There are several paths between every combination of Pickup (P) or Dropoff (D) points for the AGVs, according to our layout (see Figure 5.1). But we assume that at any time, the travel time between every two points is provided in Table 5.1 [203]. In the table the notation W/P shows Working Position of the cranes in the berth.

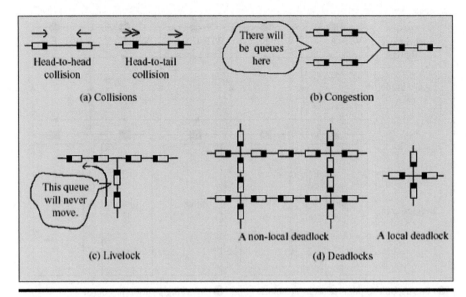

Figure 5.2   Phenomena arising in scheduling and routing of AGVs. See [153].

Table 5.1   Example of Traveling Time (Seconds) between Two Different Points in the Port

To → From ↓	Block A	Block B	Block C	Block D	Block E	W/P A	W/P B	W/P C	W/P D	W/P E
Block A	-	30	60	90	120	150	195	200	225	265
Block B	80	-	30	60	90	175	165	205	195	235
Block C	110	80	-	30	60	145	135	175	165	205
Block D	140	110	80	-	30	175	165	145	135	175
Block E	170	140	110	80	-	205	195	175	165	145
W/P A	205	175	145	175	205	-	50	90	80	120
W/P B	215	185	155	185	215	10	-	80	70	110
W/P C	225	205	175	145	175	30	20	-	50	90
W/P D	235	215	185	155	185	40	30	10	-	80
W/P E	265	235	205	175	145	60	50	30	20	-

Assumption 5-5: There are M AGVs in the container terminal. Every AGV can transport only one container. This simplification, however, ensures that the problem remains tractable and that an efficient operational plan can be devised and implemented in real time. In fact, most of the current literature focuses on AGVs with unit capacity. This is often the reality in container terminals [25]. Henceforth, we consider unit capacity for the AGVs.

Assumption 5-6: RTGCs or Yard Crane resources are always available [23], i.e., the AGVs will not suffer from delays in the storage yard location due to waiting for the Yard Cranes. This is not a restrictive assumption in the real implementation, since a good yard storage plan will be able to minimize the amount of congestion in a particular yard location, and hence reduce the amount of delays suffered by the AGVs. Furthermore, Yard Cranes or RTGCs are relatively much cheaper than QCs. Hence, YCs/RTGCs are assumed to be readily available when it is needed.

Assumption 5-7: There are N container jobs in the problem. The source and destination of these are given. Each job has an appointment time at its source/destination on the quayside. This appointment time is the time at which the job is to be unloaded/loaded from/on the vessel by a QC on the W/Ps. The appointment time, source, and destination of jobs can be as shown in Table 5.2.

Assumption 5-8: There is a predetermined crane job sequence, consisting of loading jobs, or unloading/discharging jobs, or a combination of both for every QC. Given a specified job sequence, the corresponding dropoff (for loading) or pickup (for discharging) time of the jobs on the quayside depends on the work rate of the Quay Cranes. For example, assuming an average work rate of five minutes for one container (see Table 5.2), we need the horizontal

Table 5.2 Appointment Time of Containers Jobs

Container Job (i)	Appointment time of Container Job i on the Quayside (t_i)	Source	Destination
1	00:30	W/P A	Block A
2	00:35	Block B	W/P B
3	00:40	W/P C	Block C
4	00:45	Block D	W/P A
..	..		
.	..		
N	..		

transportation system to feed a container to the Quay Crane every five minutes. This assumption for the cranes has the following two special properties that must be considered in developing any solution procedure:

- The container jobs must be carried out in the exact same order that is predetermined as in a sequence list. Planners in terminals make a discharging and loading sequence list before the ship operation begins. The sequence list is confirmed by the corresponding shipping company. Then, the ship operation is performed in the exact same order as specified in the sequence list.
- A delay in a quayside operation of a QC results in delays, by the same amount of time, to all succeeding seaside operations assigned to the same QC.

Assumption 5-9: The problem is divided into two types, static and dynamic. In the static problem, we assume that the number of vehicles, the number of jobs, and the distance between every two points in the container terminal do not change. In the dynamic problem, we assume that the number of vehicles is fixed but the number of jobs, and the distance between the source and destination of the jobs may change (since the system controller may change the route of AGVs due to congestion in the next lane or junction (see Figure 5.1)). Note that in this problem each vehicle might be in a different location of the port; on either the quayside or the yardside, or in the middle of the road between its source and destination.

Assumption 5-10: In this scheduling problem our goal is to deploy the AGVs in such a way as that all the imposed appointment time constraints are met with minimum cost. Cheng et al. (2003) minimized waiting times of the AGVs [25]. Our objectives are to minimize the following:

1. The total AGV waiting time on the quayside.
2. The total AGV traveling time in the route of the port.
3. The lateness time totals to serve the jobs.

If our objectives are achieved by a deployment scheme for the AGVs the terminal operates at the desired throughput rate.

5.3 Variables and Notations

To make a model for the problem the following variables and notations are used:

a. t_i: Appointment time of job i at the quayside.
   According to Assumption 5-7, the appointment time of the jobs are given. After the ship docked at the berth, the appointment time of the first jobs was calculated by the following expression:

$$t_i = \text{Ship\_docked\_time} + i \times W.$$

The **Ship_docked_time** is the time at which the ship is ready for discharge/loading at the berth. The time window W is the duration of discharging/loading a container. The appointment time of new jobs (after serving the first i jobs) is calculated by the following expression:

$$t_{i+k} = CT_i + k \times W$$

where CT_i denotes the actual completion time of the i-th job. Note that CT_i is available at the time of deployment of the job ($i+k$).

b. RTA_m: Ready time of AGV m at the next location (either the quayside or yardside).

TTA_{mj}: Travel Time of AGV m from the next location to the location of job j on the quayside.

In the dynamic problems (see Assumption 5-9) the AGVs can be in different locations and status. In reality, at any instant an AGV can be in one of the four states: **Waiting** on the quayside, **Going, Idle,** or **unloading/loading the job.** Each of these states, as the names suggest, corresponds to a different mode of operation for the AGV. The RTA_m for AGV m and the calculation of its traveling time to the location of container job j, TTA_{mj}, is illustrated by Figure 5.3. As an example, consider the first case in the figure (case a). The

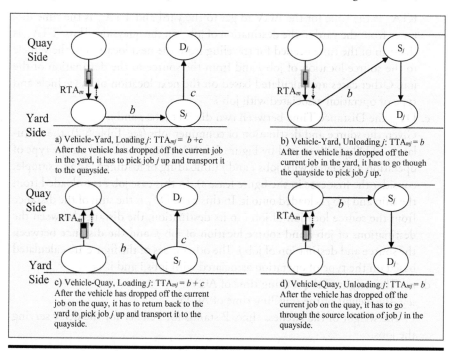

a) Vehicle-Yard, Loading j: $TTA_{mj} = b + c$
After the vehicle has dropped off the current job in the yard, it has to pick job j up and transport it to the quayside.

b) Vehicle-Yard, Unloading j: $TTA_{mj} = b$
After the vehicle has dropped off the current job in the yard, it has to go though the quayside to pick job j up.

c) Vehicle-Quay, Loading j: $TTA_{mj} = b + c$
After the vehicle has dropped off the current job on the quay, it has to return back to the yard to pick job j up and transport it to the quayside.

d) Vehicle-Quay, Unloading j: $TTA_{mj} = b$
After the vehicle has dropped off the current job on the quay, it has to go through the source location of job j in the quayside.

Figure 5.3 Traveling time computations between the next location of vehicle and the next job.

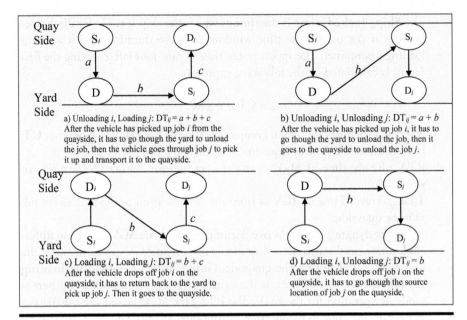

Figure 5.4   Traveling time computations between job *i* and job *j*.

RTA_m is the time for the AGV to get to the yard and TTA_{mj} is the time distance from the yard to the destination of job *j* on the quayside. Thus, TTA_{mj} is the sum of the time needed for traveling from the next location of the vehicle to the source location of job *j* and from the source to the destination of the job. Other cases are calculated based on the next location of the vehicle and type of operation associated with job *j*.

c. DT_{ij}: the Distance Time between two distinct jobs *i* and *j*.

Given the source and destination of container jobs (see Table 5.2), the calculation of DT_{ij} is illustrated by Figure 5.4. It is calculated based on the type of operation associated with jobs *i* and *j* (unloading or loading). As an example, consider the first case in the figure (case a). In this case job *i* is unloaded from the ship and job *j* is loaded onto it. In this case, DT_{ij} is the sum of the distance from the source location of job *i* to its destination, the distance between the destinations of job *i* and source location of job *j*, and the distance between the source and destination of job *j*. The other cases of the figure are calculated based on the type of operation associated with jobs i and j.

d. w_1: The weight of the waiting time of AGVs.

w_2: The weight of the traveling time of AGVs.

P: The weight of the lateness time. P stands for Penalty for the delay serving the jobs.

According to assumption 5-10, these weights are required to be considered in the objective **function.**

5.4 The Minimum Cost Flow Model

The scheduling problem of AGVs in the container terminal will be formulated as an MCF model [3]. In this section, we present the standard form of the MCF model with a few definitions systematically. These definitions are related to Graph (G), the special Graph of G for the MCF model (G_{MCF}), and the MCF model itself.

5.4.1 Graph Terminology

There are the following standard definitions in graph theory (see Carre [19], Weber (2003) [200]).

> **Definition 5-1:** A graph G = (N, A) consists of a finite set of *nodes*, N, together with a finite set of **arcs**, A.
>
> **Definition 5-2:** In an **undirected graph** the arcs are unordered pairs of nodes $\{i, j\} \in A$, $i, j \in N$. In a **directed graph** the arcs are ordered pairs of nodes (i, j).
>
> **Definition 5-3:** A **walk** is an ordered list of nodes $i_1, i_2, ..., i_t$ such that, in the case of an undirected graph, $\{i_k, i_{k+1}\} \in A$, or, in the case of a directed graph, that either $(i_k, i_{k+1}) \in A$ or $(i_{k+1}, i_k) \in A$, for $k = 1, ..., t-1$.
>
> **Definition 5-4:** A walk is a **path** if $i_1, i_2, ..., i_k$ are distinct, and a cycle if $i_1, i_2, ..., i_{k-1}$ are distinct and $i_1 = i_k$. A graph is connected if there is a path connecting every pair of nodes.
>
> **Definition 5-5:** A loop in a directed graph is an arc that goes from a node to itself.
>
> **Definition 5-6:** A network is a directed graph which is connected without loops.
>
> **Definition 5-7:** A network is **acyclic** if it contains no cycles. A network is a tree if it is connected and acyclic. A network (Ń, Á) is a subnetwork of (N, A) if Ń ⊂ N and Á ⊂ A.

5.4.2 The Standard Form of the Minimum Cost Flow Model

The MCF model deals with a directed graph. In the graph, the problem is to send flow from a set of supply nodes, through a subnetwork of the graph, to a set of demand nodes, at minimum total cost, and without violating the lower and upper bounds on flows through the arcs [3]. The MCF problem is defined as follows:

> **Definition 5-8 [3]:** For the MCF problem, let graph G = (N, A) be a directed network defined by a set of nodes, N, together with a set of arcs, A. Each arc $(i, j) \in A$ has an associated cost c_{ij} that denotes the cost per unit flow on that arc. It is assumed that the flow cost varies linearly with the amount of flow. The maximum and minimum amount of flow on each arc $(i, j) \in A$ are limited by M_{ij} and m_{ij} ($m_{ij} \leq M_{ij}$), respectively. A real number b_i is associated with

each node, representing its supply/demand. If $b_i > 0$, node i is a supply node; if $b_i < 0$, the node i is a demand node with a demand of $-b_i$; and if $b_i = 0$, node i is a transshipment node. The decision variables in the MCF problem are arc flows, which is represented by f_{ij} for an arc $(i, j) \in A$. The standard form of MCF problem is as follows:

$$MinCostFlow = \sum_{(i,j)\in A} c_{ij} \cdot f_{ij}$$

$$SubjectTo \begin{cases} \sum_{j:(i,j)\in A} f_{ij} - \sum_{j:(j,i)\in A} f_{ji} = b_i, \text{ for all } i \in N \\ m_{ij} \le f_{ij} \le M_{ij}, \text{ for all } (i, j) \in A \end{cases}$$

These constraints state that flows must be feasible and conserve each node, i.e., the flow does not exceed the supply at a node and satisfies the demand. For the feasible flows to exist the MCF problem must also have $\Sigma_{i\in N} \, b_i = 0$, which means that the network is balanced. An important special case is that of incapacitated flows, $m_{ij} = 0$ and $M_{ij} = \infty$.

We now define a special graph for the MCF problem as follows:

Definition 5-9: A graph $G_{MCF} = (G, NP, AP)$ consists of a graph G with a couple of properties for the nodes and arcs in G. The NP and AP are the Node's and Arc's Properties, respectively. The node property function NP: $N \to R$ (Real numbers; possibly negative) gives the amount of supply/demand of the nodes. This function for each node is defined as follows:

$$NP(i) = NP_i = b_i \text{ where } \begin{cases} b_i > 0 \text{ if node } i \text{ is a supply node} \\ b_i < 0 \text{ if node } i \text{ is a demand node} \\ b_i = 0 \text{ if node } i \text{ is a transshipment node} \end{cases}$$

so that $\sum_{i\in N} NP(i) = 0$

The arc property function AP: $A \to R \times R \times R$ (Real numbers; nonnegative) gives the lower bound, the upper bound, and the cost of the arcs. This function for each element in A is defined as follows:

$$AP(i, j) = AP_{ij} = \left[m_{ij}, M_{ij}, c_{ij} \right]$$

Based on Definitions 5-8 and 5-9, we define the standard MCF problem, formally as follows:

Definition 5-10: An MCF model is defined as:

$$MCF = \left(G_{MCF}, f, D, CS, FC\right)$$

where $G_{MCF} = ((N,A), NP, AP)$ is a special graph for the MCF problem;

f = a finite set of decision variables on A (*f* stands for flow*)*, $f = \{f_{ij} \mid (i, j) \in A\}$;
D = a function which determines a lower and upper bound for f;
$D: f \rightarrow R \times R$ (to be pulled out from AP); we shall take $D_{f_{ij}}$ as the lower bound and upper bound of f_{ij} by D (D stands for Domain);
CS = a finite set of Constraint S on NP and f;
FC = an objective function for the Flow's Cost on AP and f;

The task in an MCF model is to assign a value to each f_{ij} that satisfies all constraints in CS with regard to the minimum value for FC.
For the standard form of the MCF model we have:

a. For each element D and f, $D_{f_{ij}} = [m_{ij}, M_{ij}]$, for $\forall (i, j) \in A$;
b. The CS is $\sum_{j:(i,j) \in A} f_{ij} - \sum_{j:(j,i) \in A} f_{ji} = NP_i, \, for \, \forall i \in N$
c. The FC is $\sum_{j:(j,i) \in A} c_{ij} \cdot f_{ij}$

5.4.3 Applications of the Minimum Cost Flow Model

This MCF model has a rich history and arises in almost all industries, including agriculture, communications, defense, education, energy, health care, manufacturing, medicine, retailing, and transportation [3]. The MCF model is generally broad and can be used as a template to model many network problems. In this section, several applications of the MCF model along with a background are presented.

The classical transportation problem is perhaps the best known network model. A notable application of this model by Koopmans (1947) involved the reduction of cargo shipping times. Use of the model is not restricted to distribution problems, however, and it can be applied to a range of situations. Roberts (1978) applies the method to street sweeping, and to Ribonucleic Acid (RNA) mapping. Glover and Klingman (1977) solve a file aggregation problem which arose in the United States Department of the Treasury, and a crop efficiency problem. Chachra, Ghare, and Moore (1979) modeled the movement of soil from sites to fill dams or other such destinations. The authors claim that this is the oldest recorded application of Graph Theory, having been used by a French engineer named Monge (1784).

The transshipment and general MCF formulations have also been extensively applied. Glover and Klingman (1977) describe the routing of motor vehicle transportation across the United States for a major automobile manufacturer.

Kantorovich (1939) treats freight transportation, while Chachra, Ghare, and Moore (1979) formulate a highway route planning problem.

The assignment problem, as a subclass of the above problem, is very widely applicable. A variety of allocation problems, involving contracts, employees, work-groups, machines, work locations, and work crews are discussed by Chachra, Ghare, and Moore (1979).

The maximum flow problem can also be solved using the MCF framework. Chachra, Ghare, and Moore (1979) describe a formulation of this type applied to the solution of a petroleum piping problem for the Universal Oil Company.

Vehicular traffic problems on road networks are a class of problems whose network structure is readily apparent. For example, Roberts (1978) treats the problem of implementing a one-way system to increase the efficiency of a city street-plan. Chachra, Ghare, and Moore (1979) expand on the "traffic" class of problems to include situations involving the movement of people, mail, factory parts, and even court cases.

Network flow formulations also provide a very convenient method of modeling production planning and scheduling problems. Wilson and Beineke (1978) examine how production to meet varying demand can be scheduled, and also examine the similar problem of scheduling a number of related activities required to complete a large task. Kantorovich (1939) considers the distribution of the processing of various items among a number of machines in order to maximize total output. Chachra, Ghare, and Moore (1979) treat airline and railroad scheduling, as well as a rather idiosyncratic model called the "Fisherman's Problem."

The "Warehousing Problem" is that faced by an entrepreneur who seeks to maximize the profit from storing a variety of goods, prior to their sale, in a warehouse of fixed capacity. This is treated as a network problem by Ford and Fulkerson (1962).

The field of chemistry is a fertile one for the application of graph theory and network models. Applications in this field are described by Wilson and Beineke (1979) and Balaban (1976). Electrical networks and their analysis are the subjects of Minty's (1960) paper. Rockafellar (1984) deals with a range of hydraulic and mechanical applications of network flows, including a city water supply system involving pump stations and aqueducts.

5.5 The Special Case of the MCF Model for Automated Guided Vehicles Scheduling

Here, we present a special case of the MCF model for the Scheduling problem of Automated Guided Vehicles (SAGV) in the container terminal. The problem differs primarily in the arrangement of nodes and arcs with their properties. In this special case, the property function of nodes assigns integer value to every node. Additionally, the property function of arcs assigns integer values to the lower bound, the upper bound and the cost of each arc. Moreover, the lower bound and the upper bound of each arc take the binary values 0 or 1. We present the special Graph of G_{MCF} for the Automated Guided Vehicles Scheduling ($G_{MCF-AGV}$) and the special case of the MCF model for the Scheduling problem of Automated Guided Vehicles (MCF-AGV).

Based on Definition 5-9, we introduce the following definition for the G_{MCF} in a special case:

> **Definition 5-11:** A graph $G_{MCF-AGV}$ = (GS, NPS, APS) is a special case of G_{MCF} = (G, NP, AP). The graph GS = (NS, AS) is a special case of G = (N, A); the node and arcs properties of GS, NPS and APS, are also special cases of NP and AP respectively (NPS: NS→N and APS: AS→N×N×N; N is the set of Natural numbers). In this section, we formally describe the elements of $G_{MCF-AGV}$ in the two following sub-sections:

5.5.1 Nodes and Their Properties in the Special Graph

As we mentioned, there are three types of node in the standard form of an MCF model: supply nodes, transshipment nodes, and demand nodes [3]. Here, our problem is formalized with four different types of node: a supply node for each AGV, a couple of nodes for each container job as transshipment nodes (the reason is in the next section, see the Auxiliary Arcs) and a demand node. Given N jobs and M AGVs in the problem, the elements in each set, the sets themselves, and the nodes properties are defined as follows:

a. **AGVN$_m$:** A supply node corresponding to AGV m with one unit supply (AGVN stands for the AGV Node). There are M AGVs in the problem. Hence, there are M supply nodes in the $G_{MCF-AGV}$. We define the following set for these supply nodes along with their properties:
SAGVN: a set of M supply nodes in the $G_{MCF-AGV}$.

SAGVN = {AGVN$_m$ | m=1,2,...,M; NPS(m)=1}.

b. **JIN$_i$:** A node through which an AGV enters job i. It stands for the Job-Input Node. There is neither supply nor demand in this node, i.e., it is a transshipment node. We define the following set for these transshipment nodes along with their properties:
SJIN: a set of N Job-Input nodes in the $G_{MCF-AGV}$.

SJIN = {JIN$_i$ | i=1,2,...,N; NPS(i)=0}.

c. **JOUT$_i$:** A node from which an AGV leaves job i. It stands for the Job-Output Node. Like the previous nodes, there is neither supply nor demand in this node. We define the following set for these transshipment nodes along with their properties:

SJOUT: a set of N Job-Output nodes in the $G_{MCF-AGV}$

$$SJOUT = \{JOUT_i \mid i=1,2,\ldots,N; NPS(i) = 0\}.$$

d. **SINK:** It stands for a Sink node or a demand node in the $G_{MCF-AGV}$ with M units demand. This node corresponds to the end state of the process after all container jobs have been served. Hence, for the property of this node, we have: NPS(SINK) = −M.

Therefore, there are M+2×N+1 nodes in the $G_{MCF-AGV}$ so that:

$$NS=SAGVN \cup SJIN \cup SJOUT \cup SINK.$$

5.5.2 Arcs and Their Properties in the Special Graph

The following four types of arc with their properties connect the nodes in the $G_{MCF-AGV}$:

1. **Inward Arcs:** There is a directed arc from every AGV node, to the Job-Input node of job i. We define the following notation for these arcs along with their properties:
   ARC$_{inward}$: a set of arcs from SAGVN to SJIN.

   $$ARC_{inward} = \{(m, j) \mid \forall m \in SAGVN, \forall j \in SJIN, APS(m, j) = [0,1,C_{mj}]\}$$

   The number of these arcs in the $G_{MCF-AGV}$ is M×N. Each arc has the lower bound zero, and the upper bound one, i.e., only one AGV goes through each of these arcs. As we mentioned before (see Assumption 5-10), our objectives are to minimize waiting and traveling times of the AGVs and the lateness times of jobs. The cost between node m and node j is calculated as follows:

   $$C_{mj} = \begin{cases} w_1 \times (t_j - (RTA_m + TTA_{mj})) + w_2 \times (RTA_m + TTA_{mj}) \ if \ (t_j \geq RTA_m + TTA_{mj}) \\ P \times (RTA_m + TTA_{mj} - t_j) \ otherwise \end{cases}$$

   If AGV m could arrive on the quayside before the appointment time of the job associated with node j ($t_j \geq RTA_m + TTA_{mj}$), there is no lateness time to serve the job. Therefore the waiting and traveling times of AGV m to serve the job associated with node j are calculated as the cost. Otherwise, the lateness time to serving node j with a penalty (P) is considered. Note that there is neither waiting nor traveling time for the AGV in the second case.

2. **Intermediate Arcs:** There is a directed arc from every Job-Output node i to other Job-Input node j. We define the following notation for these arcs along with their properties:

$ARC_{intermediate}$: a set of arcs from SJOUT to SJIN.

$ARC_{intermediate} = \{(i, j) \mid \forall i \in SJOUT, \forall j \in SJIN, j \neq JIN_i, APS(m, j) = [0,1,C_{ij}]\}$

The number of these arcs in the $G_{MCF\text{-}AGV}$ is N×(N−1). Each arc has the lower bound zero, and the upper bound one, i.e., only one AGV goes through from one job to another. The cost between node i and node j in the $G_{MCF\text{-}AGV}$ is calculated as follows:

$$ C_{ij} = \begin{cases} w_1 \times (t_j - (t_i + DT_{ij})) + w_2 \times DT_{ij} \; if \; (t_j \geq t_i + DT_{ij}) \\ P \times (t_i + DT_{ij} - t_j) \; Otherwise \end{cases} $$

The first case shows that an AGV can serve the job associated with node j after serving the job associated with node i $(t_j \geq t_i + DT_{ij})$. In this case waiting and traveling times of the AGV are calculated without any lateness time. In the second case, there is neither waiting nor traveling time for the AGV and only the lateness time of serving node j with a penalty (P) is considered for the cost.

3. **Outward Arcs:** There is a directed arc from every Job-Output node i and AGV node m to SINK. We define the following notation for these arcs along with their properties:

$ARC_{outward}$: a set of arcs from SJOUT and SJAGVN to SINK.

$ARC_{outward} = \{(i, j) \mid \forall i \in SAGVN \; U \; SJOUT, j=SINK; APS(m, j) = [0,1,0]\}$

These arcs show that an AGV can remain idle after serving any number of jobs or without serving any job. Therefore, a cost of zero is assigned to these arcs.

4. **Auxiliary Arcs:** There is a directed arc from every Job-Input node i to its Job-Output node. We define the following notation for these arcs along with their properties:

$ARC_{auxiliary}$: a set of arcs from SJIN to SJOUT.

$ARC_{auxiliary} = \{(i, j) \mid \forall i \in SJIN, j=$a unique Job-Output node in SJOUT, corresponding to the Input-Node i; APS$(i, j) = [1,1,0]\}$

These arcs have unit lower and upper bounds. The transition cost across these arcs is zero.

These auxiliary arcs guarantee that every Job-Input and Job-Output node is visited once only so that each job is served.

Therefore, there are M×N+N×(N−1)+M+2×N arcs in the $G_{MCF\text{-}AGV}$ so that:

$$AS = ARC_{inward} \cup ARC_{intermediate} \cup ARC_{outward} \cup ARC_{auxiliary}$$

5.5.3 The MCF-AGV Model for the Automated Guided Vehicles Scheduling

Now we present the special case of the MCF model for the Automated Guided Vehicles Scheduling with the following definition.

Definition 5-12: An MCF-AGV model is a special case of the MCF (Definition 5-10) for the Scheduling problem of AGVs in the container terminals. An MCF-AGV model is defined as follows:

$$MCF - AGV = \left(G_{MCF-AGV}, f, D, CS, FC\right)$$

where:

$G_{MCF\text{-}AGV}$ = (GS, NPS, APS) is a graph for the MCF-AGV problem;

f = a finite set of integer decision variables on AS, $f = \{f_{ij} \mid (i, j) \in AS\}$;

D = a function which determines a lower and upper bound for f; D: $f \rightarrow$ N×N (to be pulled out from APS); for each element in D, corresponding to the type of arcs:

1) $D_{f_{ij}}$ = [0,1] for $(i, j) \in ARC_{inward} \cup ARC_{intermediate} \cup ARC_{outward}$
2) $D_{f_{ij}}$ = [1,1] for $(i, j) \in ARC_{auxiliary}$

CS = The constraints of the MCF-AGV are:

$$
\left\{
\begin{array}{l}
1) \displaystyle\sum_{j:(i,j)\in AS} f_{ij} = 1; \quad \forall i \in SAGVN \\[2em]
2) \displaystyle\sum_{j:(j,i)\in AS} f_{ji} = M; \quad for \; i = SINK \\[2em]
3) \displaystyle\sum_{j:(i,j)\in AS} f_{ij} - \sum_{j:(j,i)\in AS} f_{ji} = 0; \quad \forall i \in \{SJIN \cup SJOUT\}
\end{array}
\right\}
$$

The first constraint shows every node i ($i \in$ SAGVN) sends one unit flow into the network. The second constraint ensures SINK node receives M units flow (the flows sent from nodes in SAGVN set). The third constraint shows the flow balance at every Job-Input and Job-Output node.

$$FC = \sum_{(i,j)\in AS} C_{ij} \cdot f_{ij}$$

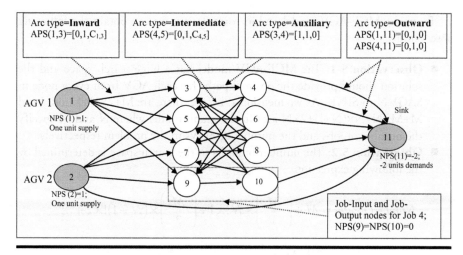

| Arc type=**Inward**
APS(1,3)=[0,1,C$_{1,3}$] | Arc type=**Intermediate**
APS(4,5)=[0,1,C$_{4,5}$] | Arc type=**Auxiliary**
APS(3,4)=[1,1,0] | Arc type=**Outward**
APS(1,11)=[0,1,0]
APS(4,11)=[0,1,0] |

Figure 5.5   An example of the MCF-AGV model for 2 AGVs and 4 jobs.

Solving the MCF-AGV model generates M paths, each of which commences from a node in SAGVN and terminates at SINK. Each path determines a job sequence for every AGV. The decision variable f_{ij} for every arc $(i,j) \in$ AS (the flow between nodes i and j in the G$_{MCF-AGV}$) is either 1 or 0. $f_{ij} = 1$ means that an AGV goes from node i to node j. Otherwise, moving the AGV from node i to node j is not possible.

The MCF-AGV model of the problem can be illustrated by Figure 5.5 for two AGVs and four container jobs. According to our definitions for nodes and arcs in the MCF-AGV model, we have the following sets with their properties:

- SAGVN = {1,2}; NPS(1) = NPS(2) = 1
- SJIN = {3,5,7,9}; NPS(j) = 0, ∀$j \in$ SJIN
- SJOUT = {4,6,8,10}; NPS(j) = 0, ∀$j \in$ SJOUT
- SINK = {11}; NPS(11) = −2
- ARC$_{inward}$ = {(1,3), (1,5), (1,7), (1,9), (2,3), (2,5), (2,7), (2,9)}; APS(m,j) = [0,1,C$_{m,j}$], ∀$m \in$ SAGVN, ∀$j \in$ JIN
- ARC$_{intermediate}$= {(4,5), (4,7), (4,9), (6,3), (6,7), (6,9), (8,3), (8,5), (8,9), (10,3), (10,5), (10,7)}; APS(i,j) = [0,1,C$_{i,j}$] ∀ $i \in$ SJOUT, ∀$j \in$ SJIN
- ARC$_{outward}$ = {(1,11), (2,11), (4,11), (6,11), (8,11), (10,11)}; APS(i,j) = [0,1,0], ∀i ∈ SJOUT, ∀$j \in$ SJIN
- ARC$_{auxiliary}$ = {(3,4), (5,6), (7,8), (9,10)}; APS(i,j) = [1,1,0]; ∀ $i \in$ SJOUT, ∀j ∈ SJIN

We showed one example for each type of arc with their properties (the lower bound, upper bound and cost, respectively) in Figure 5.5. Suppose that for some values of arc costs, the solution paths are 1→3→4→9→10→11 and 2→5→6→7→8→11. This states that AGV 1 is assigned to serve container jobs 1 and 4, and AGV 2 is assigned to serve container jobs 2 and 3, respectively.

From the MCF-AGV model and its formulation, we can obtain the following observations:

- **Observation 5-1:** The MCF-AGV model has a huge search space and the solution should provide the optimal paths for each AGV from every node in SAGVN to SINK. As we mentioned before, there are M+2×N+1 nodes and M+M×N+N×(N−1)+2×N arcs in the graph model where N and M specify the number of jobs and the number of AGVs in the problem respectively.
- **Observation 5-2:** The number of paths in the search space is determined by the following expression:

$$NumberOfPaths = M + \binom{M}{1} \times N! \times 1 + \binom{M}{2} \times (N-1)! \times 2 + \dots.$$

$$+ \binom{M}{M} \times (N - M + 1)! \times M$$

$$where \binom{P}{Q} = \frac{P!}{Q! \times (P-Q)!}$$

The expression shows that every possible path in the search space must be investigated. The first term represents paths from every node in SAGVN to SINK. The remaining terms show the number of paths when 1, 2,..., M (M ≤ N) AGVs, respectively, are selected to serve the jobs.

5.6 Summary and Conclusion

In this chapter, a scheduling problem in the container terminal was presented and formulated. The problem was to carry many container jobs from quayside to yardside or vice versa by several AGVs. Each job has an appointment time on the quayside and the jobs should be served in their appointment time by the AGVs.

The formulation was based on the MCF model. We introduced the G_{MCF} = (G, NP, AP), a graph G with a couple of functions for the Node's Properties (NP) and the Arc's Property (AP) for the MCF model. After that we presented a formal definition for the MCF model; MCF = (G_{MCF}, f, D, CS, FC), where f, D, CS, and FC were the decision variables, domain of f, constraints, and objective function, respectively.

We established the scheduling problem of AGVs on the MCF model. In order to do that, we defined a graph, $G_{MCF-AGV}$, for the problem. Then, we introduced the MCF-AGV model for the scheduling problem, as a special case of the MCF model. The decision variables with value one identified the path for the AGVs inside the graph $G_{MCF-AGV}$. There are always feasible and optimal solutions since the formulation is based on the standard form of the MCF model.

Chapter 6

Network Simplex: The Fastest Algorithm

In Chapter 5, the scheduling problem of Automated Guided Vehicles (AGVs) in the container terminals was formulated as a special case of Minimum Cost Flow model. The model was introduced as the MCF-AGV. This chapter focuses on the standard Network Simplex Algorithm (NSA) to tackle the MCF-AGV in static aspect. In this aspect the number of jobs, the distance between the source and destination of the jobs, and the number of vehicles do not change (see Assumption 5-9).

6.1 Reasons to Choose NSA

The main reasons to choose NSA are as follows:

- NSA is a solution for the Minimum Cost Flow (MCF) model. This model has a rich history and it arises in almost all industries, including agriculture, communications, defense, education, energy, health care, manufacturing, medicine, retailing, and transportation [3].
- The area of development algorithm to tackle the MCF model by NSA is under-researched and offers fertile research opportunities for large-scale problems. Several researches have been devoted to this matter [2, 4, 38, 68, 85, 110, 129, 137] in recent years.
- NSA is based on simple network operations. With simple network operations, the MCF model can be solved more than a hundred times faster than equivalently sized Linear Programs [100]. It is the fastest algorithm for solving the generalized network flow problem in practice [3].

DOI: 10.1201/9781003308386-8

6.2 The Network Simplex Algorithm

In the NSA, the linear algebra of Original Simplex Algorithm (OSA) (in Operation Research) is replaced by simple network operations. Ahuja, Magnanti, and Orlin (1993) described the NSA and gave pseudo-codes, implementation, and hints [3]. Here, the standard form of NSA is presented. More details and several other algorithms for the MCF problem can be seen in the textbook [3].

6.2.1 Spanning Tree Solutions and Optimality Conditions

Given graph $G_{MCF} = ((N, A), NP, AP)$ for the MCF problem (see Definition 5-8), the standard form of MCF problem [3] was as follows:

$$MinCostFlow = \sum_{(i, j) \in A} c_{ij} \cdot f_{ij}$$

$$SubjectTo \begin{cases} \sum_{j:(i, j) \in A} f_{ij} - \sum_{j:(j, i) \in A} f_{ji} = b_i, \text{ for all } i \in N \\ m_{ij} \leq f_{ij} \leq M_{ij}, \text{ for all } (i, j) \in A \end{cases}$$

In the NSA, it is assumed that the network is connected. Every connected graph has a spanning tree [3]. Some preliminary definitions related to the spanning tree are:

Definition 6-1: A spanning tree solution for the MCF problem is divided into three sets of arcs (T, L, U) of the graph. Given n as the number of nodes in the graph, $T \subset A$ is a set consisting of $n{-}1$ arcs. The remaining arcs are divided into the two sets L and U. For these two sets, $f_{ij} = m_{ij}$ for each arc $(i, j) \in L$ and $f_{ij} = M_{ij}$ for each arc $(i, j) \in U$.

Definition 6-2: A spanning tree solution with $m_{ij} \leq f_{ij} \leq M_{ij}$ is a feasible spanning tree solution. In Figure 6.1, the spanning tree is a feasible spanning tree solution provided that for each dotted arc $m_{ij} \leq f_{ij} \leq M_{ij}$.

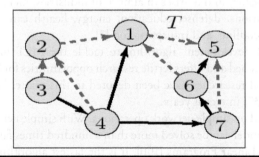

Figure 6.1 A feasible spanning tree solution (dotted).

Before stating the optimality condition of NSA, a couple of theorems and a property for the algorithm are presented.

Theorem 6-1 [3]: The MCF problem is a special form of the Linear Program (in Operation Research). Given n nodes and k arcs in the graph model, the MCF problem can be represented as follows:

$$Min\, Cost\, Flow = c_{1 \times k}\, f_{k \times 1}$$

$$Subject\, to \begin{cases} H_{n \times k}\, f_{k \times 1} = b_{n \times 1} \\ m_{k \times 1} \le f_{k \times 1} \le M_{k \times 1} \end{cases}$$

In this formulation, the matrices of b, c, f, m, and M are the same as in the MCF problem (see Section 5.4.2). The coefficient matrix, H, is called the node-arc incidence matrix. The elements of this matrix are defined as follows:

$$H_{ij} = \begin{cases} +1\ If\ node\ i\ is\ the\ start\ of\ j^{th}\ arc \\ -1\ If\ node\ i\ is\ the\ end\ of\ j^{th}\ arc \\ 0\ otherwise \end{cases}$$

Theorem 6-2 [3]: A flow vector of a basic solution for the Linear Program is a spanning tree solution of the MCF problem. Flows on non-basic arcs are either m_{ij} or M_{ij}.

Property 6-1 [3]: Suppose that a number $\pi(i)$ is associated with each node $i \in N$, which is referred to as the potential of that node. With respect to the node potentials $\pi = (\pi(1), \pi(2), \dots, \pi(n))$, the reduced cost $\overline{C}_{ij}$ of an arc (i, j) is defined as follows:

$$\overline{C}_{ij} = C_{ij} - \pi(i) + \pi(j)$$

Theorem 6-3 (Necessary Optimality Conditions): The Optimality Conditions of the spanning tree solution (T, L, U) is obtained by the Lagrangian of the MCF problem. The Lagrangian of the MCF problem is:

$$L(f, \pi) = \sum_{(i,j) \in A} c_{ij} \cdot f_{ij} - \sum_{i \in N} \pi_i \cdot \left(\sum_{j:(i,j) \in A} f_{ij} - \sum_{j:(j,i) \in A} f_{ji} - b_i \right)$$

$$= \sum_{(i,j) \in A} \left(c_{ij} - \pi_i + \pi_j \right) f_{ij} + \sum_{i \in N} \pi_i \cdot b_i$$

Minimizing $\mathbf{L}(f, \pi)$ over $m_{ij} \le f_{ij} \le M_{ij}$ gives dual feasibility and complementary slackness conditions [200]. If the reduced cost is zero, f_{ij} could have any values between m_{ij} and M_{ij}. Otherwise, the f_{ij} has the maximum (minimum) value when the reduced cost is negative (positive). Hence, the optimality conditions are:

$$\bar{C}_{ij} = C_{ij} - \pi(i) + \pi(j) \succ 0 \Rightarrow f_{ij} = m_{ij} ; (i, j) \in L$$
$$\bar{C}_{ij} = C_{ij} - \pi(i) + \pi(j) \prec 0 \Rightarrow f_{ij} = M_{ij} ; (i, j) \in U$$
$$\bar{C}_{ij} = C_{ij} - \pi(i) + \pi(j) = 0 \Rightarrow m_{ij} \leq f_{ij} \leq M_{ij} ; (i, j) \in T$$

Given n nodes in the network, the spanning tree (T) has $n-1$ arcs. The potential of each node is calculated by the last equation $(\pi(i)-\pi(j) = C_{ij})$. The potential of one node is set arbitrarily. Usually it is the root of the tree with value 0 for its potential [3].

In NSA, it is worked with the reduced cost, instead of the actual cost [3]. It is important to determine the relationship between the objective functions $z(\pi) = \sum_{(i, j) \in A} \bar{c}_{ij} \cdot f_{ij}$ and $z(0) = \sum_{(i, j) \in A} c_{ij} \cdot f_{ij}$. Suppose, initially, that $\pi = 0$, then we increase the potential of node k to $\pi(k)$. The definition of reduced cost implies that this change reduces the reduced cost of each unit of flow leaving node k by $\pi(k)$ and increases the reduced cost of each flow unit entering node k by $\pi(k)$. Thus the total decrease in the objective function equals $\pi(k)$ times the outflow of node k minus the inflow of node k. By the constraint for each node, the outflow minus inflow equals the supply/demand of the node. Consequently, increasing the potential of node k by $\pi(k)$ decreases the objective function value by $\pi(k) \times b(k)$ units. Repeating this argument iteratively for each node establishes that:

$$z(0) - z(\pi) = \sum_{i \in N} \pi(i) b(i) = \pi b$$

Given node potential π, the term $\pi.b$ is a constant. Therefore, a flow that minimizes $z(\pi)$ also minimizes $z(0)$. This result is used in **Theorem 6-4.**

Theorem 6-4 (Sufficient Optimality Conditions) [3]: Let f^* be the solution associated with the spanning tree structure (T, L, U). Suppose that some set of node potential π, together with the spanning tree structure (T, L, U) satisfy the optimality conditions.

It is needed to show that f^* is an optimal solution of the MCF problem. Previously, it was shown that minimizing $z(\pi) = \sum_{(i, j) \in A} \bar{c}_{ij} \cdot f_{ij}$ is equivalent to minimizing $z(0) = \sum_{(i, j) \in A} c_{ij} \cdot f_{ij}$. The optimality conditions stated as above imply that for the given node potential π, $z(\pi) = \sum_{(i, j) \in A} \bar{c}_{ij} \cdot f_{ij}$ is equivalent to minimizing the following expression:

$$Minimize \sum_{(i, j) \in L} \bar{c}_{ij} \cdot f_{ij} - \sum_{(i, j) \in U} |\bar{c}_{ij}| \cdot f_{ij}$$

The definition of the solution f^* implies that for any arbitrary solution f, $f_{ij} \geq f^*_{ij}$ for all $(i,j) \in L$ and $f_{ij} \leq f^*_{ij}$ for all $(i,j) \in U$. The above expression implies that the objective function value of the solution f will be greater than or equal to that of f^*.

In an economic aspect, the following interpretations can be stated [3]:

- $\bar{c}_{ij}$ is the amount of change in the objective function, if there is one unit change in f_{ij}.
- π_i is the cost of sending one unit of flow from node i to the root along the tree path.
- $c_{ij} - \pi_i$ is the cost of obtaining one unit of the commodity at node i and then shipping it to node j.

6.2.2 The Algorithm NSA

The NSA maintains a feasible spanning tree structure at each iteration and successfully transforms it into an improved spanning tree structure until it becomes optimal. The algorithm in Figure 6.2 specifies steps of this method ([3, 89]).

Figure 6.2 shows four main steps in the algorithm:

- **Step 0**: Create an initial or Basic Feasible Solution (BFS).
- **Step 1:** Select an entering arc (which is appended to the spanning tree).
- **Step 2:** Determine the leaving arc (which must be removed from the spanning tree).
- **Step 3:** Pivoting (exchange the entering and leaving arc).

Step 0: To create an initial or Basic Feasible Solution, the graph has to be connected, which corresponds to the MCF-AGV model in Chapter 5. In Line 3, creating an initial feasible spanning tree solution (see Definition 6-2) for every

```
1: Algorithm Network simplex method
2: Begin
3:      Create initial BFS; (T, L, U)  ◄──────── Step 0: Create a basic feasible solution
4:      (k, l) ◄── Entering arc ∈ {L + U} ◄──── Step 1: Select an entering arc
5: While (k, l) < > NULL Do
6:      Find cycle W ∈ {T + (k, l)}
7:      θ ◄── Flow change                     ◄──── Step 2: Determine the leaving arc
8:      (p, q) ◄── Leaving arc ∈ W
9:      Update flow in W by θ
10:     Update BFS; Tree T          ◄──── Step 3: Exchange the entering and leaving arc
11:     Update node potentials
12:     (k, l) ◄── Entering arc ∈ {L + U}
13: End while
14: End algorithm
```

Figure 6.2   The Network Simplex Algorithm.

connected graph can be made in an easy way [3]. It is obtained by adding an artificial root node '0' to N and the artificial slack arcs $(i,0)$ and $(0,i)$, respectively, to A. Each artificial slack arc has the lower bound of zero, the upper bound of infinity, and a sufficiently large cost coefficient. The initial basic tree consists of all artificial arcs, each original arc becomes non-basic at its lower bound and no arc becomes non-basic at the upper bound. We examine each node j, other than '0', one by one. If $b\,(j) \geq 0$, we include $(j,0)$ in T with a flow value of $b\,(j)$. If $b\,(j) < 0$, we include arc $(0,j)$ in T with a flow value of $-b(j)$. The set L consists of the remaining arcs, and the set U is empty.

Step 1: At each iteration of the algorithm, an entering arc is selected by some pricing schemes [89]. This arc is selected from the non-basic arcs (L + U). There are several schemes for selecting the entering arc and these determine the speed of the algorithm. A literature review of these schemes is presented later in this chapter. An arc may be admitted to the basis to improve the objective function if it violates the optimality conditions. Thus an arc $(i,j) \in A$, with the following conditions, is admissible:

$$If\ \bar{C}_{ij} \prec 0\ and\ f_{ij} = m_{ij}$$

$$or\ \bar{C}_{ij} \succ 0\ and\ f_{ij} = M_{ij}$$

If no admissible arc exists, then the current solution is optimal, and the algorithm terminates. Otherwise, Step 2 is performed.

Step 2: Appending the entering arc, (k,l), to the spanning tree forms a unique cycle, W, with the arcs of the basis. In Line 6, the algorithm finds out the cycle. In order to eliminate this cycle in the tree, one of its arcs must leave the basis. By augmenting flow in a negative cost augmenting cycle, the objective value of the solution can be improved. The cycle is eliminated when there is an augmented flow by a sufficient amount to force the flow in one or more arcs of the cycle to their upper or lower bounds. In Line 7, the flow change is determined by the following equation:

$$\vartheta = Min\left\{\Delta f_{ij} \text{ for all } (i, j) \in W\right\}.$$

The leaving arc is selected based on cycle W and ϑ, in Line 8.

Step 3: In this step, the entering arc and the leaving arc are exchanged, and the new BFS is constructed. The construction of a new basis tree is called the pivot; adjusting flows, making the new spanning tree, and updating the node potentials accordingly in the spanning tree solution (T, L, U). These operations are performed in Lines 9, 10, and 11, respectively. We refer to cycle W (see Step 2) as the basis cycle. The algorithm sends a maximum possible amount of flow in the basis cycle without violating any of the lower and upper bound constraints on arcs. An arc that blocks further increase of flow in the basis cycle is called a blocking arc. The flow in every arc of the cycle W is increased or decreased by the amount θ depending on the orientation of the arc in relation to the orientation of the cycle. Generally, a basic arc is exchanged with a non-basic arc. The algorithm drops a blocking arc, say (p,q), from T. This gives a new basis structure. Let T1 and T2 be the two sub-trees formed by deleting arc (p,q) from the previous basis T where T1 contains the root. In the new basis, potentials of all nodes in T1 remain unchanged and potentials of all nodes in T2 change by a constant amount. If (k,l) was a non-basic arc at its lower bound in the previous basis structure, then the amount of change is an increase by $|\bar{C}_{kl}|$, else it is a decrease by an amount $|\bar{C}_{kl}|$.

6.2.3 The Difference between NSA and Original Simplex

Those steps in NSA can be compared with the OSA to solve the Linear Program in Operation Research. Note that the main difference is that NSA is based on the graph and operations in the graph while the OSA needs a matrix and matrix manipulations. Step 0 is taken to find an initial solution in both algorithms. An initial basic spanning tree is created by adding the artificial node and arcs in NSA. In a similar way, OSA uses the artificial variables to generate an initial basic solution. Steps 1 and 2 in both algorithms are choosing the entering and leaving arc in NSA, which are similar to choosing the entering and leaving variable in OSA. Constructing a new spanning tree in NSA and new basic solution in OSA is Step 3 for both algorithms. In this way, OSA needs some matrix manipulation and inversion, whereas a new spanning tree can be easily constructed by some operation in the graph without any multiplication or division. Both algorithms continue Steps 1–3 until they meet the optimality conditions. Obviously, the matrix manipulations are different from graph operations, which have significant negative impacts on the performance of OSA.

6.2.4 A Literature over Pricing Rules

In order to find out an entering arc for the basic solution, there are different rules, which are called pricing schemes. The performance of the NSA is affected by these schemes. A literature review over these schemes is given below.

The standard textbook [3] provided a detailed account of the literature on those schemes. We now briefly review this literature. Bradley, Brown, and Graves (1977), used a dynamic queue, containing the indices of so-called "interesting" nodes and admissible arcs. Their method is called the **BBG Queue pricing scheme**. An "interesting" node is a node whose incident arcs have not been re-priced in recent iterations. At each iteration, the entering arc is selected from the queue. Another candidate list scheme has been described by Mulvey (1978). In the **Mulvey scheme**, there is a major and minor loop to select the entering arc. A limited number of favorably priced entering arcs are collected by scanning the non-basic arcs in a major iteration. In the minor iteration, the most favorably priced arc in the list is chosen to enter the basis. Grigoriadis (1986) describes a very simple arc **block pricing scheme** based on dividing the arcs into a number of subsets of specified size. At each iteration, the entering arc is selected from a block with the most negative price. Only the arcs of one block are re-priced at any iteration. Taha (1987) suggested **the most negative pricing scheme** for the algorithm. At each iteration, all non-basic arcs are re-priced, and the arc with the most negative price is selected as the entering arc. Kelly and Neill (1993) implemented a variation of the arc block pricing scheme, which is called **arc sample** [89]. Instead of selecting the entering arc from among the required number of consecutive arcs, this method considers arcs at constant intervals, called the skip factor, from throughout the entire arc set. Andrew (1993) studied the practical implementation of minimum cost flow algorithms and claimed that his implementations worked very well over a wide range of problems [7].

Istvan reviewed a collection of some known pricing schemes in the OSA [85]. They are **First improving candidate**, **Dantzig rule**, **Partial pricing**, **Multiple pricing**, and **Sectional pricing**. These schemes can be applied to NSA. The first improving candidate chooses the first violate arc as the entering arc. It is cheap but it usually leads to a very large number of iterations. In the Dantzig rule all non-basic arcs are checked (full pricing) and the one which violates the optimality condition the most is selected. This rule is quite expensive but overall is considerably better than the previous method. The Partial pricing scans only a part of the non-basic arcs and the best candidate from this part is selected. In the next step, the next part is scanned, and so on. In Multiple pricing, some of the most profitable candidates (in terms of the magnitude) are selected during one scanning pass. They are updated and a sub-optimization is performed involving the current basis and the selected candidates using the criterion of greatest improvement. The Sectional pricing behaves as a kind of partial pricing, but in each iteration sections or clusters of arc are considered.

In recent years, several pieces of research have been devoted to the NSA. Muramatsu (1999) used a **primal-dual symmetric pivoting rule** and proposed a new scheme in which the algorithm can start from an arbitrary pair of primal and dual feasible spanning trees [129]. Eppstein (1999) presented a **clustering technique** for partitioning trees and forests into smaller sub-trees or clusters [38]. This technique has been used to improve the time bounds for optimal pivot selection in the primal NSA for the minimum cost flow problem. Lobel (2000) developed and implemented the **multiple pricing rules** to select an entering arc, a mixture of several sizes for the arc block [110]. A **general pricing scheme** for the simplex method has been proposed by Istvan (2001). His pricing scheme is controlled by three parameters. With different settings of the parameters, he claimed that it creates large flexibility in pricing and is applicable to general and network simplex algorithms [85]. Ahuja et al. (2001) developed an NSA with $O(n)$ consecutive degenerate pivot [4]. They presented an **anti-stalling pivot rule** based on the concept of a strong feasible spanning tree, which is described in the following section. Their rule uses a negative cost augmenting cycle to identify a sequence of entering variables. Paparrizos et al. (2009) presented a new Network Exterior Point Simplex Algorithm (NEPSA) for the minimum cost network flow problem [140]. NEPSA belongs to a special simplex type category and is a modification of the classical NSA. The main idea of the algorithm is to compute two flows. One flow is basic but not always feasible and the other is feasible but not always basic. The authors also presented a complete proof of correctness for the proposed algorithm. Moreover, the computational behavior of NEPSA is shown by an empirical study carried out for randomly generated sparse instances created by the well-known GRIDGEN network problem generator.

6.2.5 Strongly Feasible Spanning Tree

The definition of the strongly feasible solution for NSA and a property are given below:

Definition 6-3 [3]: The basis structure (T, L, U) is strongly feasible if we can send a positive amount of flow from any node to the root along arcs in the spanning tree without violating any of the flow bounds. An equivalent way of stating this property is that no upward pointing arc of the spanning tree can be at its upper bound and no downward pointing arc can be at its lower bound. An example of a strongly feasible basis is given in Figure 6.3. Note that the current flow and upper bound of every arc are given on each arc in the figure. The Lower bound of the arcs is zero.

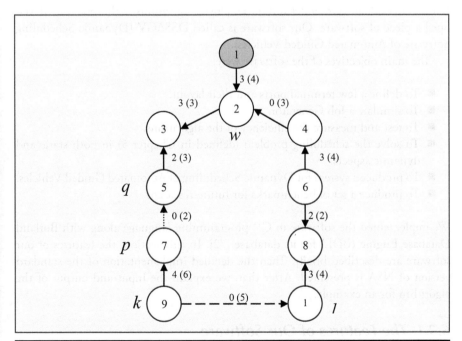

Figure 6.3   An example of a strongly feasible spanning tree. See [3].

The NSA can maintain a strongly feasible basis at every iteration. In order to do this, the initial basic solution, which was described in the previous section, should be strongly feasible. The algorithm may also select the leaving arc appropriately so that the next basis would be also strongly feasible. Suppose that the entering arc (k,l) is at its lower bound and node w is the first common predecessor of nodes k and l. Let W be the basis cycle formed by adding arc (k,l) to the basis tree. This cycle consists of the basis path from node w to node k, the arc (k,l), and the basis path from node l to node w. After updating the flow, the algorithm identifies blocking arcs. If the blocking arc is unique, then it leaves the basis. If there is more than one blocking arc, then the algorithm should select the leaving arc to be the last blocking arc encountered in traversing W along its orientation starting at node w. For example, in Figure 6.3, the entering arc is (9,10), the blocking arcs are (2,3) and (7,5), and the leaving arcs is (7,5). It can be shown that the above rule guarantees that the next basis is strongly feasible [3]. A strongly feasible basis has the following property.

> **Property 6-2 [3]:** Due to degeneracy, cycling may occur in the NSA. By maintaining a strongly feasible basis due to Cunningham (1976, 1979), cycling can be prevented without restrictions on the entering variable.

6.3 Simulation Software

In order to evaluate our model and the employed algorithms in this book, we developed a piece of software. Our software is called DSSAGV (Dynamic Scheduling Software of Automated Guided Vehicles).

The main objectives of the software were:

- To define a few terminal ports and their layout.
- To simulate a Job Generator.
- To test and measure the efficiency of the algorithms.
- To solve the scheduling problem (defined in Chapter 5) in both static and dynamic aspects.
- To produce a system for Dynamic Scheduling of Automated Guided Vehicles.
- To produce a set of benchmarks for future research.

We implemented the software in C^{++} programming language along with Borland Database Engine (BDE) for its database [72]. In this section, the features of our software are described briefly. Then the detailed implementation of the standard version of NSA is presented. After that, we explain the input and output of the algorithm for an example.

6.3.1 The Features of Our Software

Figure 6.4 shows the main screenshot of the software. It shows a couple of vessels, five Quay Cranes (QCs), one Rubber Tyred Gantry Crane (RTGC) in each block

Figure 6.4   The main screenshot of the software.

of the Storage Area, and several AGVs. Figure 6.4 also shows the main menu as well as several buttons including "Port," "Route," "Containers," "Vehicles," and "Process." These buttons have been shown under the main menu and designed as hotkeys to facilitate the software execution.

Some important features of DSSAGV are described briefly as follows:

■ The user can define a few ports, a number of blocks in the yard, a number of working positions or cranes in the berth, and a number of AGVs in each port. The "port" button activates this feature.

■ A facility to generate a random distance between every two points in the yard or berth has been considered. The user can change the distance. The "route" button activates this feature.

■ At the beginning of the process, the start location of each vehicle may be any point of the port. The user can define or change the ready time of the vehicles at the start location and the location as well. But at the first stage, the software generates them randomly. The "vehicle" button activates this feature.

■ A Job Generator was designed and implemented in the software. For static and dynamic fashion, a few container jobs may be generated to transport from their source to their destination. Either the source or destination of each job is the quayside, which can be chosen randomly by the Job Generator. There are three options for Quay Cranes: single crane and multiple cranes, randomly and circular. In the first option, crane number 1 is selected to handle the jobs whereas in the second option one crane, among different cranes in the berth, will be selected to handle the jobs. In the last option, choosing the crane number will be circular; the first job for the first crane, the second job for the second crane, and so on. After the next job is allocated for the last crane, it is the turn of the first crane again.

- The initial time of the operation and the time window for the cranes and vehicles are defined by the user. The first parameter plays a role as the ship's arrival time; the second one determines the processing time of a container job by the crane (namely the time between two consecutive jobs). The last one is the time taken by a vehicle to pickup/dropoff the job from/to the crane. We assume some default values for these parameters.

- The user can monitor some indices to measure the efficiency of the model and algorithm. The waiting or delay time for every job, the number of jobs, and the total traveling and waiting times for every vehicle, are calculated in the static and dynamic problems. The "process" button activates another screenshot of the software. In the screenshot, several panels and facilities for verification and validation of the software have been designed and implemented to help the user. These panels are "Static," "Model," "Dynamic," "Result," "Graph," "Algorithm," and "Performance." The "Static" and "Dynamic" panels are used for the static and dynamic problems. The input and output of the algorithm, before and after solving a problem, can be observed by the user. The "Model" panel shows the input and output of the algorithm. The "Algorithm" panel shows the employed algorithms from which the user can choose one. The "Performance" panel shows the CPU-Time and the number of iterations required to solve the model. The "Graph" panel shows and compares the "Quay Crane time" (when the crane is ready to pickup/dropoff the job from/on the vehicle), the "Vehicle time" (when the vehicle is ready to deliver/pickup the job to/from the crane), and the "Actual time" (the maxima of "Quay Crane time" and "Vehicle time").

- A real-time analogue clock has been designed and implemented. In dynamic aspect, the performance of different parts of the software can be monitored by the clock.

- A relational database has been designed and implemented, alongside the software by Borland Database Engine (BDE). The relationships between tables or the Entity Relationship Diagram (ERD) of the database have been illustrated by Figure 6.5.

There are six tables in the database and their fields are shown in Figure 6.5. The relationships between the tables have been illustrated by one or two fields into the diamond. The DB-Table 1 is considered to store port specification, including

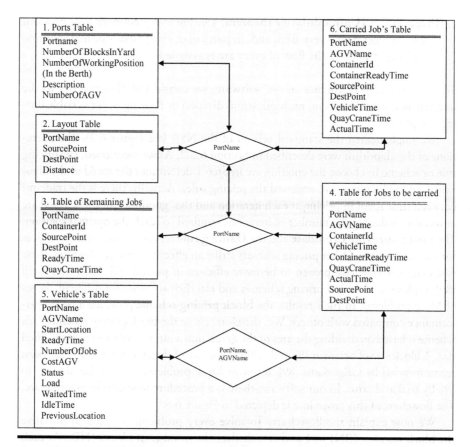

Figure 6.5 **Relationships between the tables of the database.**

the name of ports, the number of blocks in the yard, the number of cranes or working positions, the number of AGVs, and a description for the port. The distance between every different two points either in the yard or in the berth will be stored in DB-Table 2. While the system is doing its processes, the remaining jobs, the jobs to be carried for each vehicle, and the vehicles status are updated in DB-Tables 3, 4, and 5, respectively. The start location, previous location, time traveled, and time waited of the vehicles are stored and updated in DB-Table 5. The ready time of the vehicles to pickup/deliver the job from/to the crane, the time that the crane picks up/delivers the job from/to the vehicle and the "Actual time" of the job served (maximum of the two former times) are stored in DB-Table 4.

6.3.2 The Implementation of NSA in Our Software

Before going to the detail of our implementation, Unimodularity theorem in network flow problem is stated.

Theorem 6-5 (Unimodularity theorem) [3]: For every network flow problem with integer data, every BFS, and, in particular, every basic optimal solution, an integer value to the flow of every arc is assigned.

To get a higher performance in our software, we considered Theorem 6-5 in the implementation. There is no multiplication, division or floating-point variable during the process.

We implemented the standard version of the NSA (see Figure 6.2). The operations of the algorithm were described in Section 6.2.2. As we mentioned, the pricing rule or scheme to choose the entering arc in Step 1 determines the speed of the algorithm. In the literature, we reviewed the pricing rules. Actually, there is the trade-off between time spent in pricing at each iteration and the "goodness" of the selected arc in terms of reducing the number of iterations required to reach the optimal solution. The **First improving candidate** and the **Dantzig rule** represent two extreme choices for the entering arc. Other pricing schemes strike an effective comprise between these two extremes and have proven to be more efficient in practice [3]. Kelly and Neill [89] implemented several pricing schemes and ran their software for different classes of MCF problems. In their results, the **block pricing scheme** provided a better performance compared with others. We, therefore, chose the block pricing scheme. This scheme is based on dividing the arcs of the graph into a number of subsets of specified size. A block size of between 1% and 8.5% of the size of the arcs in the graph has been recommended by Grigoriadis [89], for large MCF problems. We set the number to 5% by trial and error. In our software, there is a procedure to select the entering arc. The flowchart of this procedure is depicted in Figure 6.6.

We now explain the flowchart. To solve every problem, we need to initialize the block number (BN) to 1 and to calculate the number of blocks (NB). At each iteration, the reduced cost of the arcs in a block, identified by BN, is calculated and the optimality condition is checked. Only the arcs of one block are re-priced. Then, the most violated arc within the block is selected as the entering arc. If there is no violated arc in the block, the block number (BN) is increased circularly (1, 2, …, NB, 1, …). If there is no violated arc in the graph (BN=SBN), then the current solution is optimal.

6.3.3 How the Program Works

As we mentioned in Section 5.5, the container jobs to be served and the AGVs to be deployed were considered as nodes in the MCF-AGV model. There were M AGV nodes, 2×N job nodes, and a Sink node, altogether M+2N+1 nodes in the model. The AGV nodes were considered as supply nodes and the Sink was a demand node. Each job was considered with a couple of nodes, Job-Input and Job-Output nodes (see Section 5.5).

A graph $G_{MCF-AGV}$ = (GS, NPS, APS) is made by the software. In the graph, NS is a set of nodes and AS is a set of arcs; NPS, APS are the properties of the nodes

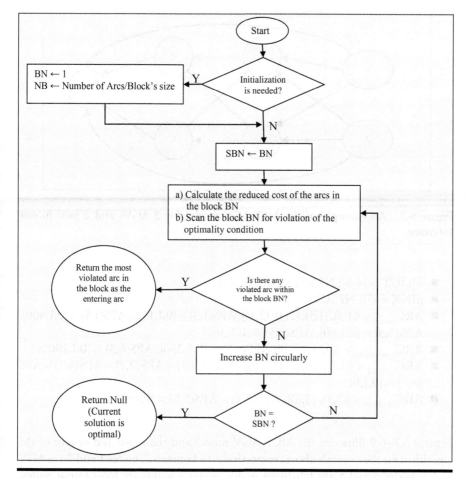

Figure 6.6 Flowchart of Network Simplex Algorithm (Block pricing scheme) to select an entering arc.

and arcs, respectively. We defined the NS and AS and their elements (see Section 5.5 of Chapter 5) as below:

$$NS = SAGVN \cup SJIN \cup SJOUT \cup SINK$$

$$AS = ARC_{inward} \cup ARC_{outward} \cup ARC_{auxiliary} \cup ARC_{intermediate}$$

As an example, assume there are two AGVs to be deployed and two jobs to be served. The nodes and arcs with their properties are:

- SAGVN = {1,2}; NPS(1) = NPS(2) = 1
- SJIN = {3,5}; NPS(3) = NPS(5) = 0

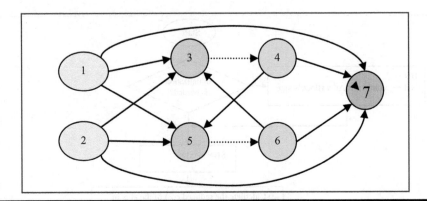

Figure 6.7 An example of the MCF-AGV model for 2 AGVs and 2 jobs in our software.

- SJOUT = {4,6}; NPS(4) = NPS(6) = 0
- SINK = {7}; NPS(7) = −2
- ARC_{inward} = {(1,3), (1,5), (2,3), (2,5)}; APS(1,3) = [0,1,132], APS(1,5) = [0,1,400], APS(2,3) = [0,1,80], APS(2,5) = [0,1,360]
- $ARC_{intermediate}$ = {(4,5), (6,3)}; APS(4,5) = [0,1,280], APS(6,3) = [0,1,10000]
- $ARC_{outward}$ = {(1,7), (2,7), (4,7), (6,7)}; APS(1,7) = APS(2,7) = APS(4,7) = APS (6,7) = [0,1,0]
- $ARC_{auxiliary}$ = {(3,4), (5,6)}; APS(3,4) = APS(5,6) = [1,1,0]

Figures 6.7–6.9 illustrate the MCF-AGV model and the input and output of the algorithm for the example above, respectively. In Figure 6.7, nodes 1 and 2 are AGV nodes, nodes 3 and 5 are Job-Input nodes, nodes 4 and 6 are Job-Output nodes, and node 7 is the Sink node.

In Figure 6.8, the prefixes of 'p', 'c', 'n', and 'a' identify defining the problem, comments, nodes, and arcs in the graph, respectively. The first line in the figure defines a problem with seven nodes and twelve arcs, which has to be minimized. Lines 3 and 4 define supply nodes with the amount of flow to be sent into the network. Line 6 defines the Sink node with the amount of its demand. Other lines in the figure specify the arcs with their tail and head nodes, lower and upper bounds, and transition cost.

Figure 6.9 shows the output of the algorithm. In the figure, the prefixes of 's' and 'f' identify the objective function and solution for the problem. The numbers after prefixes of 'f' determine which arcs have been chosen as the optimal paths for the vehicles. According to the solution for this example, jobs 1 and 2 are served by AGV 2 and there is no job for AGV 1.

```
1 : p min 7   12
2 : c Create Supply nodes
3 : n    1    1
4 : n    2    1
5 : c Create Demand node
6 : n    7   -2
7 : c Create Inward arcs from every vehicle node to every Job-Input node
8 : a    1    3    0  1   132
9 : a    1    5    0  1   400
10: a    2    3    0  1    80
11: a    2    5    0  1   360
12: c Create Outward arcs from every vehicle nodes to the Sink node
13: a    1    7    0  1      0
14: a    2    7    0  1    0
15: c Create Auxiliary arcs from every Job-Input node to its Job-Output node
16: a    3    4    1  1    0
17: a    5    6    1  1    0
18: c Create Outward arcs from every Job-Output node to the Sink node
19: a    4    7    0  1    0
20: a    6    7    0  1    0
21: c Create Intermediate arcs from every Job-Output node to others Job-Input nodes
22: a    4    5    0  1   280
23: a    6    3    0  1  10000
```

Figure 6.8   The input of the algorithm (NSA) in DIMACS (Centre for Discrete Mathematics and Theoretical Computer Science) format.

```
1 :  c Output to Minimum Cost Flow problem
2 :  c The problem was solved with the
3 :  c standard version of the Network Simplex
4 :  c Algorithm.
5 :  c
6 :  c It needed 6 iteration(s) in 0 second(s).
7 :  s Objective function: 360
8 :  f 2 3 1
9 :  f 1 7 1
10: f 3 4 1
11: f 5 6 1
12: f 6 7 1
13: f 4 5 1
14: c
15: c All other flow variables are zero
```

Figure 6.9   The output of the algorithm (NSA) in DIMACS format.

6.3.4 The Circulation Problem

There is a special case for the MCF model, which has no supply nodes and demand nodes. Given $G = (N, A)$ and b_i $(i \in N)$ as the amount of supply/demand flow at node i, for the MCF problem (see Definition 5-8), the circulation problem is defined as follows:

> **Definition 6-4** [3]: The circulation problem is an MCF problem with only transshipment nodes; that is, $b_i = 0$ for all $i \in N$.

The circulation problem may occur in the solutions for the MCF-AGV model. If every AGV could not arrive before the appointment times of the Job-Input nodes (the transition cost from every AGV to the Job-Input node incurs the Penalty) and the cost between any two distinct jobs has not Penalty, the circulation will happen. This problem can be demonstrated by an example in Figure 6.10. In the figure, the number on each arc is its cost and P shows the Penalty (see Section 5.5.2 for the cost and Penalty).

In Figure 6.10, there are two AGVs and two container jobs. In order to send two units flow from AGV nodes 1 and 2 to the Sink node with minimum cost, the solution is 1→7 and 2→7. Other nodes have one unit input and one unit output flow (3→4→5→6→3), according to the constraints. The cost of the problem is 100 + P, which is less than any other possible solution in the network. In this case, neither job1 nor job2 is served.

Although the circulation problem has never happened in our experience (in the static aspect), the following operations are performed to fix the problem. When the solution became ready, the status of every job was checked to see whether it was assigned to a vehicle or not. There are two solutions for the problem. The

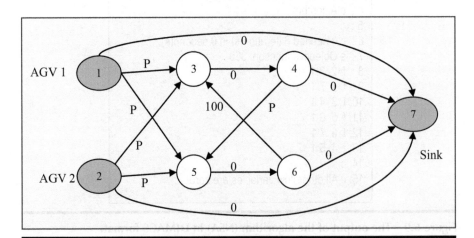

Figure 6.10   An example of the circulation problem (P = penalty).

first solution is to assign the remaining jobs to an idle vehicle. This scheme has a higher priority because moving the vehicles is preferred over their stopping. Among the idle vehicles, a vehicle with minimum cost is assigned to the job. This process continues until there is no remaining job. If the first solution could not solve the problem (no idle vehicle), the second solution is to distribute the remaining jobs among the vehicles randomly.

6.4 Experimental Results

In this section, the results of our implementation and running the algorithm to tackle the static problem of the MCF-AGV model are presented. In the static problem the number of jobs, the distance between source and destination of the jobs, and the number of vehicles do not change (see Assumption 5-9). The values in Table 6.1 were used as parameters in the objective function, for the port specification and to generate the jobs. We considered ECT (European Container Terminal) [36] for the port specification. It includes seven Quay Cranes, thirty-two automatic stacking cranes, and a maximum of fifty AGVs in operation.

Some outputs of running the program in a static fashion were taken. Table 6.2 shows the result, including the number of jobs, the number of nodes, and the

Table 6.1   Values of Parameters for the Simulation

Parameters	Values
Weight of waiting times for the AGVs (W_1 in the costs of the objective function)	1
Weight of traveling times for the AGVs (W_2 in the costs of the objective Function)	5
Number of AGVs in the port	50
Number of Quay Cranes	7
Number of blocks in the yard (Storage area inside the port)	32
Time window of the cranes (the duration of discharging/loading a container)	120 seconds
The distance table (see Table 4.1)	Uniform random distribution between 1 and 100
Time window of the vehicles, time to unload/load a job	2 seconds
P as a penalty (see the costs of the MCF-AGV model in Chapter 5)	10,000

Table 6.2   Experimental Results of Network Simplex Algorithm in Static Fashion

Problem	Number of Jobs	Number of Nodes	Number of Arcs	CPU-Time (Second)
1	500	1,051	275,550	1
2	700	1,451	525,750	2
3	1,000	2,051	1,051,050	4
4	1,200	2,451	1,501,250	6
5	1,300	2,651	1,756,350	7
6	1,400	2,851	2,031,450	6
7	1,500	3,051	2,326,550	9
8	1,500	3,051	2,326,550	11
9	1,600	3,251	2,641,650	13
10	1,700	3,451	2,976,750	15
11	1,800	3,651	3,331,850	17
12	2,000	4,051	4,102,050	27
13	2,100	4,251	4,517,150	28
14	2,200	4,451	4,952,250	33
15	2,300	4,651	5,407,350	47
16	2,500	5,051	6,377,550	49
17	2,700	5,451	7,427,750	59
18	2,710	5,471	7,482,360	64
19	2,715	5,481	7,509,740	65
20	2,718	5,487	7,526,192	66
21	2,800	5,651	7,982,850	68
22	2,900	5,851	8,557,950	86
23	2,930	5,911	8,734,380	100
24	2,940	5,931	8,793,590	99
25	3,100	6,201	9,768,150	122
26	3,200	6,401	10,403,250	136
27	3,300	6,601	11,058,350	137

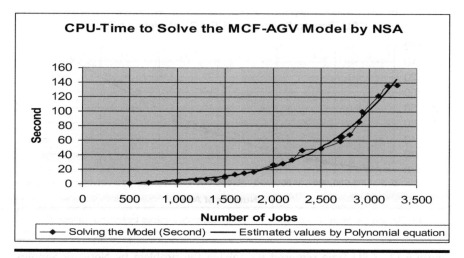

Figure 6.11 CPU-Time required for solving the problem by Network Simplex Algorithm, based on the number of jobs.

number of arcs in the MCF-AGV model. The CPU-Time required solving the MCF-AGV problems is also shown in Table 6.2.

Note that those results have been collected by running our software on a Pentium PC with a 2.4 GHz processor and 1GB of RAM. Obviously, on different computers, CPU-Time is not the same.

The CPU-Time required to solve the MCF-AGV model is demonstrated by Figures 6.11 and 6.12, according to both the number of jobs and number of arcs in the graph model. Based on our observations the estimated values by a polynomial equation for the CPU-Time are also shown on the figures. We assumed degrees 3 and 2 for the polynomial equations respectively in Figure 6.11 and Figure 6.12.

From the figures, we can observe that:

Observation 6-1: The NSA is fast and efficient. It could find out the global optimal solution for the problem of three thousand jobs and ten million arcs in the MCF-AGV model within two minutes.

Observation 6-2: From the figures, it seems that NSA is run in polynomial time to solve the MCF-AGV model in practice.

There are two different types of iteration in NSA, degenerate and non-degenerate [3]. In every non-degenerate iteration, the value of the objective function is decreased whereas degenerate iterations do not change the objective function's value. In the degenerate iterations, a flow change of zero causes cycling. In the literature, Grigoriadis experienced that cycling is rare in practical application [89]. Observation 6-1 confirms the experience.

In order to confirm that NSA is run in polynomial time to solve the MCF-AGV model (Observations 6-2), we estimated the complexity of the algorithm in the next section.

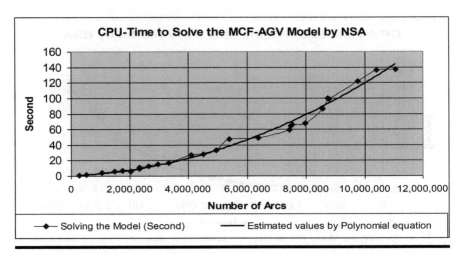

Figure 6.12 CPU-Time required for solving the problem by Network Simplex Algorithm, based on the number of arcs.

6.5 An Estimate of the Algorithm's Complexity in Practice

The time complexity can be expressed in CPU-Time required solving the MCF-AGV model. The CPU-Time is estimated based on the number of jobs and number of arcs in the graph model. Based on Observations 6-1 and 6-2, we considered the following equations to estimate the CPU-Time:

$$CPU-Time_{NSA} = a_1 \times NumberofJobs^3 + a_2 \times NumberofJobs^2 + a_3 \times NumberofJobs$$

$$CPU-Time_{NSA} = b_1 \times NumberofArcs^2 + b_2 \times NumberofArcs$$

The experimental results in Table 6.2 were used to estimate the parameters of 'a1', 'a2', 'a3', 'b1', and 'b2' in the equations. The estimation's results for the parameters have been shown in Tables 6.3 and 6.4. The Coefficient section of the tables specifies values for 'a1', 'a2', 'a3', 'b1', and 'b2' in the equations.

Based on the Coefficients in Tables 6.3 and 6.4 for values of the parameters, we have the following equations for the CPU-Time to solve the MCF-AGV model:

$$CPU-Time_{NSA} = 8.11 \times 10^{-9} \times NumberofJobs^3 - 1.83 \times 10^{-5}$$
$$\times NumberofJobs^2 + 0.154 \times NumberofJobs$$

$$CPU-Time_{NSA} = 1.05 \times 10^{-12} \times NumberofArcs^2 + 1.4 \times 10^{-6} \times NumberofArcs$$

The degree of the second equation is less than the first one, because the number of arcs is extremely greater than the number of jobs.

Table 6.3 Regression Result for CPU-Time Required Solving the Problem by NSA (Based on the Number of Jobs)

Multiple R	R-Square	Adjusted-R-Square	Standard Error	Observations	
0.99	0.99	0.94	5.24	27	
	DF	SS	MS	F	Significance-F
Regression	3.00	47310.45	15770.15	574.17	0.00
Residual	24.00	659.18	27.47		
Total	27.00	47969.63			
	Coefficients	Standard-Error	t-Stat	P-value	Lower 95%	Upper 95%
X Variable 1	1.54E-02	6.14E-03	2.50	1.95E-02	2.71E-03	2.81E-02
X Variable 2	−1.83E-05	5.52E-06	−3.31	2.94E-03	−2.96E-05	−6.87E-06
X Variable 3	8.11E-09	1.19E-09	6.83	4.58E-07	5.66E-09	1.06E-08

Table 6.4 Regression Result for CPU-Time Required Solving the Problem by NSA (Based on the Number of Arcs)

Multiple R	R-Square	Adjusted-R-Square	Standard-Error	Observations	
0.99	0.99	0.95	5.07	27	
	DF	SS	MS	F	Significance-F
Regression	2	47327.497	23663.75	921.29	2.0415E-23
Residual	25	642.1324	25.68		
Total	27	47969.63			
	Coefficients	Standard-Error	t-Stat	P-value	Lower 95%	Upper 95%
X Variable 1	1.40E-06	6.30E-07	2.23	3.50E-02	1.07E-07	2.70E-06
X Variable 2	1.05E-12	7.41E-14	1.41	1.98E-13	8.95E-13	1.20E-12

Note that for any prediction the equation for the CPU-Time in practice depends on other factors, such as the speed of the processor, other active programs when the problem is being solved in multi-task operating systems, and so on. Our program has been run on a Windows 2000 computer with a Pentium 2.4 GHz processor in the normal situation.

More details about the information in the two tables and their explanations follow:

- **DF:** It stands for the degrees of freedom. There are twenty-seven samples in this experiment.
- **SS**: It refers to the Sum of Squares differences between the values of curve fitted and the average of the dependent variable (for Regression), and the Sum of Squares differences between the actual values of the dependent variable and the values of curve fitted (for Residual).
- **MS:** It stands for the Mean Square, which is calculated by dividing the SS over the DF.
- **F:** This is a test statistic. A large value indicates that the estimated equation is significant in the sense that it is unlikely to have resulted from random variation.
- **Significance-F:** It gives us the probability that we would get this result by random chance. This value for both estimations is zero.
- **R-Square:** This is the percentage of the SS of Regression over the SS of Total. It reveals how closely the values of the estimated curve correspond to the actual data. Its value is 0.99 for both estimations.
- **Multiple-R:** This is the square root of the R-Square. It is the correlation between the dependent variable and the curve fitted.
- **Adjusted-R-Square:** This indicates the percentage of the variations explained by the model. Its value for both estimations is 0.99. This is useful because we assumed two independent variables in the model.
- **Standard-Error:** This is the square root of the Residual Mean Square discussed above. It is essentially the standard deviation of the points around the regression curve. This is very useful in evaluating how big a mistake we are likely to make when using the model for prediction. Its value is 5.24 and 5.07, respectively, for both estimations.
- **t-Stat:** This is a statistic for a null hypothesis that the coefficient is zero. The "t-Stat" value is calculated by dividing the coefficient by its standard error. The large value of "t-Stat" indicates that it is of a low probability to have occurred by chance. Usually, a "t-Stat" greater than two is considered to indicate a model is significant.
- **P-value:** This gives a probability that the coefficient is zero. Its value for each coefficient of both estimations is almost zero.
- **Lower and Upper 95%:** These give an upper and lower bound on a 95% confidence interval for the coefficients. Given α as a coefficient, S_α as its standard

error, and *t* as the critical value of the *t* distribution at 95% confident limit, the values are calculated as follows:

$$\alpha \pm t \times (S_\alpha)$$

6.6 Limitation of the NSA in Practice

The question is how big (the number of vehicles, the number of jobs) of a problem can be solved by NSA within time *t*, a minute for example? The answer is that there is no limitation in NSA theoretically. In practice, the answer is based on the platform and implementation. Given the number of jobs and number of vehicles, N and M respectively in our formulation, there are M+2×N+1 nodes and M+M×N+N×(N−1)+2×N arcs in the MCF-AGV model. The limitation is due to the available memory to put the MCF-AGV model into. The largest problem, which has been solved by our software, was an MCF-AGV model consists of 11,058,350 arcs (M=50; N=3,300; see Table 6.2). Based on this maximum number of arcs and the related formula, the number of vehicles (M) and the number of jobs (N) can have different values. Hence, we have another observation from the experiment:

Observation 6-3: Although NSA is efficient and provides the optimal solution, it can only work on a problem with certain limits in size. The limitation is due to the available memory to put the MCF-AGV model into.

6.7 Summary and Conclusion

In this chapter, the steps of NSA were reviewed. To select the next basic solution at each step of the algorithm, the literature over different pricing schemes was presented. Then, the standard version of NSA with the block pricing scheme was applied to the MCF-AGV model (defined in Chapter 5). To test the program, random data were generated and fed to the model for fifty vehicles.

Based on our experiment, we can now conclude that with simple network operation in the graph and specializations, NSA is efficient. Our software, which has been implemented in Borland C++ and run on a 2.4 GHz Pentium PC, could find the global optimal solution for three thousand jobs and ten million arcs in the MCF-AGV model within two minutes. Although the algorithm is efficient and provides the optimal solution, it can only work on problems with certain limits in size. When the size of the problem goes beyond the limit, incomplete solution methods should be used.

Chapter 7

Network Simplex Plus: Complete Advanced Algorithm

In Chapter 6, the static scheduling problem of Automated Guided Vehicles (AGVs) in container terminals was solved by the standard version of Network Simplex Algorithm (NSA). In this chapter, some modifications are applied to NSA to obtain a novel version of the algorithm. The new algorithm is then applied to the dynamic scheduling problem of AGVs in container terminals (the problem defined in Chapter 5 and modeled as the MCF-AGV).

7.1 Motivations

Although NSA is efficient, cycling may occur in the algorithm. Additionally, to tackle the dynamic scheduling problem in Chapter 5, we need more efficient algorithms. In dynamic problems, new jobs arrive continually, the fulfilled jobs are removed, and the distance between the source and destination of jobs may be changed. The objective of this chapter is to develop a new version of NSA, which avoids cycling and is faster. We call it Network Simplex plus Algorithm (NSA+). Like NSA, NSA+ is a complete algorithm, which means it guarantees optimality of the solution if it finds one within the time available.

DOI: 10.1201/9781003308386-9

7.2 The Network Simplex Plus Algorithm (NSA+)

NSA+ is an extension of NSA. Compared with the standard version of NSA, it has two features. Firstly, it deals with the concept of strongly feasible solution [3]. Secondly, a mixture of heuristic approach and memory technique is used in NSA+. These features are explained below.

7.2.1 Anti-Cycling in NSA+

The first feature is related to maintaining the strongly feasible basis at each iteration (see Definition 6-3 in Chapter 6). At the beginning, NSA+ chooses a strongly feasible solution (see Step 0 of NSA in Chapter 6). In each pivot, the leaving arc is selected appropriately by the last blocking arc in the cycle so that the next basis is also strongly feasible (see Figure 6.3 as an example). We avoid cycling in NSA+ by this feature (see Property 6-2 in Chapter 6).

7.2.2 Memory Technique and Heuristic Approach in NSA+

The second feature of NSA+ is concerned with the entering arc (Step 1 in Figure 6.2). In order to find the entering arc, there is a procedure in our software. The flowchart of this procedure is depicted by Figure 7.1.

The arcs in the graph are divided into several blocks with the same size. At each iteration, a packet of the violated arcs are collected. The capacity of the packet is more than the block's size, and the most violated arcs are kept at the top of the packet. The memory technique uses a few elements at the top of the packet for the next iteration. Clearly, the size of memory must not be too big since it prevents from collecting new violated arcs. To get a higher performance in solving large-scale problems, we set the block's size and the size of memory to two hundred and twenty-five, respectively. In our software, DSSAGV, the blocks are identified by a Block-Number, and the first one is chosen Randomly or by a Heuristic method (based on the location of the largest cost in the graph, for example). To solve every problem, we need to initialize the Block-Number and calculate the number of blocks. At the initial stage, the packet is empty. Then, scanning of the arcs for violation of the optimality conditions among the blocks is performed circularly. At each scan, one violated arc (at most) from each block is put in the packet.

At the beginning of the entering arc procedure, the reduced costs of the most violated arcs in the previous stage are recalculated. If they violate the optimality conditions again, they are kept in the packet. Otherwise, they could be replaced by new violated arcs. Then, some new violated arcs, based on the scanning of arcs from the blocks, are put into the packet so long as it has an empty place. At the end of the procedure if the packet is empty (there is no violated arc in the graph), then the current solution is optimal. Otherwise, the packet will be sorted decreasingly, based on the absolute value of the reduced costs, and the most violated arc (at the top of the packet) will be chosen as the entering arc.

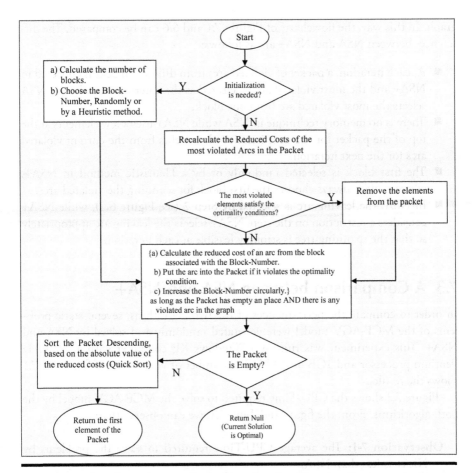

Figure 7.1   Flowchart of network simplex plus algorithm to select an entering arc.

As we mentioned, there are two options available in choosing the first block, Randomly or Heuristically. With this aspect, NSA+ has two extensions:

■ **NSA+R:** The entering arc procedure chooses the first block by Random selection.
■ **NSA+H:** The entering arc procedure chooses the first block by a Heuristic method (based on the location of the largest cost in the graph).

7.2.3 *The Differences between NSA and NSA+*

The main difference between NSA and NSA+ are in the pricing scheme and the entering arc procedure. As we mentioned (see Section 6.2.4), the role of the pricing scheme impacts how the entering arc is to be selected from the violated arcs in the graph. In this way, the flowcharts of Figures 7.1 and 6.6 can be compared. The differences between NSA and NSA+ are as follows:

- At each iteration, a packet of violated arcs from different blocks is collected in NSA+ and the most violated arc is selected as the entering arc, whereas NSA selects the most violated arc from one block.
- There is no memory technique in NSA while NSA+ uses a few elements at the top of the packet for the next iteration. It benefits from the current violated arcs for the next iteration.
- The first block is selected randomly or by a Heuristic method in NSA+, whereas NSA always chooses the first block for scanning the violated arcs.
- In NSA, the leaving arc is selected by Step 2 (see Figure 6.2), while NSA+ considers a restriction on the step. NSA+ selects the leaving arc appropriately so that the spanning tree is strongly feasible at each iteration.

7.3 A Comparison between NSA and NSA+

In order to compare the performances of the two algorithms, several static problems of the MCF-AGV model were generated randomly and solved by NSA and NSA+. This experiment was run on a Windows XP computer with a 2.2 GHz Pentium processor and 1GB of RAM. The number of vehicles was fifty. Table 7.1 shows the results.

Figure 7.2 shows the CPU-Time required to solve the MCF-AGV model by the both algorithms. From the figure and Table 7.1, we can observe that:

Observation 7-1: The average CPU-Time required to solve the problems by NSA+ is less than NSA.

In order to calculate the average CPU-Time required to solve the problems and to compare performance of the algorithms in this experiment, we introduce the following terms:

T_i^{NSA}: The CPU-Time used to solve the problem i by NSA.

T_i^{NSAH}: The CPU-Time used to solve the problem i by NSA+H.

T_i^{NSAR}: The CPU-Time used to solve the problem i by NSA+R.

PIH_i: The Percentage of Improvement in CPU-Time used to solve the problem i by NSA+H compared with NSA.

PIR_i: The Percentage of Improvement in CPU-Time used to solve the problem i by NSA+R compared with NSA.

TPIH: The Total Percentage of Improvement in CPU-Time used to solve the problems by NSA+H compared with NSA.

TPIR: The Total Percentage of Improvement in CPU-Time used to solve the problems by NSA+R compared with NSA.

Table 7.1 Experimental Results for a Comparison between NSA and NSA+

Problem	Number of Jobs	CPU-Time by NSA (second)	CPU-Time by NSA+H (second)	CPU-Time by NSA+R (second)	Problem	Number of Jobs	CPU-Time by NSA (second)	CPU-Time by NSA+H (second)	CPU-Time by NSA+R (second)
1	50	0.005	0.005	0.005	17	1100	6.741	3.2532	4.644
2	60	0.005	0.005	0.005	18	1200	8.217	3.5577	6.885
3	70	0.009	0.0047	0.005	19	1300	11.996	5.1795	8.180
4	80	0.009	0.0048	0.005	20	1400	11.039	12.3	10.500
5	90	0.009	0.0045	0.010	21	1500	12.548	7.092	7.092
6	100	0.024	0.0093	0.011	22	1600	15.980	14.208	17.208
7	150	0.033	0.0327	0.033	23	1700	20.592	10.734	18.246
8	200	0.061	0.0468	0.050	24	1800	26.462	12.342	18.426
9	300	0.103	0.117	0.113	25	1900	36.526	17.081	27.294
10	400	0.600	0.225	0.525	26	2000	30.951	21.651	30.810
11	500	0.394	0.3795	0.381	27	2100	37.152	23.301	24.816
12	600	1.415	0.6984	0.745	28	2200	48.683	25.546	28.242
13	700	1.003	0.8298	0.950	29	2300	46.588	36.069	39.609
14	800	1.307	0.9981	1.298	30	2400	57.050	33.613	35.113
15	900	4.566	1.7718	3.272	31	2500	64.084	40.018	61.179
16	1000	5.259	2.5359	3.849	32	2600	70.553	62.952	55.735

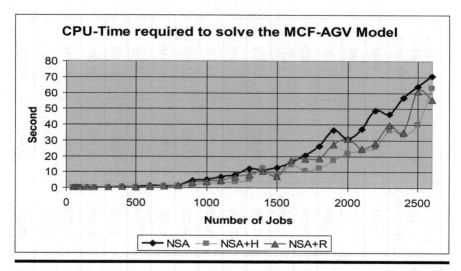

Figure 7.2 A comparison of CPU-Time required solving the same problems by NSA and NSA+.

W_i: The Weight of improvement for the problem i. In this experiment we consider the number of arcs in the MCF-AGV model for the weight. Given N jobs and M AGVs in the problem, the number of arcs is M+M×N+N×(N-1)+2×N.

Now we calculate the percentage of improvements in the CPU-Time used for problem i by the following terms:

$$PIH_i = \frac{100 * (T_i^{NSAH} - T_i^{NSA})}{T_i^{NSA}}$$

$$PIR_i = \frac{100 * (T_i^{NSAR} - T_i^{NSA})}{T_i^{NSA}}$$

The total percentage of improvements in the CPU-Time used to solve the problems by NSA+H and NSA+R, compared with NSA, is calculated by the following equations:

$$TPIH = \frac{\sum_{i=1}^{32} W_i \times PIH_i}{\sum_{i=1}^{32} W_i} = -35.16\%$$

$$TPIR = \frac{\sum_{i=1}^{32} W_i \times PIR_i}{\sum_{i=1}^{32} W_i} = -21.28\%$$

Table 7.2   The Result of *t*-Test for the Two Algorithms, NSA and NSA+

Statistical Parameters	NSA+H vs. NSA	NSA+R vs. NSA
Observations	32	32
t-Test (paired two sample for means)	–4.1799	–3.3617
Degree of freedom	31	31
Critical T-value	–1.6955	1.6955

In order to determine which factor, from the two features, made these improvements, we disabled the first feature (maintaining the strongly feasible spanning tree) and ran the software for some problems. We got the following observation:

> **Observation 7-2:** There was no significant change in the improvement for the non-strongly feasible spanning tree. In the literature, Grigoriadis had experienced that cycling is rare in practical application [89]. Therefore, the second feature has significant impact on the CPU-Time required to solve the problems. In fact, the memory technique and scanning method are the most important features of NSA+.

7.4 Statistical Test for the Comparison

The CPU-Time required to solve the problems by the two algorithms, NSA and NSA+, were analyzed statistically. We tested the null hypothesis so that the means produced by the two algorithms were statistically indifferent. Table 7.2 provides the test's result along with the critical values of T-distribution for the particular degree of freedom. The *t*-test confirms that NSA+ is significantly better than NSA with 95% degree of confidence.

The values and hypotheses to do the test between the means of NSA+H and NSA are demonstrated by Figure 7.3. The hypotheses are on whether the mean

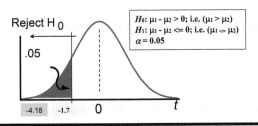

Figure 7.3   The *t*-test acceptance and reject regions (NSA and NSA+H).

CPU-Time for NSA+H is greater than NSA or not. The values of "*t*-test" and "Critical T-value" are shown in Figure 7.3. As we can see the result of the *t*-test is inside the reject region. The same examination is performed to do statistical test analysis between the means of NSA+H and NSA. The result of this test also shows the mean of CPU-Time for NSA+H is less than NSA.

7.5 Complexity of Network Simplex Plus Algorithm (NSA+)

Assume that the Maximum Flow (MF) in each of the m arcs, at maximum cost, C, for the Minimum Cost Flow model. So there is an upper bound on the value of the objective function. This upper bound is given by $m \cdot C \cdot MF$. There are two different types of pivots in the algorithm, non-degenerate and degenerate pivots. The former is bounded by $m \cdot C$ because the number of non-degenerate pivots in the algorithm is bounded by $m \cdot C \cdot MF$ (MF = 1 in the MCF-AGV model). The number of degenerate pivots is determined by the sum of nodes potential and maintaining the strongly feasible spanning tree. Given n as the number of nodes in the graph model, the sum of nodes potential is bounded by $n^2 \cdot C$. It is decreased at each iteration when the spanning tree is strongly feasible [3]. A series of degenerate pivots may occur between each pair of non-degenerate pivots, and thus a bound on the total number of iterations is $m \cdot n^2 \cdot C^2$. Find the entering arc is $O(m)$ and sorting the packet is $O(K \cdot LogK)$ operation (K is size of the packet, K = 225). Finding the cycle, amount of flow change, leaving arc and updating the tree are $O(n)$ operations. Hence the complexity of each pivot is $O((m + n) K \cdot LogK)$. Based on the complexity of the number of iterations and the complexity of each pivot, the total complexity of this algorithm is determined as follows:

$$O\left((m+n)mn^2C^2KLogK\right)$$

Given N and M (M < N), respectively, as the number of jobs and AGVs in the MCF-AGV model (see Section 5.5 in Chapter 5), we have the following results:

$$m = O(N^2); \quad n = O(N)$$

Therefore, the total complexity of NSA+ Algorithm to tackle the MCF-AGV model is:

$$O(N^6)$$

We estimated the performance of NSA+ by the experimental results of Table 7.1 (see Section 6.5). The results support this complexity.

7.6 Software Architecture for Dynamic Aspect

The architecture of the main part of the software for the dynamic scheduling problem of AGVs is demonstrated in Figure 7.4. At the start of the process, the Job Generator generates a few jobs for each crane. These jobs will be appended to the remaining jobs, which are empty at the beginning. The remaining jobs are used to make up an MCF-AGV model. Then the model will be tackled by NSA+. The output of this algorithm is a few job sequences for the vehicles. Based on these sequences the software will prepare a job list for each vehicle.

Flowchart of Figure 7.5 demonstrates what is done in the real-time processing and dynamic aspect while the time is being progressed. Note that the termination condition for the end of simulation is determined by meeting a specific time, ten hours or a day for example.

At the beginning, based on the solution to the current problem, a job is assigned to each vehicle and crane. During the simulation, the handling of the jobs by the cranes and vehicles are executed in parallel.

Briefly, the software does two tasks. The first task is related to updating the status of the vehicles and cranes whereas the second one takes influence from any change in the problem or any idle crane.

As depicted in the flowchart, the status of each crane and the traveling and waiting times of every vehicle are updated while the time is being progressed. At the same time, if the vehicles pick up the job from the quayside, the job will be removed from the crane, list of jobs for the vehicles and the remaining jobs. After that, the new job will be assigned to the vehicles and cranes. If a job has to be delivered to the crane on the quayside, it could not be removed until the meeting time between the crane and the vehicle. Note that, the appointment place of the jobs is on the quayside, not the yardside.

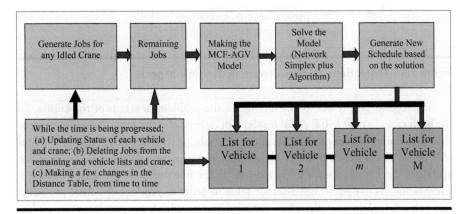

Figure 7.4 Block diagram of the software and algorithm (NSA±) for dynamic aspect.

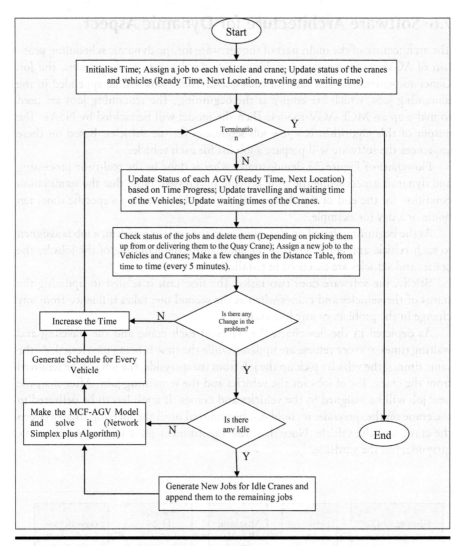

Figure 7.5   Operations of the software in dynamic aspect.

The second task refers to any change in the problem or status of the cranes. In the both cases, a new MCF-AGV model will be made by the remaining jobs (except the current job for every vehicle) and the new jobs (if there are any). The new model will be tackled by NSA+ from scratch. Then, the new solution will be used for updating the list of jobs for every vehicle. Every five minutes, the software makes a few random changes in the distance table in order to produce dynamic problems (see Table 5.1). Additionally, when the Job Generator finds out any idle crane, it has to generate a few jobs for the crane.

Note that generating jobs for any idle crane, making the MCF-AGV model, solving the model and generating new schedule for the vehicles are performed sequentially. These tasks are not preemptive, i.e., when a task starts execution on the processor it finishes to its completion.

One important question remained. How many new jobs should be generated for any idle crane and what is the best situation for the problem? The answer to this question depends on the stability of the schedule and the software's performance. Generally, the first factor is related to any change in the problem and traffic in the routes such as congestion, collision, livelock, and deadlock. Since we assume that the vehicles are moving with an average speed so that there is no traffic problem, the answer to this question is determined by the rate of change in the problem and software's performance.

7.7 Experimental Results from the Dynamic Aspect

In order to evaluate the result of NSA+ for the Scheduling problem of AGVs in dynamic aspect, we did a simulation for six hours. In this simulation, the distance between every two points in the port as well as the source and destination of jobs were chosen randomly. During the simulation, the Job Generator generated five jobs for any idle crane. Other parameters were the same as Table 6.1.

We put some parts of the simulation's results in Figures 7.6 and 7.7. Figure 7.6 shows the traveling and waiting times of the vehicles as well as the waiting times of the cranes.

Figure 7.7 shows three attributes of the carried jobs based on "Appointment time" of jobs. These attributes are "QCraneTime" (when the crane is ready to pickup/dropoff the job from/on the vehicle), "VehicleTime" (when the vehicle is

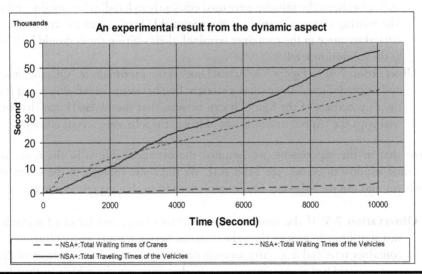

Figure 7.6 An experimental result from the dynamic scheduling problem of AGVs (NSA± solved the problem).

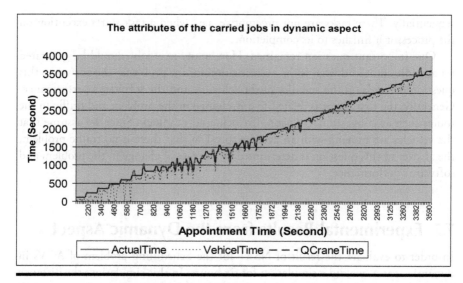

Figure 7.7 The attributes of the carried jobs in the dynamic scheduling problem of AGVs.

ready to deliver/pickup the job to/from the crane), and "ActualTime" (when the job has been served).

In this experiment, our observations were:

Observation 7-3: As we can see in Figure 7.6, the traveling times of the vehicles are significantly greater than their waiting times after 2,700 seconds. This indicator shows the vehicles were used efficiently to handle the container jobs. The waiting times of cranes are at a reasonable level. Since the cranes are a critical resource in the container terminal, their waiting times should be kept at the minimum level.

Observation 7-4: In Figure 7.7, "ActualTime" is the maximum of "QCraneTime" and "VehicleTime." If we draw a straight line between the left-down and the right-up corners of the figure, it can be seen that the "ActualTime" has fits well with the "Appointment times." Hence, the jobs were served efficiently.

Note that in the experiment, we assumed the distance table is in the range of the time window of cranes (see Table 6.1). We did some changes in the values of Table 6.1 and ran the software. Our observations from that experiment were:

Observation 7-5: If the time window of cranes (e.g., two hundred seconds) was significantly greater than the distance between every two points in the container terminal (e.g., fifty seconds on average), then waiting times of the cranes would be less than our results. In this situation, the vehicles waited for the cranes more, and therefore the jobs were served with more delay.

Observation 7-6: If the time window of cranes (e.g., twenty seconds) was significantly less than the distance between every two points in the container terminal (e.g., two hundred seconds on average), then waiting times of the cranes would be greater than our results. In this situation, the cranes waited for the vehicles more, and therefore the jobs were served with more delay.

7.8 Summary and Conclusion

In this chapter, some modifications were applied to NSA to obtain a new version of the algorithm, NSA+. The main features of NSA+ deal with the entering arc and leaving arc. In order to find an entering arc, the algorithm uses a mixture of memory techniques and heuristic method. Additionally, the leaving arc is chosen appropriately so that the spanning tree of the graph always becomes strongly feasible. NSA+ prevents cycling by this feature.

Then, the same static problems were solved by both algorithms NSA and NSA+, and CPU-Time required to solve the problems were compared. Our experiments showed that NSA+ can solve the problems faster than NSA.

NSA+ is a complete and polynomial algorithm. We employed NSA+ to solve the dynamic scheduling problem of AGVs in a container terminal (defined in Chapter 5 and presented by the MCF-AGV). The result of a six-hour simulation showed the "Actual time" of jobs, during which they had been handled by the vehicles and cranes, fitting well with their "Appointment times." Based on our experiments, NSA+ is a practical algorithm for dynamic Automatic Vehicle Scheduling.

Chapter 8

Dynamic Network Simplex: Dynamic Complete Advanced Algorithm

In this chapter, we extend Network Simplex Algorithm in dynamic aspect. In this aspect Dynamic Network Simplex Algorithm (DNSA) and Dynamic Network Simplex plus Algorithm (DNSA+) are presented. Then, NSA+ and DNSA+ are applied to the dynamic scheduling problem of Automated Guided Vehicles in container terminals (the problem defined in Chapter 5) and their results are compared.

8.1 Motivations

The objectives of DNSA are to solve the new problem faster, to use some parts of the previous solution for the next problem, and to respond to changes in the problem. These objectives are explained below:

Firstly, although Network Simplex Algorithm is much faster than the traditional simplex algorithm for Linear Programs, for dynamic scheduling with large-scale problems, it still takes time to make a new MCF-AGV model and to solve it. The dynamic problem arises when new jobs are introduced, fulfilled jobs are removed, and the distance between the source and destination of the jobs is changed. The dynamic problems need more efficient algorithms [156].

DOI: 10.1201/9781003308386-10

Secondly, in most practical environments, scheduling is an ongoing reactive process where the presence of real-time information continually forces reconsideration and revision of pre-established schedules. The second goal of DNSA is to repair the solution based on dynamic changes, rather than having to resolve it from scratch each time.

Thirdly, in many applications of graph algorithms, including communication networks, graphics, assembly planning, and scheduling, graphs are subject to discrete changes, such as additions or deletions of arcs or nodes. In the last decade, there has been a growing interest in such dynamically changing graphs, and a whole body of algorithms and data structures for dynamic graphs has been discovered [159]. In a typical dynamic graph problem, one would like to respond to the changes in the graph that are undergoing a sequence of updates, for instance, insertions and deletions of arcs and nodes.

8.2 Classification of Graph Algorithms and Dynamic Flow Model

Given the powerful versatility of dynamic algorithms, it is not surprising that these algorithms and dynamic data structures are often more difficult to design and analyze than their static counterparts. Rauch (1992) classified dynamic graph problems according to the types of updates allowed [159]. A graph is said to be fully dynamic if the update operations include unrestricted insertions as well as deletions of arcs and nodes. A graph is called partially dynamic if only one type of update, either insertions or deletions, is allowed. If only insertions are allowed, the graph is called incremental; if only deletions are allowed, it is called decremental. In this chapter, our graph is fully dynamic.

The dynamic flows networks over time and their variations are very challenging problems. These types of problems are arising in various real applications such as communication networks, air/road traffic control, and production systems. Some examples and further applications of the problems are found in the references (see [8, 44, 74, 147, 176]). Below we survey the results most closely related to the dynamic network flows and problems.

Shen et al. (2007) [171] and Zheng and Chiu (2011) [220] worked on a dynamic problem and made simplified System Optimal Dynamic Traffic Assignment (SO-DTA) model. The model is based on the concept of Cell-Transmission Model (CTM), which requires the links in the graph model to be decomposed into cells in space and time. Both works gave definitions on traffic holding in CTM based on a single commodity and single destination problem. Shen et al. (2007) utilized a network flow structure and solved a simplified SO-DTA, thus losing the ability to capture wave propagation and queue spillback effects. They suggested a post-processing algorithm to remove traffic holding from a solution generated by the Linear Programming, but this algorithm depends on the fact that the traffic holding does not improve the objective function value. Zheng and Chiu observed that the definition on diverge node may lead to a suboptimal solution [220], and for the diverge links, it may be better to hold instead of discharging all flow early. So they only applied the definition of holding-free solution to merge ordinary links. Then, they proved that an augmenting path algorithm produces holding-free solutions at non-diverge links. Therefore, the definitions of holding-free in [171] and [220] are too strict for diverging nodes; the algorithms may lead to suboptimal and are not appropriate for most dynamic problems.

Nasrabadi and Hashemi (2007) present a general minimum cost dynamic flow problem in a discrete time model with time-varying transit times, transit costs, transit capacities, storage costs, and storage capacities [134]. For this problem, the authors develop an algorithm, which is a discrete-time version of the successive shortest path. The time complexity of the algorithm is O $(V \times n \times T \times (n + T))$ where V is an upper bound on the total supply, n is the number of nodes, and T denotes the given time horizon of the dynamic flow problem.

Parpalea (2011) presents an approach for solving bi-criteria minimum cost dynamic flow problem with continuous flow variables [142]. The approach is to transform a bi-criteria problem into a parametric one by making a single parametric linear cost out of the two initial cost functions. The approach iteratively finds efficient extreme points in the decision space by solving a series of minimum parametric cost flow problems with different objective functions. On each of the iterations, the flow is augmented along a minimum path from the source node to the sink node in the time-space network avoiding the explicit time expansion of the network.

Based on the previous research, Parpalea and Ciurea (2011) represent a generalization of the maximum flow of minimum cost problem for the case of minimizing the traveling cost (minimum cost flow) and traveling time (quickest flow). On this generalization, the research states a multi-criteria maximum flow problem in discrete dynamic networks with two objective functions [144]. Then a solution method is based on generating efficient extreme points in the objective space by iteratively solving a series of maximum flow problems with different single objective functions. Each time, the dynamic flow is augmented along a minimum cost path from the source node to the sink node in the time-space network while avoiding the explicit time expansion of the network. Parpalea and Ciurea (2011) also study the generalization of the maximum flow of minimum cost problem for the case of maximum discrete dynamic flow of minimum traveling cost and time [144]. Their approach is very similar to the one used in [142].

Hosseini (2011) introduces another class of dynamic network flows in which the flow commodity is dynamically generated at source nodes and dynamically consumed at sink nodes [77]. As a basic assumption in this research, the source nodes produce the flow according to time generative functions and the sink nodes absorb the flow according to time consumption functions. In the general form and some special cases, the dynamic problems arise when the capacities and costs are time varying. This research formulates the problem as the minimum cost dynamic flow problem for a pre-specified time horizon. To solve the problems, some simple and efficient approaches based on the minimum cost static flow models are developed.

Ciurea and Parpalea (2010) present a dynamic solution method for dynamic minimum flow networks [30]. The solution method solves the problem for a special parametric bipartite network. Instead of directly working on the original network, the method uses the parametric residual network and finds a particular state of the residual network from which the minimum flow and the maximum cut for any of the parameter values are obtained. The research implements a round-robin algorithm looping over a list of nodes until an entire pass ends without any change of the flow.

Fonoberova (2010) presents other classes of dynamic flow networks with the cases of nonlinear cost functions on arcs, multi-commodity flows, and time- and flow-dependent transactions on arcs of the network [43]. All parameters of the networks are assumed to be dependent on time. To formulate the problems, the classical optimal flow problems on networks are extended and generalized. The algorithms for solving such kinds of problems are developed by using special dynamic programming techniques based on the time-expanded network method together with classical optimization methods. To solve the problem, the author proposes an approach based on the reduction of the dynamic problem to a static problem. This approach is employed for solving some power systems problems by using optimal dynamic flow problems.

Fathabadi (2011) proposes a minimum flow problem on network flows in which the lower arc capacities in the graph model vary with time [167]. For a set of time points, this problem is solved by at most n minimum flow computations. The solution method is based on combining of pre-flow-pull algorithm and re-optimization techniques. The complexity of the presented algorithm is $O(n^2m)$ where m is the number of arcs in the graph model.

Sherbeny (2012) proposes a new version of the minimum cost flow problem on a time varying and time windows [37]. For each vertex in the network, three integer parameters are considered. These parameters are waiting cost, vertex capacity, and time windows. In order to obtain dynamic networks, all these parameters are functions of the time. The objective is to find an optimal schedule to send a flow from the source vertex to it's the sink vertex satisfies a time window constraint with minimum cost and minimum waiting times at vertices, subject to the constraint that the flow must arrive at the sink vertex before a deadline. In this paper, the developed algorithm does search, successively, for the shortest paths from the source vertex s to the sink vertex in a dynamic residual network and then transmit as much as possible flow along the paths so that satisfies the time window constraint..

Geranis et al. (2012) develop a new Dual Network Exterior-Point Simplex Algorithm (DNEPSA) for the Minimum Cost Network Flow Problem (MCNFP) [50]. The algorithm starts from an initial dual feasible tree-solution, and, after a number of iterations, it reaches an optimal solution by producing a sequence of tree solutions that can be both dual and primal infeasible. In following the work, Geranis and Sifaleras (2013) utilize the dynamic trees data structure in the DNEPSA algorithm, in order to achieve an improvement of the amortized complexity per pivot [35]. In extensive computational studies, DNEPSA performed better than the classical Dual Network Simplex Algorithm (DNSA). Although the authors consider a dynamic tree data structure, the problem does not change over time and the algorithm is not dynamic.

Afshari and Taghizadeh (2013) consider a dynamic version of the maximum flow network in the simplest kinds of interdiction problem [1]. In the problem, they assume that a positive number is assigned to each arc in the graph model which indicates the traversal time of the flow through the arcs. Moreover, they assume that an intruder uses a single resource with a limited budget to interrupt the flow of a single commodity through the arcs in the network graph within a given limited time period. So the arcs in the graph model are either vital or non-vital. To formulate the problem, a mixed-integer mathematical programming model is presented, based on the concept of Temporally Repeated Flow (TRF). The model is then tackled by a couple of algorithms, an algorithm based on the Benders' decomposition and another based on the algorithm of Ratliff et al. (1975) for the most vital arcs. Although they consider a dynamic problem of the network flow model, the algorithms are not dynamic, i.e., without having any exploitations the current solution to respond to the dynamic changes.

8.3 The Dynamic Network Simplex Algorithm

In this section, the DNSA with some examples is presented. The data structures of the problem and graph are basic components of the algorithm. Additionally, efficient memory management plays an important role in the algorithm. Before presenting details of the algorithm, the data structures and memory management are explained.

8.3.1 Data Structures

The defined problem in Chapter 5 is considered to be solved by the algorithm. We formulated the problem and presented it as the MCF-AGV model (see Section 5.5). The MCF-AGV model was established on a directed graph. There are three dynamic data structures for the algorithm and problem. The memory is allocated for these structures based on the maximum number of jobs in the dynamic problem. These main structures are explained briefly below:

a. The first structure maintains the status of nodes in the graph model and its spanning tree. For each node we considered the Node number, Predecessor, first Child, Right sibling (next Child of the Predecessor), Left sibling (previous

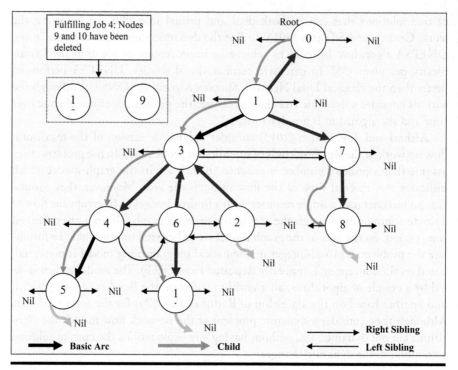

Figure 8.1   A sample of the spanning tree and its attributes (fix = 'fixed', ufd = 'unfixed').

Child of the Predecessor), Balance (amount of supply or demand of the node), Sub-tree's size, Basic arc of the node, Orientation of the Basic arc, Flow value of the Basic arc and Potential of the node. We explain these attributes with an example.

Figure 8.1 shows an example of the spanning tree [3, 110] for a small problem like Figure 5.5 when nodes 9 and 10 (the Job-Input and Job-Output nodes for Job 4) have been deleted. Given a graph G = (N, A), let $T_t \subset A$ be a spanning tree in G at time *t*. The Root is identified with node '0'. Consider some node $v \in N-\{0\}$:

■ There is a unique (undirected) path, denoted by P (v), from v to the Root node '0'. The arc in P (v), which is incident to v, is called the Basic arc of v.
■ The Orientation of the Basic arc is called Upward/Downward if v is the tail/ head node of its Basic arc.
■ The other terminal node *u* of the Basic arc is called the Predecessor (node) of v. If v is the Predecessor of some other node *u*, we call *u* a Child (node) of v.
■ The number of nodes in the sub-tree, rooted by v, including itself, is called the Sub-tree size of v.

- Every node may have a Right and/or Left sibling, but it has at most one Child reference. The other children of the node are accessible by traversing the Siblings.
- The Sub-tree's size and Predecessor variables are used to find a cycle and pivoting. The Orientation, Child, and Sibling variables are used for the computation of the node Potentials (see the main loop in Figure 6.2).

The Predecessor, Child, Left sibling, Right sibling, Sub-tree's size, Basic arc of each node, and Orientation of the Basic arc are shown in Figure 8.1.

Node number	0	1	2	3	4	5	6	7	8	9	10	11
Predecessor	Nil	0	3	1	3	4	3	1	7	–	–	8
Child	1	3	Nil	4	5	Nil	11	8	Nil	–	–	Nil
Right sibling	Nil	Nil	7	7	6	Nil	2	Nil	Nil	–	–	Nil
Left sibling	Nil	Nil	6	Nil	Nil	Nil	4	3	Nil	–	–	Nil
Sub-tree' size	9	8	1	6	2	1	2	2	1	–	–	1
Orientation	–	Up	Up	Down	Down	Down	Up	Down	Down	–	–	Down
Identification	FIX	FIX	FIX	FIX	FIX	FIX	FIX	FIX	FIX	UFD	UFD	FIX

For the status of the nodes, we introduce the following property.

> **Property 8-1:** Every node has an Identification flag. At any time, the Identification of a node specifies whether the node belongs to the model or not. There are two cases for the Identification of nodes, "FIXED" and "UNFIXED." At each stage of the dynamic problem, the "FIXED" nodes are considered by the algorithm whereas the "UNFIXED" nodes are ignored. We introduce the following notations for these sets:
>
> FN_t: The set of "FIXED" nodes of the current graph model at time t.
> DN_t: The set of "UNFIXED" nodes after repairing the solution at time t.

At each stage of the dynamic problem, a few existing jobs are fulfilled and a few new jobs arrive. Based on the fulfilled jobs, a set of nodes for deletion is collected (we call it the "DELETION" nodes). The elements of this set are a couple of nodes associated with every fulfilled job (we called them the Job-Input and Job-Output nodes; see Section 4.5). The nodes of this set have to be removed from the graph model in the next stage. Additionally, when a new job arrives, a set of new nodes associated with the job are collected (we call it the "INSERTION" nodes). These nodes have to be inserted into the graph model in the next stage of the dynamic problem.

When a node is removed from the graph model, the arcs associated with the node are marked as the "DELETION" arc (we use the notation D to show these arcs after repairing the solution). When a node must be inserted into the model, the arcs associated with the node are marked as the "INSERTION" arc.

  b. The second data structure is considered for arcs in the MCF-AV model, including the Tail node, Head node, Lower bound, Upper bound, Cost, and Value of the arcs. For the status of the arcs, we introduce another property below.

  Property 8-2: Every arc has an Identification flag. The Identification of an arc specifies which set of the spanning tree structure the arc is in. There are four cases for the Identification of an arc at time t; the arc is in the T_t set, the L_t set, the U_t set (according to the spanning tree structure (T, L, U); see Definition 6-1 in Section 6.2.1) or in the D_t set.

Suppose that the paths in the solution for the problem in Figure 5.5 are $1{\to}3{\to}4{\to}5{\to}6{\to}11$ and $2{\to}7{\to}8{\to}11$. According to Figure 8.1 for the solution, those sets at time t are as follows:

$T_t = \{(1,0), (1,3), (3,4), (4,5), (6,3), (6,11), (2,3), (1,7), (7,8)\}$
$L_t = \{(1,5), (2,5), (1,11), (2,11), (4,7), (4,11), (6,7), (5,6), (8,3), (8,5), (2,0), (0,3),$
$\quad (4,0), (0,5), (6,0), (0,7), (8,0), (0,11)\}$
$U_t = \{(2,7), (8,11)\}$
$D_t = \{(1,9), (9,10), (2,9), (10,3), (10,5), (10,7), (10,11), (4,9), (6,9), (8,9), (0,9),$
$\quad (10,0)\}$

Note that the flow on every Basic arc in the spanning tree is between the Lower bound and the Upper bound of the arc. The flow of every arc in the set L is at the Lower bound of the arc. The flow of every arc in the set U is at the Upper bound of the arc. Moreover, we considered the Artificial arcs that connect the Root to the other nodes in the sets. These Artificial arcs were explained in Section 6.2.2 (Step 0).

  c. The third data structure is a Job Buffer. There is a direct mapping between the Job-Input and Job-Output nodes in the MCF-AGV model and a particular location in the buffer for every job. For example, the nodes 3 and 4 in Figure 8.1 are associated with the first location in the Job Buffer. When a job is fulfilled, its location in the Job Buffer is marked as empty or "hole." According to Figure 8.1, we have a hole in the Job Buffer. The nodes 9 and 10 associated with the job 4 were the "DELETION" nodes in the MCF-AGV model. When a new job arrives, it is put into a hole in the Job Buffer.

8.3.2 Memory Management

A small memory management facility has been designed, implemented, and embedded in the software. The objectives of this facility are to make independent software, to get a higher performance (most programming languages, including C/C++, have the Garbage Collection facility in dynamic memory allocation which has negative impacts on the efficiency) and prevent any missing job (when the Job Generator generates a job and the memory cannot be allocated).

There are two aspects of memory management in the software. The first one is relevant to the jobs whereas the second one refers to the graph model. There is a buffer for the jobs, which is allocated at the start of operation. Once a job is fulfilled, a hole will be created in the buffer, and when the Job Generator generates a job, it puts the job into the first hole. For the arcs and nodes in the graph model, an Identification flag has been considered. The Identification flag associated with each arc identifies whether the arc is in the T_t set, L_t set, U_t set, or D_t set (see Property 8-2) at time t. There is a one-to-one mapping between every location in the Job Buffer and the nodes associated with the job in the graph model. When a job is fulfilled, the nodes associated with this job are marked for "DELETION." For each node belonging to the fulfilled jobs, the node and the relevant arcs are removed from the spanning tree of the graph. In order to make a new spanning tree, we use a **Remove-Node-Algorithm,** which will be presented in the next section. When a new job arrives the relevant nodes, which have been deleted from the graph model, will be marked for "INSERTION." The "INSERTION" nodes and the arcs associated with the new jobs are inserted into the spanning tree consistently. This task is performed by an **Insert-Node-Algorithm,** which will be presented later in the next section.

As stated before (Section 5.5 in Chapter 5), given N jobs and M AGVs in the problem, there are $M+2\times N+1$ nodes and $M+M\times N+N\times(N-1)+2\times N$ arcs in the MCF-AGV model. The challenge here is to control them correctly. The memory management routine allocates the memory based on the maximum number of jobs. This parameter is determined by the user and here is represented as MNJ. Table 8.1 shows a memory map of the allocated space. There were four different types of arc in the MCF-AGV model: Inward Arcs, Outward Arcs, Auxiliary Arcs, and Intermediate Arcs (see Figure 5.5). Additionally, we needed the Artificial Arcs to generate an initial Basic Feasible Solution (see "Step 0" in Section 6.2.2). Two blocks of the memory are allocated for these arcs and two pointers are used to access them; the first one is for arcs in the MCF-AGV model and the second one is for the Artificial Arcs. In order to address a certain type of arc, it is necessary to have an offset. The offset is the difference in the address from the beginning of the block.

8.3.3 The Algorithms DNSA and DNSA+

We base the Dynamic Network Simplex Algorithms on the Network Simplex Algorithm. DNSA is a standard dynamic form of NSA, and DNSA+ is

Table 8.1 Memory Allocation for the Arcs of the MCF-AGV Model and Its Algorithm

Type of Arcs	Specification	Offset	Size (the Number of Arcs)	Example for 2 AGVs and 2 Jobs (see Figure 5.7)
ARC_{inward}	Arcs from every vehicle node to Job-Input nodes	0	$M \times MNJ$	(1,3); (1,5); (2,3); (2,5)
$ARC_{outward}$	Arcs from every vehicle node to the Sink	$M \times MNJ$	M	(1,7); (2,7)
	Arcs from every Job-Output node to the Sink	$M \times MNJ + M$	MNJ	(4,7); (6,7)
$ARC_{auxiliary}$	Arcs from every Job-Input node to its Job-Output node	$M \times MNJ + M + MNJ$	MNJ	(3,4); (5,6)
$ARC_{intermediate}$	Arcs from every Job-Output node to other Job-Input node	$M \times MNJ + M + MNJ + MNJ$	$MNJ \times (MNJ - 1)$	(4,5); (6,3)
$ARC_{artificial}$	Artificial Arcs to generate initial feasible solution	0	$2 \times MNJ + M + 1$	(1,0); (2,0); (0,3); (4,0); (0,5); (6,0); (0,7)

DNSA with the features of NSA+ (see Section 7.2). The inputs of the dynamic algorithms are:

- **s:** Stage for the dynamic problem, which is increased by the algorithm.
- **Set of "DELETION" Nodes**: it determines which nodes have to be removed from the model.
- **Set of "INSERTION" Nodes**: it determines which nodes have to be put into the new model.

Figure 8.2 shows the DNSA. At the beginning, when the container or Job buffer became full and the software made an MCF-AGV model, an initial feasible solution is generated by the **Generate-Initial BFS** procedure. The operation of

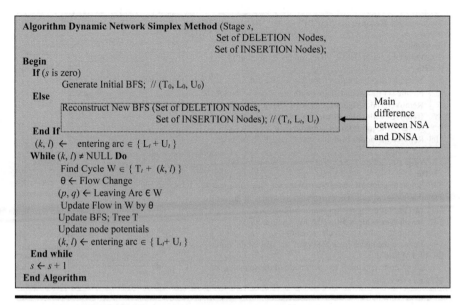

Figure 8.2   The dynamic network simplex algorithm.

this procedure was described in Section 6.2.2 (Step 0). In fact, an initial feasible spanning tree solution (T_0, L_0, U_0) is created (see Definition 6-1). The difference between NSA and DNSA is the **Reconstruct New BFS**. When s is zero, the **Generate Initial BFS** is called. Otherwise, the **Reconstruct New BFS** procedure repairs the current solution, and the spanning tree at time t; (T_t, L_t, U_t) is reconstructed. The main body of the algorithms, NSA and DNSA, is the same. The operation of the main body was described in Section 6.2.2.

Here, we describe the **Reconstruct New BFS**. Figure 8.3 shows the algorithm for reconstructing the new spanning tree. There are three main steps in the algorithm: Step 01, Step 02, and Step 03.

In Step 01, all "DELETION" nodes and their arcs are removed from the model, spanning tree of the graph and the solution paths. After that, the "INSERTION" nodes and their arcs are put into the model, its spanning tree, and solution in the second step (Step 02). In Step 03, according to the current solution, a value is assigned to the potential of each node in the new spanning tree. There is no challenge in Step 03 since it is an easy task. The Steps 01 and 02 are elaborated by some examples as follows:

Step 01: There is a loop for this step. At first, a couple of nodes associated with every fulfilled job (from the "DELETION" set) are selected and transferred into the D_t set. These two tasks are performed in Lines 5 and 6, respectively. Then, in Lines 7 and 8 a procedure, which is called **Remove-Node-Algorithm**, is used to remove the nodes from the spanning tree consistently. After that in Line 9, the fulfilled job associated with the nodes is removed from the solution paths. Based

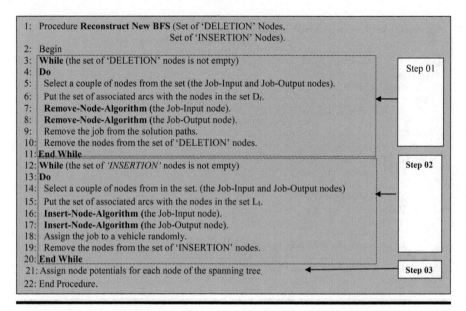

```
1:   Procedure Reconstruct New BFS (Set of 'DELETION' Nodes,
                          Set of 'INSERTION' Nodes).
2:   Begin
3:   While (the set of 'DELETION' nodes is not empty)
4:   Do
5:     Select a couple of nodes from the set (the Job-Input and Job-Output nodes).
6:     Put the set of associated arcs with the nodes in the set D_t.
7:     Remove-Node-Algorithm (the Job-Input node).
8:     Remove-Node-Algorithm (the Job-Output node).
9:     Remove the job from the solution paths.
10:    Remove the nodes from the set of 'DELETION' nodes.
11:  End While
12:  While (the set of 'INSERTION' nodes is not empty)
13:  Do
14:    Select a couple of nodes from in the set. (the Job-Input and Job-Output nodes)
15:    Put the set of associated arcs with the nodes in the set L_t.
16:    Insert-Node-Algorithm (the Job-Input node).
17:    Insert-Node-Algorithm (the Job-Output node).
18:    Assign the job to a vehicle randomly.
19:    Remove the nodes from the set of 'INSERTION' nodes.
20:  End While
21:  Assign node potentials for each node of the spanning tree
22:  End Procedure.
```

Step 01
Step 02
Step 03

Figure 8.3   The pseudo-code of reconstructing the spanning tree in dynamic network simplex algorithm.

on removing the job from the solution, some arcs may be transferred into the set L_t or U_t.

Figure 8.4 shows the operation of the **Remove-Node-Algorithm.** Removing a node from the spanning tree, splits T_t into several clusters, say T1, T2, … and so on. Depending on whether the deleted node has a Child or not, there is a branch in the algorithm. Based on the location of the deleted node in the spanning tree, appropriate operations are done.

If the "DELETION" node does not have any Child (Line 3) and its Predecessor does not have any other Child (Line 4), then the Child of the Predecessor is set

```
1: Procedure Remove-Node-Algorithm (Node)
2: Begin
3:   If (the Node has not any Child)
4:       Set the Child of the Predecessor of node to Nil (if its parent had only one Child).
5:       Set the Right sibling, Left sibling of the other nodes if it is necessary.
6:       Set the Sub-tree's size of the new spanning Tree.
7:   Else
8:       Set the Right sibling, Left sibling of the other Nodes.
9:       Find the last Child of the root.
10:      Set the Sub-trees (Children of the deleted node) as the new Children for the root.
11:      Set a Basic-arc for every root-node of the sub-trees using Artificial arcs.
12:      Set Predecessor, Sub-tree's size of the nodes in the new spanning tree.
13:  End If
14: End Procedure.
```

Figure 8.4   The pseudo-code of removing a node from the spanning tree in dynamic network simplex algorithm.

to Nil. After that in Lines 5 and 6, the Right and Left siblings of other nodes are adjusted and the Sub-tree's size of the new spanning tree is updated. If the "DELETION" node has a Child, the Right and Left siblings of other nodes are adjusted in Line 8. In Lines 9 and 10, the last Child of the Root is found out and the sub-trees (Children of the "DELETION" node) are connected to the root with the Artificial arcs. Then in Lines 11 and 12, the Basic arc of the root in the sub-trees, and their Predecessor as well as the sub-tree's size is adjusted. Some examples for a "DELETION" node are demonstrated below:

Example 8-1: Suppose that the job associated with nodes 7 and 8 is fulfilled. Imagine the node 8 in Figure 8.1 must be deleted, first. In this case, the "DELETION" node does not have any Child, Right sibling or Left sibling. In this case, T1 is the rooted spanning tree, and T2 is empty. What is necessary to do is to delete the Child of its Predecessor and then update the Sub-tree's size from the Predecessor of the deleted node to the Root. The spanning tree after removing node 8 is shown in Figure 8.5. The same operation is done for deleting the node 7. After these operations, the solution paths are

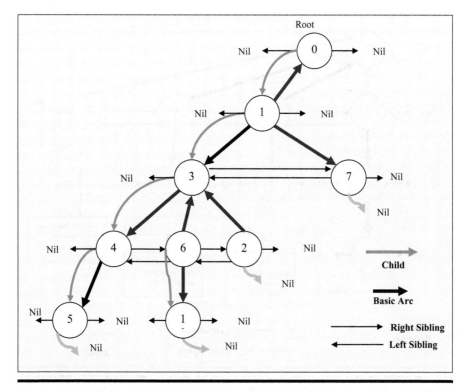

Figure 8.5   The new spanning tree after removing nodes 8 (see Figure 8.1).

1→3→4→5→6→11 and 2→11. According to Property 8-1, the sets of nodes in the graph at time *t* are:

$$FN_t = \{1, 2, 3, 4, 5, 6, 11\}$$
$$DN_t = \{9, 10, 7, 8\}$$

According to Property 8-2, the sets of arcs in the current graph are:

$T_t = \{(1,0), (1,3), (3,4), (4,5), (6,3), (6,11), (2,3)\}$
$L_t = \{(1,5), (2,5), (1,11), (4,7), (4,11), (5,6), (2,0), (0,3), (4,0), (0,5), (6,0)\}$
$U_t = \{(2,11)\}$
$D_t = \{(1,9), (9,10), (2,9), (10,3), (10,5), (10,7), (10,11), (4,9), (6,9), (8,9), (0,9),$
$(10,0), (0,11), (1,7), (2,7), (7,8)\ (0,7), (6,7), (7,8), (8,11), (8,0), (8,3), (8,5)\}$

Example 8-2: Suppose that the job associated with nodes 3 and 4 is fulfilled in Figure 8.1. Imagine the node 3 is deleted first. The spanning tree after removing node 3 and the reconstruction operation is shown in Figure 8.6. In this

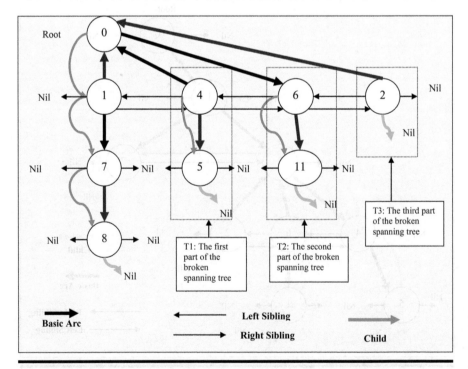

Figure 8.6   The new spanning tree after removing node 3 (see Figure 8.1).

case, the "DELETION" node had a Child and its Right sibling exists. The following operations were necessary for this case:

- Adjust the Child of node 1 to node 7.
- Connect the sub-trees T1 (node 4 and 5), T2 (node 6 and 11), and T3 (node 2) to the Root.
- Adjust the Right and Left siblings from the most left side (node 1) to the most right side (node 2).
- Recalculate the Sub-tree size for the node 1 and Root.

Note that in our experience, the best and fastest way to recover the spanning tree is to connect the minor fragmented sub-trees to the Root. We used the artificial arcs for reconnecting T1, T2, and T3 to the Root or main part of the spanning tree. The Orientation of the Artificial-Basic arc depends on the amount of supply/demand of the node. For the node j, if j is a Job-Output node we include $(j,0)$ in T_r. If j is a Job-Input node, we include arc $(0,j)$ in T_r.

After deleting the node 3, the node 4 in Figure 8.6 must be deleted. The spanning tree after removing node 4 and the reconstruction operation are shown in Figure 8.7. After these operations, the solution paths are $1\rightarrow5\rightarrow6\rightarrow11$ and $2\rightarrow7\rightarrow8\rightarrow11$. According to Property 8-1, the sets of nodes in the graph at time t are:

$$FN_t = \{1, 2, 5, 6, 7, 8, 11\}$$
$$DN_t = \{9, 10, 3, 4\}$$

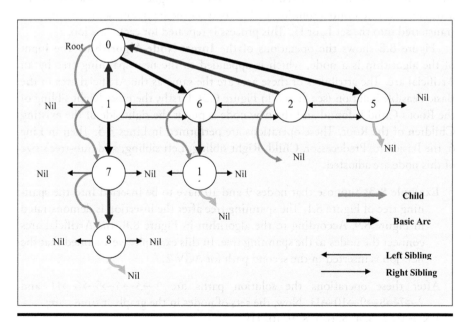

Figure 8.7 The new spanning tree after removing node 4 (see Figure 8.6).

```
1: Procedure Insert-Node-Algorithm (Node)
2: Begin
3:     Find the Child of the root.
4:     Find the most right sibling of the Child.
5:     Set the node as a new Child for the Root by an Artificial arc.
6:     Set Basic-arc, Predecessor, Child, Right-sibling, Left-sibling and Sub-tree's size for this node and the
           root.
7: End Procedure.
```

Figure 8.8 The pseudo-code of inserting a node into the spanning tree in dynamic network simplex algorithm.

According to Property 8-2, the sets of arcs in the graph are:

T_t = {(1,0), (6,11), (1,7), (7,8), (2,0), (0,5), (6,0)}
L_t = {(2,5), (1,11), (2,11), (4,7), (4,11), (6,7), (5,6), (8,3), (8,5), (0,7), (8,0), (0,11)}
U_t = {(1,5), (2,7), (8,11)}
D_t = {(1,9), (9,10), (2,9), (10,3), (10,5), (10,7), (10,11), (4,9), (6,9), (8,9), (0,9), (10,0), (1,3), (3,4), (4,5), (6,3), (0,3), (4,0), (2,3)}

Step 02: In this step, every new job is inserted into the spanning tree and the solution paths. At first, a couple of nodes associated with a new job (from the "INSERTION" set) are selected and transferred into the L_t set. Then, a procedure called **Insert-Node-Algorithm** is used to insert the nodes into the spanning tree. After that, the new job associated with the nodes is assigned to a vehicle randomly. This job is inserted into a solution path. Based on the insertion, some arcs may be transferred into the set L_t or U_t. This process is repeated for each new job.

Figure 8.8 shows the operations of the **Insert-Node-Algorithm.** The input of the algorithm is a node, which is appended to the new spanning tree by an Artificial arc. The attributes of these arcs are the same as the Artificial arcs in the Basic Feasible Solution (see Step 0 in Figure 6.2). Firstly, the most Right sibling of the Root's Child is found and the new node is put at the right side of the existing Children of the Root. These operations are performed in Lines 3-5. Then in Line 6, the Basic-arc, Predecessor, Child, Right sibling, Left sibling, and Sub-tree's size of this node are adjusted.

> **Example 8-3:** Suppose that nodes 9 and 10 have to be inserted into the spanning tree of Figure 8.1. The spanning tree after the insertion is demonstrated in Figure 8.9. According to the algorithm in Figure 8.8, the Artificial arcs connect the nodes to the spanning tree. In this example, we assumed that the new job is inserted in the second path for AGV 2.

After these operations the solution paths are 1→3→4→5→6→11 and 2→7→8→9→10→11. Now, the sets of nodes in the graph at time *t* are:
FN_t = {1, 2, 3, 4, 5, 6, 7, 8, 9, 10, 11}
DN_t = {}

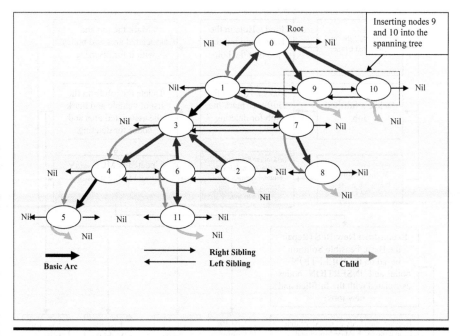

Figure 8.9 The new spanning tree after inserting nodes 9 and 10 (see Figure 8.1).

According to Property 8-2, the sets of arcs in the current graph are:

T_t = {(1,0), (1,3), (3,4), (4,5), (6,3), (6,11), (2,3), (1,7), (7,8), (0,9), (10,0)}
L_t = {(1,5), (2,5), (1,11), (2,11), (4,7), (4,11), (5,6), (2,0), (0,3), (4,0), (0,5), (6,0),
    (10,3), (10,5), (10,7), (0,7), (6,7), (7,8), (8,11), (8,0), (8,3), (8,5), (1,9), (2,9),
    (4,9), (6,9)}
U_t = {(2,7), (8,9), (9,10), (10,11)}
D_t = {}

8.4 Software Architecture for Dynamic Aspect

At the start of the process, a few jobs are generated for each crane and the memory for the jobs and graph are allocated. Then, the MCF-AGV model is made and tackled by Network Simplex plus Algorithm. The output of this algorithm is a few job sequences for the vehicles. Based on these sequences, the software will prepare a job list for each vehicle.

The main architecture of the software is demonstrated in Figure 8.10 for the dynamic aspect. Note that this architecture is for the time when $s > 0$ (see the algorithm in Figure 8.2).

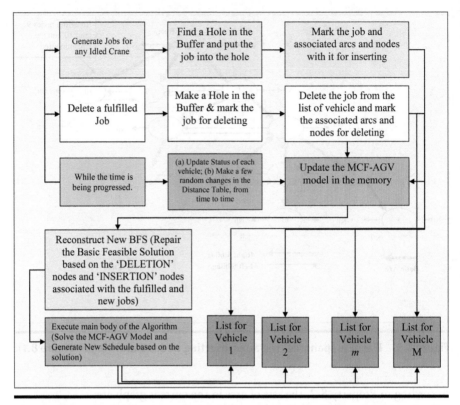

Figure 8.10 Block diagram of the software and algorithm (DNSA+) in the dynamic aspect.

While the time is being progressed, the vehicles and cranes are carrying and handling the containers. From time to time, the software makes a few random changes in the distance table (see Table 5.1) in order to produce dynamic problems. The Job Generator has to generate a few new jobs, when it finds out any crane is in an idle state.

As we see in Figure 8.10, every event is recorded in order to be processed later. The events include modification of the vehicle's position, the fulfilled jobs and new jobs, and any change in the distance table. As we mentioned (see Section 8.3.2), a hole will be created in the Job Buffer when a job is fulfilled. After the Job Generator generates a job, it puts the job into a hole of the buffer. The software marks the nodes and arcs associated with the fulfilled and new jobs. The most important events that affect the spanning tree are the fulfilled and new jobs. The fulfilled jobs are removed from the list of vehicles and model whereas the new jobs are appended to the remaining jobs and inserted into the model. Note that any change in the problem, without any fulfilled or new job, does not affect the spanning tree. In this case, only the body of the algorithm is executed and finds out the optimal solution.

The software processes the recorded events and updates the MCF-AGV model. After removing the nodes and arcs (associated with the fulfilled jobs) from the model and omitting the jobs from the vehicle's lists, a new spanning tree is made. Next, the nodes and arcs associated with the new jobs are put into the new model and then the spanning tree is repaired. These jobs are assigned to one or more vehicles, randomly. These two tasks are made by **Reconstruct New BFS**. After repairing the spanning tree, the main body of the algorithm is executed and it finds out the optimal solution. Note that these tasks are not pre-emptive, i.e., when a task starts execution on the processor it finishes to its completion.

8.5 A Comparison between DNSA+ and NSA+

To test and compare the performance of the algorithms, many jobs in dynamic fashion have been generated. Their sources, destinations, and the distance between every two points in the port have been chosen randomly. During three hours simulation, about ninety problems with the condition of generating five jobs for any idle crane have been solved by DNSA+ and NSA+H. In these samples, we assumed that there were fifty AGVs and seven cranes in the port (see Table 6.1). It was very difficult to isolate the CPU-Times required to tackle the problems by the algorithms and the CPU-Time required for memory management. Hence, we considered the number of iterations as an indicator to compare the algorithms. The number of iterations required to solve the problems has been drawn in Figure 8.11. A sample was collected whenever there were changes in the problem and the algorithms had to solve the new problem.

From Figure 8.11, we can observe that:

Observation 8-1: As we can see in the figure, the number of iterations in DNSA+ has been greatly decreased compared with NSA+. Therefore, the average number of iterations in DNSA+ is less than NSA+ for the dynamic problem. Since the major process of the algorithms is performed in the body and the operations of the body are identical (see Figures 6.2 and 8.2), the CPU-Time required to solve the problems is also decreased practically.

In these results for ninety problems, there was about a 40% reduction in the number of iterations by DNSA+ compared with NSA+. The percentage of improvement, in reduction of the number of iterations, is calculated by the following terms and equation:

NSA_i^+: The number of iterations in NSA^+ for the dynamic problem at stage i.
$DNSA_i^+$: The number of iterations in $DNSA^+$ for the dynamic problem at stage i.
TPR: The Total Percentages of Reduction in the number of iterations in the experiment.

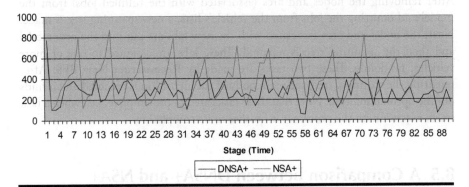

Figure 8.11   A comparison of the number of iterations in DNSA+ and NSA+.

$$TPR = \frac{\sum_{i=1}^{90}(DNSA_i^+ - NSA_i^+)}{\sum_{i=1}^{90}DNSA_i^+} * 100 = -38.79\%$$

8.6 Statistical Test for the Comparison

The number of iterations of running the two algorithms, DNSA+ and NSA+ (Figure 8.11), has been analyzed statistically. We tested the null hypothesis that the means produced by the two algorithms were statistically indifferent ($\alpha = 5\%$). Table 8.2 provides the test's result along with the values of T-distribution for a particular degree of freedom. Since we cared if the change (the difference between the two means) was positive or negative, 'One-tail' test was chosen. The Paired t-test determines the two means are significantly different at a 95% degree of confidence since the test's result is in the reject region (see Figure 7.3 for the acceptance and reject regions).

Table 8.2   The Result of t-Test for the Two Algorithms, DNSA+ and NSA+

Statistical Parameters	Values
Observations	90
t-Test (paired two sample for means)	−5.0936
Degree of freedom	89
Critical T-value	−1.662

8.7 Complexity of the Algorithm

The complexity of Network Simplex plus Algorithm was calculated in Section 7.5. In this section, it is shown that Network Simplex plus Algorithm and Dynamic Network Simplex plus Algorithm have the same complexity. Both the algorithms run the BFS procedure, which finds a Basic Feasible Solution at the beginning. The Dynamic Network Simplex plus Algorithm then calls the Reconstruct New BFS procedure to repair the spanning tree and current solution when s (the input of the algorithm) becomes greater than zero. Given n as the number of nodes in the graph, it is easy to understand that the complexity of both BFS and Reconstruct new BFS are n and $3n^2$, respectively. Based on the number of iterations and the complexity of each pivot (see Section 7.5), the total complexity of this algorithm is determined as follows:

$$O\left(3n^2 + (m+n)mn^2C^2 KLogK\right)$$

Note that m is the number of arcs in the graph model. In Section 7.5, we had the following equations:

$$m = O(N)^2; \; n = O(N)(N \text{ is the number of jobs})$$

Therefore, the total complexity of the algorithm for the problem is:

$$O(N^6)$$

8.8 Summary and Conclusion

In this chapter, the dynamic extensions of NSA and NSA+ were presented. These extensions are DNSA and DNSA+. To evaluate the performance of the algorithms, we considered the dynamic scheduling problem of AGVs in the container terminal (the problem defined in Chapter 5). Many random problems have been solved by both DNSA+ and NSA+. The comparison showed that the number of iterations is significantly improved.

To conclude Network Simplex Algorithm and its three extensions (NSA+, DNSA, and DNSA+), we made a summary. Table 8.3 shows this summary, including the important features of these algorithms as well as their advantages and disadvantages.

In dynamic problems, NSA and NSA+ start from scratch and reconsider the pre-established schedules. Memory management in these two algorithms is an easy task since a block of memory is allocated for the whole of the graph. Also, there is no partitioning in the graph and its spanning tree to solve the problem by those algorithms. The disadvantage of these algorithms lies in taking time to rebuild

Table 8.3   A Comparison between NSA and Its Extensions

Algorithms	Data Structure	Features	Memory Management	Advantages	Disadvantages
NSA	Graph and operations on the graph	The standard version of the algorithm	Easy: One block of memory is allocated for the whole graph	Faster than equivalently size Linear Program	Time-consuming to rebuild the graph in dynamic problem
NSA+		NSA with enhanced features		Faster than NSA	
DNSA		Dynamic version of NSA; Repairs the solution and spanning tree	Difficult: Partitioning of the graph and its spanning tree	Faster than NSA and NSA+ in dynamic problems	Needs memory management; adding, removing and updating nodes and arcs
DNSA+		Dynamic version of NSA+; Repairs the solution and spanning tree		Faster than DNSA in dynamic problems	

the graph and putting it into the memory. DNSA and DNSA+ repair the solution rather than starting from scratch. The main advantage of these dynamic algorithms over NSA and NSA+ is the performance. On the other hand, DNSA and DNSA+ deal with memory management, partitioning of the graph, and its spanning tree. However, they are disadvantages that have to be paid in return for the performance.

Chapter 9

Greedy Vehicle Search: An Incomplete Advanced Algorithm

In this chapter, an incomplete algorithm for the scheduling problem of Automated Guided Vehicles (AGVs) is presented. We called it Greedy Vehicle Search (GVS). To evaluate the relative strength and weakness of Network Simplex plus Algorithm (NSA+) and GVS, the results of the two algorithms are compared.

9.1 Motivations

In the previous three chapters, the scheduling problem of AGVs, the problem in Chapter 5, was solved by NSA and its extensions. Although these complete solutions are efficient, they can only work on problems with certain limits in size (see Section 6.6). When the size of the problem goes beyond the limits or the time available for computation is too short, incomplete search methods are used. To complement the solutions, GVS method is designed and implemented in this chapter. This incomplete search method can be applied to both static and dynamic problems.

9.2 Problem Formalization

The problem here is the problem defined in Chapter 5, but we model it as an incomplete case of the MCF-AGV model (see Definition 5-12). The MCF formulation requires this incomplete model. Given M AGVs and N jobs in the problem, there

DOI: 10.1201/9781003308386-11

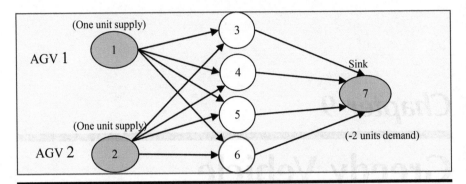

Figure 9.1   An example of the incomplete case of the MCF-AGV model with two AGVs and four jobs.

are M vehicle nodes, N job nodes, and one Sink node in the model. The graph model is illustrated by Figure 9.1 for two AGVs and four container jobs.

The MCF-AGV model and its incomplete case can be compared. There were four different types of arcs in the MCF-AGV model: the Inward arcs, Intermediate arcs, Auxiliary arcs, and Outward arcs. In the incomplete case of the MCF-AGV model, there are only Inward and partial Outward arcs. Moreover, in the MCF-AGV model we considered two nodes for each job. In the incomplete case of the MCF-AGV model, there is only one node for each job (see Figures 9.1 and 5.5 for the differences). We formalize this incomplete case with two definitions.

Based on Definitions 5-11, we introduce the following definition:

Definition 9.1: A graph $G_{MCF-AGV-I}$ = (GSI, NPSI, APSI) is an Incomplete graph of $G_{MCF-AGV}$ = (GS, NPS, APS). The elements of $G_{MCF-AGV-I}$, nodes, and arcs in the GSI = (NSI, ASI) are formally defined in the two following subsections.

9.2.1 Nodes and Their Properties in the Incomplete Graph

There are three types of nodes in the $G_{MCF-AGV-I}$. The elements in each set and the sets themselves with their properties are defined as follows:

a. **AGVN$_m$:** A supply node corresponding to vehicle m. Each node has one unit supply. Hence, there are M supply nodes in the model. We define the following set for these supply nodes:
SAGVN: A set of M supply nodes in the $G_{MCF-AGV-I}$.

$$SAGVN = \{AGVN_m \mid m = 1,2,...,M; NPS(m) = 1\}$$

b. **JN$_j$:** A node for job j. There is neither supply nor demand in this node, i.e. it is a transshipment node. We define the following set for these transshipment nodes:

SJN: A set of N job nodes in the G$_{MCF\text{-}AGV\text{-}I}$.

$$SJN = \{JN_j \mid j = 1,2,\ldots,N; \ NPS(j) = 0\}$$

c. **SINK:** This is a demand node in the G$_{MCF\text{-}AGV\text{-}I}$ with M units demand. This node corresponds to the end state of the process. For the property of this node, we have:

$$NPS(SINK) = -M$$

Therefore, there are M+N+1 nodes in the G$_{MCF\text{-}AGV\text{-}I}$:

$$NSI = SAGVN \cup SJN \cup SINK$$

9.2.2 Arcs and Their Properties in the Incomplete Graph

The following two types of arcs connect the nodes in the G$_{MCF\text{-}AGV\text{-}I}$:

1. **Inward Arcs:** There is a directed arc from every vehicle node, to the node of job i. We use the following notation for these arcs:

ARC$_{inward}$: A set of arcs from SAGVN to SJN.

$$ARC_{inward} = \{(m,j) \mid \forall m \in SAGVN, \forall j \in SJN, APS(m,j) = [0,1,C_{mj}]\}$$

The number of these arcs is M×N. Each arc has the lower bound zero, and the upper bound one, i.e., only one AGV goes through each of these arcs. Given the appointment time of container job j, t_j, the ready time of AGV m to get the next location, RTA$_m$, and the travel time of the AGV from its next location to the source/destination of job j on the quayside, TTA$_{mj}$, the cost of arc (m,j) is calculated as:

$$C_{mj} = \begin{cases} w_1 \times \left(t_j - (RTA_m + TTA_{mj})\right) + w_2 \times (RTA_m + TTA_{mj}) \\ \quad if\,(t_j \geq RTA_m + TTA_{mj}) \\ P \times (RTA_m + TTA_{mj} - t_j)\,otherwise \end{cases}$$

Note that this cost is exactly the same as what we calculated in Chapter 5 (see Section 5.5.2 and Assumption 5-10); $w1$ and $w2$ are the weight of waiting and traveling times of the vehicles, and P is a penalty.

2. **Outward Arcs:** There is a directed arc from every job node i to SINK. We use the following notation for these arcs:
$ARCI_{outward}$: A set of arcs from SJN to SINK.

$$ARCI_{outward} = \{(i,j) \mid \forall i \in SJN, j = SINK, APS(i,j) = [0,1,0]\}$$

The number of these arcs is N. Each arc has the lower bound zero; the upper bound one and the cost zero, i.e., the AGV (that visited a job node in SJN) goes through each of these arcs.

Therefore, there are M×N+ N arcs in the $G_{MCF\text{-}AGV\text{-}I}$:

$$ASI = ARC_{inward} \cup ARCI_{outward}$$

9.2.3 The Special Case of the MCF-AGV Model for Automated Guided Vehicles Scheduling

Now we present an incomplete version of the MCF-AGV model for the AGVs Scheduling with the following definition.

Definition 9.2: An MCF-AGV-I model is defined on the graph of $G_{MCF\text{-}AGV\text{-}I}$ as an Incomplete case of the MCF-AGV (Definition 5-12) for the Scheduling problem of AGVs. The elements of D, CS, and FC in the MCF-AGV-I = $(G_{MCF\text{-}AGV\text{-}I}, f, D, CS, FC)$ are introduced as follows:

a. For each element in D, we have:

$$D_{f_{ij}} = [0,1] \text{ for } (i,j) \in ARC_{inward} \cup ARCI_{outward}$$

b. The constraints of CS in the MCF-AGV-I are:

$$
\left\{
\begin{array}{l}
1) \displaystyle\sum_{j:(i,j)\in ASI} f_{ij} = 1, \forall i \in SAGVN \\[2em]
2) \displaystyle\sum_{j:(j,i)\in ASI} f_{ji} = M, i = SINK \\[2em]
3) f_{is} = \left\{
\begin{array}{l}
1 \text{ if } \displaystyle\sum_{m:(m,i)\in ARC_{inward}} f_{mi} = 1 \\[1.5em]
0 \text{ otherwise}
\end{array}
\right\}, \forall i \in SJN, s = SINK
\end{array}
\right\}
$$

The first constraint shows that every node i ($i \in$ SAGVN) sends one unit flow into the network. The second constraint ensures SINK node receives M units flow (the flows sent from nodes in SAGVN set). The third constraint shows that one unit flow can be sent from every node in SJN to SINK provided that it received one unit flow.

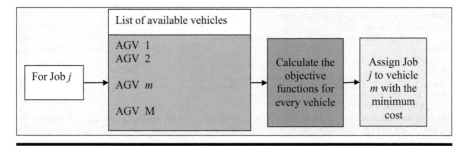

Figure 9.2   The block diagram of Greedy Vehicle Search.

c. The objective function is:

$$FC = \underset{\substack{m=1,2,..,M \\ j=1,2,..,N}}{Min} \; C_{mj} \times f_{mj}$$

Solving the MCF-AGV-I model generates M paths, each of which commences from a node in SAGVN and terminates at SINK. Each path determines a job for every AGV. The decision variable f_{ij} for every $(i,j) \in$ ASI (the flow between nodes i and j in the $G_{MCF-AGV-I}$) is either 1 or 0. $f_{ij} = 1$ means that an AGV goes from node i to node j. Otherwise, moving the AGV from node i to node j is not possible.

9.3 Algorithm Formalization

The block diagram of GVS method is demonstrated in Figure 9.2.

There are N container jobs and M vehicles in the problem (the same as Chapter 5). In this simple search method a job needs to be served every time, like a Taxi Service System (TSS) does. In fact, for any unassigned job and the list of idles AGVs, a job is assigned to a vehicle with minimum cost, including waiting and traveling times of the vehicles as well as the lateness of the jobs.

The pseudo-code of GVS in the dynamic aspect is demonstrated by Figure 9.3. This pseudo-code is divided into two parts. In the first part, the cost for any combination between the remaining jobs and the idle vehicles is calculated. In the second part, one vehicle is assigned to a job, based on the minimum cost.

9.4 Software Architecture for Dynamic Aspect

The architecture of the main part of the software is demonstrated in Figure 9.4. At the start of the process, the Job Generator generates a few jobs for the cranes. These jobs will be appended to the set of remaining jobs, which is empty at the beginning. The remaining jobs are used by GVS and the output of this method is an individual job for every vehicle.

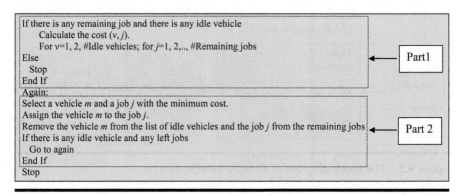

Figure 9.3   The pseudo-code of Greedy Vehicle Search in dynamic aspect.

The software does two tasks in the real-time processing and dynamic fashion. The first task is related to updating the vehicle's status and assigning a job to any available vehicle whereas the second one takes influence from any idle crane. While the time is running, the amount of time traveled and waited for every vehicle is updated. At the same time, if a vehicle picks up a job from the quayside, the assigned job will be deleted from the list of jobs for the vehicle and will be removed from the list of remaining jobs. If the job has to be delivered to the crane on the quayside, it could not be removed until the meeting time between the crane and the vehicle (note that the appointment place is on the quayside, not the yardside). The second task refers to any change in the crane's status. The Job Generator has to generate a few new jobs when it finds out any idle crane.

From time to time, the software makes a few random changes in the distance table (see Table 5.1) in order to produce dynamic problems. These changes are

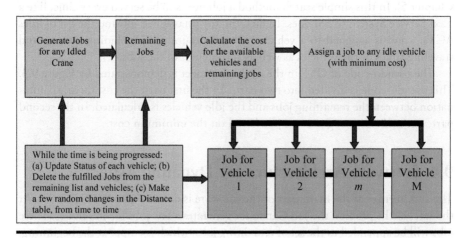

Figure 9.4   The block diagram of the software and algorithm (GVS) in dynamic aspect.

applied to the problem directly. Since the algorithm is reactive, it finds out a solution for the new problem in each run.

9.5 A Comparison between GVS and NSA+ and Quality of the Solutions

To evaluate the relative strength and weakness of GVS and NSA+ in the dynamic scheduling problem, we used randomly generated problems. The distance between every two points in the port as well as the source and destination of jobs were chosen randomly. We did a simulation for six hours subject to generating five jobs for any idle crane. Other parameters for this simulation were the same as Table 6.1. We compared solutions of both the algorithms, NSA+H and GVS. The components in the objective function, the number of carried jobs, and the delay from the appointment time were compared in this experiment. Our observations were:

Observation 9.1: Figure 9.5 shows components in the objective function, the waiting and traveling times of vehicles for both the algorithms. As we can see from the figure, waiting times of the vehicles for GVS are significantly greater than waiting times of the vehicles in NSA+, although traveling times of the vehicles for both algorithms are almost the same during the six hours. The main reason for the result is that NSA+ solves the MCF-AGV model (in Chapter 5) and produces the global optimum solution for the problem whereas GVS does a search in the search space and finds out a local optimum for the MCF-AGV-I model.

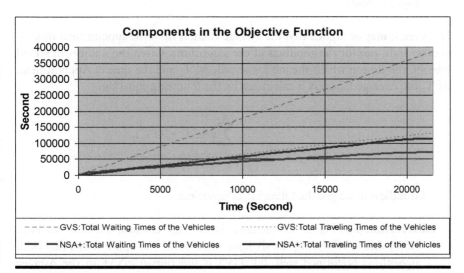

Figure 9.5 A comparison of NSA± and GVS for traveling and waiting times of the vehicles.

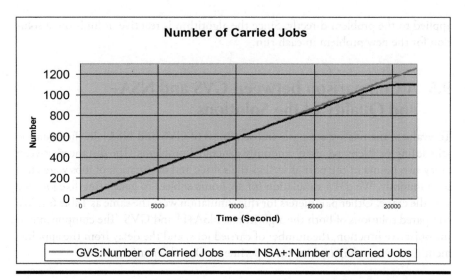

Figure 9.6 The number of carried jobs by NSA± and GVS during six-hour simulation.

Observation 9.2: Figure 9.6 shows the number of carried jobs during the six-hour simulation ($21,600 = 6 \times 3,600$). As we can see in the figure, the number of carried jobs for both algorithms, NSA+ and GVS, is approximately the same. Generally, due to the tight schedules of the Quay Cranes, it is undesirable for containers to be served early or too late for the appointment.

However, it may be argued that the average lateness from the appointment times is another indicator for the goodness of the algorithms. Given the number of served jobs, N, the time at which the job i is served, ACT_i, and the time of Appointment, APT_i, the Average Lateness is calculated by the following equation:

$$Average\ Lateness = \frac{\sum_{i=1}^{N}(ACT_i - APT_i)}{N}$$

For this indicator, we got the following observation:

Observation 9.3: Figure 9.7 presents the Average Lateness indicator for both NSA+ and GVS during the six-hour simulation. The figure shows that both algorithms performed well, but GVS is superior to NSA+ in the Average Lateness. GVS sacrifices the waiting and traveling times of the vehicles to the Average Lateness.

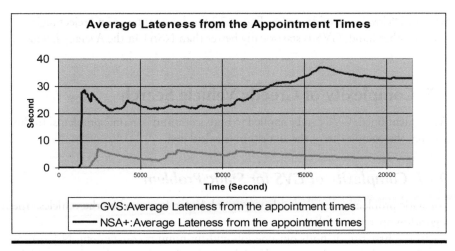

Figure 9.7 A comparison of NSA± and GVS for the average lateness from the appointment time.

9.6 Statistical Test for the Comparison

The waiting and traveling times of the vehicles as well as the average lateness of jobs, produced by NSA+ and GVS, were analyzed statistically. During the simulation, the samples were collected at regular thirty-second intervals. We tested the null hypothesis that the means produced by the two algorithms were statistically indifferent ($\alpha = 5\%$). Table 9.1 provides the test's result along with the Critical t-value for a particular degree of freedom.

Since we cared if the change (the difference between the two means) was positive or negative, "One-tail" test was chosen. The Paired t-test confirms that NSA+ is significantly better than GVS in both traveling and waiting times of the vehicles

Table 9.1 The Result of t-Test for the Two Algorithms, GVS and NSA+

Statistical Parameters	Total Waiting Times of the Vehicles	Total Traveling Times of the Vehicles	Average Lateness from the Appointment Times
Observations	720	720	720
t-Test (paired two sample for means)	–43.4054744	–43.5902651	73.6809406
Degree of freedom	719	719	719
Critical T-value	–1.646972	–1.646972	–1.646972

with a 95% level of confidence (see Figure 7.3 for the acceptance and reject regions). On the other hand, GVS is statistically better than NSA+ in the Average Lateness.

9.7 Complexity of Greedy Vehicle Search

As we mentioned, GVS can be applied to both static and dynamic problems. In this section, the complexity of the algorithm is calculated.

9.7.1 Complexity of GVS for Static Problem

For static problems, we assume that every job has to be served by the vehicles. The algorithm operates as follows:

In the first run, it finds out one job with minimum cost (among N jobs) for a vehicle. In the second run, another job among N-1 jobs is assigned to a vehicle, which could be the selected vehicle in the first run or others. This process is continued until there is no remaining job. Hence, given N jobs and M vehicles in the problem, the complexity of the algorithm is calculated by the following equation:

$$M \times N + M \times (N-1) + M \times (N-2) + \cdots + M \times 1 = \frac{M \times N \times (N+1)}{2}$$

Therefore, the complexity of GVS is O(M·N²). It is less than the complexity of NSA+ (see Section 7.5).

We got some samples to show the performance of GVS. The CPU-Time required to solve the problems by GVS is shown in Figure 9.8.

The estimated values by a polynomial equation (with degree 2) have also been shown in Figure 9.8. As we can see when the number of jobs is eight thousand, it

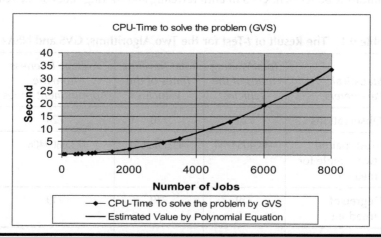

Figure 9.8 CPU-Time required solving the static problems by GVS.

takes thirty-five seconds CPU-Time to solve this large problem (M = 50). Note that these samples have been collected by running GVS on a Windows XP computer with a 2.2 GHz processor and 1GB of RAM.

From a comparison between Figures 9.8 and 6.11, we can observe that:

> **Observation 9.4:** GVS is faster than NSA and NSA+. Moreover, GVS could solve the larger problems, which are beyond the limits of NSA and NSA+. GVS could find a local optimum for the problem of eight thousand jobs within thirty-five seconds whereas NSA and NSA+ solve the problem with three thousand jobs within two minutes. The reason is that GVS is an incomplete algorithm while NSA and NSA+ are complete.

We estimated the time complexity of the algorithm by the experimental results in Figure 9.8. The time complexity can be expressed in the CPU-Time required to find a local optimum. The CPU-Time is estimated based on the number of jobs. We considered the following equation to estimate CPU-Time required finding a local optimum:

$$CPU - Time_{GVS} = f(Number\ of\ Jobs) = a \times NumberofJobs + b \times NumberofJobs^2$$

The estimation's results for the CPU-Time have been shown in Table 9.2. The coefficients of 'a' and 'b' have been calculated and put in the Coefficients section of the table.

Table 9.2 Regression Result for CPU-Time Required to Finding a Local Optimum by GVS for Static Problem

Multiple R	R-Square	Adjusted-R-Square	Standard Error	Observations		
0.99988	0.99977	0.92832	0.1640	16		
	DF	SS	MS	F	Significance-F	
Regression	2	1656.086	828.043	30780.79811	1.28×10^{-24}	
Residual	14	0.3766	0.0269			
Total	16	1656.46				
	Coefficients	Standard-Error	t-Stat	P-value	Lower 95%	Upper 95%
X Variable 1	-7.488×10^{-5}	4.121×10^{-5}	-1.8171	0.0906578	-0.00016	1.35×10^{-5}
X Variable 2	5.33383×10^{-7}	6.332×10^{-9}	84.242	2.40409×10^{-20}	5.198×10^{-7}	5.46×10^{-7}

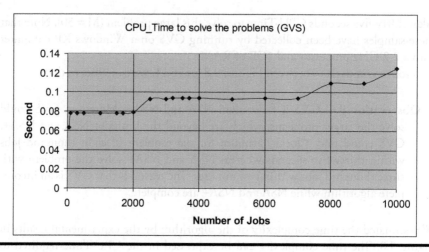

Figure 9.9   CPU-Time required solving the dynamic problems by GVS.

Based on the Coefficients in Table 9.2, we have the following equation for the CPU-Time to find a local optimum:

$$CPU - Time_{GVS} = -7.488 \times 10^{-5} \times Numberof Jobs + 5.33 \times 10^{-7} \times Numberof Jobs^2$$

More details about information in Table 9.2 are the same as in Section 6.5.

9.7.2 Complexity of GVS for Dynamic Problem

In dynamic problems, we assume that only one job is assigned to an idle vehicle. Here, there is no doubt that GVS is very fast. We got some samples to show its performance. The CPU-Time required to solve the problems by GVS is shown in Figure 9.9. As we can see when the number of jobs is ten thousand, it doesn't get too much CPU-Time to solve the large problems (less than 1 second). Note that these samples have been collected by running the software on a Windows XP computer with a 2.2 GHz Pentium processor and 1GB of RAM for fifty vehicles.

Given the number of jobs and vehicles in the problem, N and M, respectively, for this algorithm, its complexity is O(N·M). It is easy to understand this complexity in Figure 9.3 (pseudo-code of the algorithm).

9.8 A Discussion over GVS and Meta-Heuristic

A discussion could arise over using GVS compared to some well-known meta-heuristics (stochastic search methods) such as Genetic Algorithms, Tabu Search, Simulated Annealing method, and others when the problem is too big or when the time available to tackle the problem is too short. In the literature, we reviewed these solutions methods, including general considerations and major specific considerations in them (see Section 3.7). In this section, we have a short discussion on the matter

According to the literature, GVS could be considered as a heuristic. Voβ (2000) [196] defines heuristic as follows: "A heuristic is a technique (consisting of a rule or a set of rules) which seeks (and hopefully finds) good solutions at a reasonable computational cost. A heuristic is approximate in the sense that it provides (hopefully) a good solution for relatively little effort, but it does not guarantee optimality." We based GVS on two simple rules, the idle vehicles and jobs remained. Moreover, GVS doesn't get too much CPU-Time to tackle the problem, and for that reason, it finds out a local optimum solution.

We had the problem with memory to put the MCF-AGV model into (see Section 6.6). One of the reasons to use GVS is that it has no memory technique. In the literature, we studied that "the meta-heuristics manipulate a complete (or incomplete) single solution or a collection of solutions at each iteration" [196]. In order to do that, they require memory. Although we didn't provide any numerical comparison for the matter, our judge is that the memory usage of GVS is nil compared with the meta-heuristics.

Our work shows that GVS solves a huge problem in a short time. The problem of ten thousand jobs and fifty AGVs could be solved in a second (see the previous section). Additionally, GVS is effective in the average lateness to serve the jobs (see Section 9.5). The weakness of the meta-heuristics is that effectiveness could be sensitive to the choice of parameters values and operators [186]. Basically, finding out a set of suitable parameters for the meta-heuristics and their training to tackle the problem will be beyond the scope of the research reported in this book.

9.9 Summary and Conclusion

In this chapter, a greedy method, GVS for the scheduling problem of AGVs was presented. Then, we compared some solutions of GVS and NSA+ for the Dynamic Automated Vehicle scheduling problem. Many random problems with the same distribution were generated and solved by both algorithms. Given the results of the six-hour simulation, we claim that NSA+ is efficient and effective in both waiting and traveling times of the vehicles. GVS is useful when the problem is too big for NSA+ to solve or when the time available to tackle the problem is too short. Being an incomplete algorithm, GVS sacrifices completeness.

9.9 Summary and Conclusion

Chapter 10

Multi-Load and Heterogeneous Vehicles Scheduling: Hybrid Solutions

When the capacity of the vehicles is one container, the problem is a Minimum Cost Flow (MCF) model. This model was solved by the highest performance Algorithms, developed in Chapter 6 through Chapter 9, i.e., Network Simplex Algorithm (NSA) and its extensions. If the capacity of the vehicles increases, the problem is an NP-hard problem. This problem has a huge search space and must be tackled by some heuristic algorithms. In this chapter, the problem is tackled by the Simulated Annealing Method (SAM). Three approaches for its initial solution and a neighborhood function to the search method are implemented. A hybrid of SAM and NSA also is made and applied to the heterogeneous vehicle scheduling problem in container terminals. Several of the same random problems are generated, solved by the hybrid with the proposed approaches, and the simulation results are compared. The experimental results show that NSA provides a good initial solution for SAM when the capacity of vehicles is heterogeneous.

10.1 Motivation

In the past few decades, much research has been devoted to the technology of Automated Guided Vehicle (AGV) systems, both in hardware and software (see [148, 153]). Nowadays they have become popular over the world for automatic

DOI: 10.1201/9781003308386-12

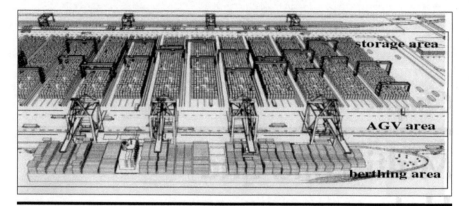

Figure 10.1 Layout of a seaport container terminal. See [53].

material-handling and flexible manufacturing systems. These unmanned vehicles are also increasingly becoming a common mode of container transport in the seaport. In this chapter, we consider a highly automated seaport container terminal, which consists of a berthing area (quayside), an AGV area, and a storage area (yardside). Figure 10.1 illustrates the layout of one of the latest seaport container terminals. The berthing area is equipped with Quay Cranes for the loading and unloading of vessels. The storage area is divided into blocks each of which is serviced by one or more stacking cranes. The transportation of the containers from the berthing area to the storage area is realized by AGVs, which can carry up to two 20 ft containers or alternatively one 40 or 45 ft container at a time. In the container terminal considered, AGVs are operated in single-carrier mode, but shall be used as multi-load carriers in the future.

10.2 Assumptions and Formulation

In this section, the Multi-Load and Heterogeneous AGVs scheduling problem in the container terminals is defined and formulated.

10.2.1 Assumptions

The major assumptions used here are the same as the assumptions in Chapter 5. In that chapter, we assumed that the AGVs are homogeneous with unit capacity, but here we assume that they are heterogeneous. In formal, we substitute the Assumption 5-5 in Chapter 5 with the following:

> **Assumption 5-5:** We are given a fleet of $V = \{1,2,\ldots,|V|\}$ vehicles. The vehicles are heterogeneous and every vehicle transports a few containers. At the start of the process, the vehicles are assumed to be empty.

10.2.2 Formulation

The Assumption 5-5 converts the problem defined in Chapter 5 into an NP-hard problem. The formulation in Chapter 5 was a MCF model whereas the problem and its formulation, here, are somewhat different. The problem, here, is formulated as Constraint Satisfaction and Optimization (CSOP).

A directed graph or network is considered for this transportation system. Given n for the number of jobs, let node i and node n + i represent the pickup and delivery location of the ith job in the network, respectively. In this network, different nodes obviously may represent the same physical location in the yard or berth. By adding node 0 and node 2n + 1, as the depot, to the network, the node set becomes N = {0, 1, 2,...,n, n + 1, n + 2,...,2n, 2n + 1}. The pickup and delivery points are, respectively, included into two sets P^+ = {1, 2,...,n} and P^- = {n + 1, n + 2,...,2n}. Obviously, P = P^+ U P^- is the set of nodes other than the depot node.

The following parameters are known:

AT_j: The appointment time of the jth job.
TS_{v0}: The times at which the vehicle v leaves the depot.
q_v: The capacity of vehicle v.
TT_{ij}: The travel time from the physical location of node i, L_i, to the physical location of node j, L_j (for each pair of i, j in N).

10.2.3 Decision Variable

X_{ijv}: This variable indicates the movement of vehicle v from node i to node j. In fact, this variable is one if vehicle v moves from node i to node j; otherwise, it is zero. So, its domain is {0,1}.

10.2.4 Constraints and Objective Function

The constraints and objective function of the problem are formulated in equations (10.1) to (10.6). In the formulation, we make a couple of auxiliary variables. The first one, Y_{vi}, is the load of vehicle v when it leaves node i. At the start of the process $Y_{v0} = 0$. This variable is determined by equation set (10.1). The first statement in equation set (10.1) represents the load of a vehicle when it leaves the first pickup point after the depot. The second statement in equation set (10.1) has a similar meaning but for when each vehicle goes to any pickup or dropoff point after the first pickup. If a vehicle goes to any pickup (dropoff) point, its load is increased (decreased) by one. The second auxiliary variable, TS_{vi}, is the time at which the vehicle v starts service at node i ($TS_{v0} = 0$). This variable is determined by equation set (10.2).

(a) IF $(X_{0jv} = 1) \Rightarrow Y_{vj} = 1; v \in V, j \in P^+,$

(b) IF $(X_{ijv} = 1) \Rightarrow$
$$\left\{ \begin{array}{l} Y_{vj} = Y_{vi} + 1; v \in V, j \in P^+, i \in P, i \neq j \\ Y_{vj} = Y_{vi} - 1; v \in V, j \in P^-, i \in P, i \neq j \end{array} \right\} \quad (10.1)$$

(a) IF $(X_{0jv} = 1) \Rightarrow TS_{vj} = TS_{v0} + TT_{L0,Lj}; j \in P^+, v \in V,$

(b) IF $(X_{ijv} = 1) \Rightarrow TS_{vj} = TS_{vi} + TT_{Li,Lj}; i, j \in P, v \in V \quad (10.2)$

(c) IF $(X_{i(2n+1)v} = 1) \Rightarrow TS_{v(2n+1)} = TS_{vi} + TT_{Li,L(2n+1)}; i \in P^-, v \in V$

(a) $\displaystyle\sum_{v \in V}\sum_{j \in N} X_{ijv} = 1, i \in P^+$

(b) $\displaystyle\sum_{j \in N} X_{ijv} - \sum_{j \in N} X_{jiv} = 1, i \in P, v \in V \quad (10.3)$

(c) $\displaystyle\sum_{j \in N} X_{ijv} - \sum_{j \in N} X_{j(n+i)v} = 1, i \in P^+, v \in V$

(a) $\displaystyle\sum_{j \in P^+} X_{0jv} = 1, v \in V$

$\qquad\qquad\qquad\qquad\qquad\qquad\qquad (10.4)$

(b) $\displaystyle\sum_{i \in P^-} X_{i(2n+1)} = 1, v \in V$

$$Y_{vi} \leq q_v, v \in V, i \in P \quad (10.5)$$

$$MinCosts = \sum_{v \in V} \left\{ \begin{array}{l} w1 \displaystyle\sum_{i \in P}\sum_{j \in P, j \neq i} X_{ijv} \cdot TT_{ij} + \\ \underbrace{\displaystyle\sum_{\text{jobs on the Quay-Side}} \left(w_2 \sum_{i \in P} |AT_i - TS_{vi}|^+ + w_3 \sum_{i \in P} |TS_{vi} - AT_i|^+ \right)} \end{array} \right\}$$

$\qquad\qquad\qquad\qquad\qquad\qquad\qquad (10.6)$

The first statement in equation (10.2) represents leaving the depot where the vehicles are followed by a pickup point. The second statement in equation (10.2) shows that the vehicles can go to any pickup or delivery point after the first pickup. The last statement in equation (10.2) represents going to the depot where the vehicles have delivery before that. To calculate the starting service time at each node, the service time of the current node and the traveling time between the previous and current nodes have to be considered.

Equation (10.3) shows the constraints set on pickup and delivery points of the vehicles. The first constraint in equation (10.3) ensures that each pickup point is visited once by one of the vehicles. The second constraint in equation (10.3) indicates that if a vehicle enters a node, it will exit the node. The third constraint in equation (10.3) ensures that if a vehicle visits a pickup node, then it has to visit the associated delivery node.

Equation (10.4) shows the constraint set on the first and last visit points of the vehicles. The first constraint in equation (10.4) ensures that the first visit of every vehicle is a pickup node. The second constraint in equation (10.4) ensures that the last visit of the vehicles is a delivery node. Equation (10.5) shows the constraint on the capacity of the vehicles. The load of vehicle v when it leaves the node i must not exceed the capacity of the vehicle. Equation (10.6) presents the objective function of the problem. The first term in equation (10.6) is the sum of traveling time of the vehicles. The second and third terms in equation (10.6) are the cost of waiting of vehicles and the cost of lateness time to serve the jobs, respectively. These two terms have impacts on the objective function provided that they are only positive. Note that w_1, w_2, and w_3 are the weights of those three terms in the objective function.

10.3 Solutions to the Problem

In this section, a couple of solutions for the problem are presented; (a) SAM for Multi-Load AGVs and (b) a hybrid of NSA and SAM for heterogeneous capacity of AGVs. These solutions are applied to the problems for the first time.

10.3.1 Simulated Annealing Method for the Multi-Load AGVs

The problem has a huge search space and must be tackled by one of the meta-heuristics search methods. Although Meta-heuristics usually also require relatively long computation times in order to provide good quality solutions, in some real-world applications meta-heuristics like Tabu Search and SAM might prove to be a good choice of method. This is due to the fact that these methods for the most part will be able to find a feasible solution within few seconds (see [153, 157]).

More research efforts were observed recently on the SAM to improve their running times (see [34, 46, 157). This method could have a significant impact on the speed up and the performance of the solutions. We, therefore, restrict ourselves to SAM in this research.

The SAM is analogous to the physical annealing process of obtaining a solid material in its ground state. A pseudo-code for the SAM is demonstrated in Figure 10.2. For a description of the steps in this method and more details on parameters refer to [34] and [46].

```
Initial Feasible Solution R
Let temp = Initial Temperature
Repeat
    Repeat
                Repeat R` = move ( ) until feasible
                Let ΔC = cost(R`) - cost(R)
                r = U [0,1]
                If (ΔC < 0) then
                        Accept R`
                Else If (r < exp(-ΔC /T)) then
                            Accept R`
                        End If
                End If
        Until (max temperature iterations)
        temp = Cooling Rate * temp
    Until (temp <= End Temperature) or (Max Iterations)
```

Figure 10.2   A pseudo-code for SAM. See [46].

In order to represent the neighborhood for the SAM, three alternatives including String Relocation, String Exchange, and String Mix (a string is a subsequence of the jobs for each vehicle) are considered. The String Relocation method tries to insert a stop (a job) or a string of stops (a sequence of jobs served by a vehicle) from one route into another route. The String Exchange attempts to improve the solution for the VRP by exchanging stops or strings of stops between two routes. The String Mix method is a mixture of the previous two methods. It tries to relocate or exchange stops or strings of stops and evaluates which yields the greatest savings. For our implementation, the String Relocation method was used, which provided a better solution in [46].

10.3.2 The Hybrid of SAM and NSA for Heterogeneous AGVs

The NSA and SAM are solutions for the Single-Load and Multiple-Load AGVs problem, respectively. NSA provides the global optimum solution whereas SAM finds a local optimum for the problem. These two methods can be combined to produce a hybrid method for heterogeneous AGVs. Three following methods are considered to get an initial feasible solution for the SAM:

■ **Deterministic Initial Feasible Solution**: In this case, the tour length for each vehicle equals the total number of jobs divided by the total number of vehicles.
■ **Random Initial Feasible Solution**: Some random jobs can be chosen so those satisfy our feasibility constraints. This approach allows the process to begin at different neighborhoods.

- **Solutions from Network Simplex Algorithm**: The optimal solution from NSA for Single-Load AGVs provides an initial solution for SAM. Then, SAM can continue to find a better solution for Multi-Load AGVs.

The hybrid of SAM and NSA is based on the last option for the initial feasible solution. Regarding the high performance of NSA, one can use the algorithm to produce an initial feasible solution for SAM.

10.4 Experimental Results

To test the model and the algorithms, a hypothetical port was designed. The parameters in our experiment are the same as what we used in Chapter 6 (see Table 6.1). The software was implemented in Borland C++ and then was run to solve several random problems on a Pentium 2.4 GHz PC with 1 GMB RAM. This section presents the experimental results for the problems of fifty AGVs and seven Quay Cranes.

We ran the Hybrid Method for Multi-Load AGVs. The values used for the parameters to run the hybrid method are shown in Table 10.1.

Table 10.2 demonstrates the number of container jobs and the values of the objective function (traveling and waiting times of the vehicles as well as the lateness time to serve the jobs) by different options for the initial feasible solution of SAM. The number of iterations in NSAWBP (Network Simplex Algorithm With Block Pricing, See Chapter 6, Section 6.2.4) to solve the model for Single-Load AGVs is also shown in the table. Note that the number of iteration of running the NSA for the Single-Load AGVs (the 3rd column in Table 10.2) is not considerable compared with the number of iterations of SAM for Dual-Load AGVs (the last row in Table 10.1). The percentages of increase in the objective function for the Deterministic Initial Feasible Solution and Random Initial Feasible compared with Initial Feasible Solution by NSAWBP are also calculated and provided in the table.

The value of the objective function in Table 10.2 was analyzed statistically, according to 5% rejection on the "True Hypothesis" (the two means are equal).

Table 10.1   Simulated Annealing Parameters

Parameters	Values
Initial temperature	1
End temperature	4
Cooling rate	0.999
Minimum string limit	3
Iterations per temperature	1000
Total iterations	30,000

Table 10.2 A Comparison between Different Options for the Initial Points of SAM

Problem	Number of Jobs	Number of Iterations in NSAWBP for Single-Load AGVs	(1) Initial Feasible Solution by NSAWBP	The Values of Objective Function by Simulated Annealing Method for Dual-Load AGVs Capacity along with the differences				
				Deterministic Initial Feasible Solution		Constructive Random Initial Feasible Solution		
				Objective Function	Percentage of Increase, Compared with (1)	Objective Function	Percentage of Increase, Compared with (1)	
1	10	98	2452	11884093	99.98	2548	3.77	
2	15	124	5444	61736113	99.99	5240	-3.89	
3	20	160	7184	32438256	99.98	6617513	99.89	
4	25	183	9905	190180985	99.99	3231285	99.69	
5	30	243	1512972	258873766	99.42	2664134	43.21	
6	35	299	926109	339936300	99.73	2617294	64.62	
7	40	350	1520243	463498316	99.67	13250455	88.53	
8	45	346	933279	678490771	99.86	8436397	88.94	
9	50	560	1377087	29832	4516.14	26769356	94.86	
10	55	471	942830	3701579	74.53	27073631	96.52	
11	60	541	1115226	30874299	96.39	27767825	95.98	
12	65	613	5732181	55866349	89.74	21771211	73.67	
13	70	681	3536178	142518848	97.52	32274173	89.04	
14	75	632	2521881	192762995	98.69	68571331	96.32	
15	80	827	4325901	298072454	98.55	100107503	95.68	
16	85	842	6248466	392395471	98.41	83278606	92.50	
17	90	1304	2514134	510167424	99.51	57437507	95.62	
18	100	1148	7013900	28445220	75.34	152630562	95.40	

Table 10.3 The Result of *t*-Test from SAM with Different Options for Initial Solution

Statistical Parameters	Initial Solutions by NSAWBP and Deterministic Initial Solution	Initial Solutions by NSAWBP and Random Initial Solution
Observations	18	18
t-Test (paired two sample for means)	−4.22193	−3.486049
Degree of freedom	17	17
T-Distribution	2.109819	2.1098185

Table 10.3 provides the test's result along with the values of T-distribution for a particular degree of freedom. The student's *t*-test determines the means are significantly different at a 95% degree of confidence.

In this experiment, we got the following observations:

Observation 10-1: If we choose some initial points for SAM by the Deterministic Initial Feasible Solution (DIFS) and Random Initial Feasible Solution (RIFS), then the objective function will become approximately 100% and 78% deteriorated, respectively compared with an Initial Feasible Solution by NSAWBP (see the 6th and 8th columns in Table 10.2). Therefore, NSAWBP provides a significantly better initial point for SAM. It is because NSA escapes from any local optimum and reaches the global solution of the problem of Single-Load AGVs. Then, the hybrid method continues to find more optimal local solutions for the problem of heterogeneous AGVs.

Observation 10-2: The Multi-Load AGVs problems have huge search space and few pieces of research have been devoted to that. In comparison, the size of problems solved for the Dual-Load AGVs, here, is very larger than on which [53] focused (there are only six AGVs in [53] for the experiment). This observation shows that the Multi-Load AGVs need more research and efficient algorithms in the future.

10.5 Summary and Conclusion

In this chapter, a couple of solutions for the Multi-Load and Heterogeneous AGVs scheduling problem in container terminals are proposed. These solutions are SAM for Multi-Load AGVs and a hybrid of NSA (Network Simplex Algorithm With Block Pricing-NSAWBP) and SAM for heterogeneous capacity of AGVs. The String Relocation as a neighborhood function and three options for the initial feasible solutions for the method (the solution from NSAWBP, deterministic, and random job) were considered. Then, several of the same random problems were generated and solved by the method. The experimental results showed the hybrid of NSAWBP and SAM provides a significantly better result when the capacity of the vehicles is increased to dual-load containers.

Chapter 11

Integrated Management of Equipment in Automated Container Terminals

11.1 Introduction

The efficiency of ports and container terminals is strongly related to the process of loading containers onto and unloading containers from the docked ships. In this chapter, an issue of integrated equipment management in automated container terminals with the aim of increasing efficiency has been studied. Due to this issue falls into NP-Hard problems, it was divided into two sub-problems: Allocating resources to containers and arranging the containers serviced by automated guided vehicles. Both sub-problems were formulated and expressed using the linear integer-programming model. The first sub-problem is solved by the allocation of random process resources with uniform distribution and the second part is solved using a Sorting Genetic Algorithm. The main parameters of the proposed solution methods were determined with Minitab software and Taguchi techniques [178]. In order to evaluate the efficiency and effectiveness of the proposed solution methods, many numerical experiments have been examined and evaluated. The experimental results show that the proposed solutions are efficient for estimating the service time and the number of automated guided vehicles required to transporting the containers in the container ports.

DOI: 10.1201/9781003308386-13

11.2 Motivations

International trade and exchanging commodities between countries are increasing and are continued exponentially in the current age. Depending on their needs, each country imports the commodities it needs and exports its surplus to other countries. The automated container terminals (ACT) are developed to transport commodities by cargo ships on which loading containers or unloading containers from them. The main functions of these terminals are delivering containers to consignees and receiving containers from shippers, loading containers onto and unloading containers from ships, and storing containers temporarily to account either for the efficiency of the equipment or for the difference in arrival times of the sea and land carriers. Containers are usually handled in two important compartments. Figure 11.1 shows the layout of the automated container terminal with two main compartments. The first compartment is called the quay-side and the second one is the yard-side. Between the yard-side and quay-side, the automated guided vehicles transport the containers. Anchoring of ships in an ACT spends high costs because of the expensive equipment used loading, unloading, and transporting the containers as well.

Figure 11.2 shows the loading and unloading process of containers. In the quay-side, there are a number of berths where the ships are docked for loading and unloading operations by the Quay Cranes (QC). Only one ship is allowed to dock at the same time in a berth. Each QC has three important parts: the main trolley, the transfer platform, and the portal trolley. The main trolley is responsible for getting the container from the ship and put it on the platform or vice versa. The transfer platform is responsible for maintaining the container. The trolley is responsible for getting the container from the transfer platform and put it onto the automated guided vehicle or vice versa. These trucks can move just one container in each operation.

In the yard-side, there are many storage locations and yard cranes. Each storage location has separate parts called blocks. Each block contains two short-term and long-term storage locations. Each storage area has a yard crane. For example, the front crane is in short-term storage and the back crane is in long-term storage.

The compartment between the beach and the yard is the place where automated guided vehicles (AGV) move. This middle part of the terminal is called the

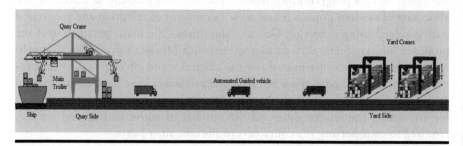

Figure 11.1   Layout of the automated container terminal. (Adopted from [94].)

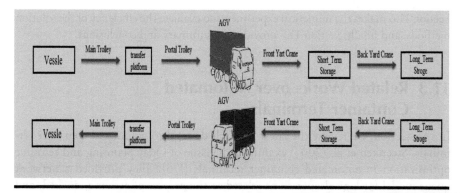

Figure 11.2   Loading and unloading process. (Adopted from [94].)

transmission location. This section encompasses rails and automated guided vehicles. The AGVs move in the rails. They are unmanned vehicles that are responsible for transporting and moving containers from the quay-side to the yard-side or vice versa. Each AGV is capable of carrying one container at the same time.

The process of loading inbound containers is transmitting containers from the ship to the storage area. At first cargo ship docked at the berth for doing operations. Several QCs start working on the ship. Then, on the shore, the main trolley of each crane picks the container from the ship and puts it on the transfer platform. The portal trolley picks the container from the transfer platform and puts it to the AGV. Trucks carry the container from the quay-side to the yard-side. On the yard-side, the front yard crane picks up the container from the AGV and places it in short-term storage. Then the backyard crane removes the container from the short-term storage area and places it in the long-term storage area.

The process of loading the outbound containers is transmitting containers from the storage place onto the ship. At first, the backyard crane puts the container from the long-term storage place to the short-term storage place. Then, the front yard crane picks up the container from the short-term storage area and delivers it to the AGV. The AGV transfers the container from the yard-side to the quay-side. On the quay-side, the portal trolley puts the container from the AGV and places it on the transfer platform. Then the main trolley in the crane lifts the container dock from the moving platform and places it on the ship.

The efficiency of each ACT depends on the time each docked ship spent on the quay-side for service. To increase this efficiency, the speed of sending the import containers from the docked ships to the yard-side or from the yard-side to the docked ships in the terminal must be improved. This chapter presents an integrated planning for the equipment available in the container terminals with the aim of reducing the service time of ships. The rest of this chapter is organized as follows. Section 11.3 presents the related works and reviews the latest researches devoted to the container terminals. Section 11.4 formulated the problem. Section 11.5 proposes the solution methods.

Section 11.6 makes the numerical experiments to evaluate the efficiency of the solution methods, and finally Section 11.7 provides the summary and conclusions.

11.3 Related Works over Automated Container Terminals

In this section, we review the latest research devoted to automated container terminals. Steenken et al. (2004) examined the issue of Quay planning and resource optimization in automated container terminals [176]. They provided a network queue model for logical operations related to the process of arriving, docked, and leaving ships at container terminals. To solve the problem, they used the "what if" optimization approach for the dock planning problem.

Chen et al. (2013) studied the interactions between crane handling and truck transportation in a maritime container terminal by addressing them simultaneously [24]. Yard trucks are shared among different ships, which helps to reduce empty truck trips in the terminal area. The problem was formulated as a constraint programming model and a three-stage algorithm was developed. At the first stage, crane schedules were generated by a heuristic method. At the second stage, the multiple-truck routing problem was solved based on the precedence relations of the transportation tasks derived from the first stage. At the last stage a complete solution was constructed by using a disjunctive graph. The three procedures are linked by an iterative structure, which facilitates the search for a good solution. The computational results indicated that the three-stage algorithm is effective for finding high-quality solutions and can efficiently solve large problems.

Tang et al. (2014) addressed the joint QC and truck scheduling problem at a container terminal, considering the coordination of the two types of equipment to reduce their idle time between performing two successive tasks [181]. For the unidirectional flow problem with only inbound containers, in which trucks go back to quay-side without carrying outbound containers, a mixed-integer linear programming model is formulated to minimize the makespan. Several valid inequalities and a property of the optimal solutions for the problem are derived, and two lower bounds are obtained. An improved Particle Swarm Optimization (PSO) algorithm is then developed to solve this problem, in which a new velocity updating strategy is incorporated to improve the solution quality. For small-sized problems, this research compared the solutions of the proposed PSO with the optimal solutions obtained by solving the model using the CPLEX software. The solutions of the proposed PSO for large-sized problems are compared to the two lower bounds because CPLEX could not solve the problem optimally in a reasonable time. For the more general situation considering both inbound and outbound containers, trucks may go back to quay-side with outbound containers. The model is extended to handle this problem with bidirectional flow. The experiment shows that the improved PSO proposed is efficient to solve the joint QC and truck scheduling problem.

He et al. (2015) addressed the problem of integrated QC scheduling, IT scheduling, and YC scheduling. Firstly, this problem is formulated as a mixed integer programming model (MIP), where the objective is to minimize the total departure delay of all vessels and the total transportation energy consumption of all tasks. Furthermore, an integrated simulation-based optimization method is developed for solving the problem, where the simulation is designed for evaluation and optimization algorithm is designed for searching solution space. The optimization algorithm integrates the genetic algorithm (GA) and particle swarm optimization (PSO) algorithm, where the GA is used for global search and the PSO is used for local search. Finally, numerical experiments are conducted to verify the effectiveness of the proposed method. The results show that the proposed method can coordinate the scheduling of the three types of handling equipment and can realize the optimal trade-off between time-saving and energy-saving.

Roy and Koster (2018) developed a new integrated stochastic model for analyzing the performance of overlapping loading and unloading operations that capture the complex stochastic interactions among quay-side, vehicle, and stack-side processes [164]. This research used a network of open and semi-open queues to make an analytical model. The model was solved using an iterative algorithm based on the parametric decomposition approximation approach. The system performance is tested at varying container traffic levels. This research found that the percent absolute errors in throughput times compared to simulation are less than 10% for all cases. The model was used to generate design insights and also rapidly analyze what-if scenarios. For example, this research showed that the best yard layout configurations for single (either loading or unloading) operations and the best for overlapping (both loading and unloading) operations largely overlap. The best configurations have relatively few stack blocks and many rows per block. The model is generic and amenable to obtain other design and operational performance insights.

Yang et al. (2018) proposed an integrated scheduling method for routing AGVs at container terminals [205]. In this case, the goal was to reduce the duration of the ship's deployment and the process of loading or unloading containers. They formulated the problem with an integer linear programming model and proposed a two-level genetic algorithm to solve it.

Vahdani et al. (2019) integrated the assignment of QCs in container terminals and internal truck sharing assignment among them [192]. For this purpose, a bi-objective optimization model was developed. In the proposed model, several assignment phases, including the assignments of the vessel to container terminals, cranes to terminals, cranes to vessels, and trucks to cranes, were performed. The model also aimed to increase and improve the efficiency and effectiveness of internal trucks by sharing them among different terminals, so that there was an appropriate balance between the volume of workloads of the terminals and the trucks in question. The first objective function in the proposed model was to minimize operational costs, and the second objective function was to minimize the maximum overflowed workload in the terminals. Furthermore, in order to solve the proposed model, two meta-heuristic multi-objective algorithms, including modified non-dominated sorting genetic algorithm-II (MNSGA-II) and modified multi-objective particle swarm optimization (MMOPSO), were presented. Several numerical examples have been investigated and analyzed to show the accuracy of the proposed model and the methods. In addition, the results demonstrated that the simultaneous consideration of the assignments and the sharing of trucks would reduce the remaining workload in the terminals.

Zhao et al. (2019) developed a collaborative scheduling model for automated quay-side cranes (AQCs) and AGVs [219]. In the model, the capacity limitation of the transfer platform on AQCs was considered. The minimum total energy consumption of AQCs and AGVs was taken as the objective function. A two-stage taboo search algorithm was adopted to solve the problem of collaborative scheduling optimization. This algorithm integrated AQC scheduling and AGV scheduling. The optimal solution to the model was obtained by feedback from the two-stage taboo search process. Finally, the Qingdao Port was taken as an example of a data experiment. Ten small-size test cases were solved to evaluate the performance of the proposed optimization methods. The results showed the applicability of the two-stage taboo search algorithm since it can find near-optimal solutions, precisely and accurately.

Castilla et al. (2020) developed an intelligent system that integrates Artificial Intelligence techniques and simulation tools to aid terminal managers [21]. The system combines an intelligent evolutionary algorithm to generate high-quality schedules for the cranes with a simulation model that incorporates uncertainty and the impact of internal delivery vehicles. The joint use of these tools provides managers with enhanced information to decide on the quality and robustness of the proposed schedules, resulting in better solutions for everyday situations. The intelligent system based on the optimization-simulation model provides clear benefits to maritime terminal management. The system efficiently identified high-quality schedules and can be used to evaluate its robustness. It was also flexible and can easily be adapted if other elements need to be introduced, which may affect the goodness of a schedule.

Kizilay et al. (2020) proposed constraint-programming models for integrated container terminal operations [95]. The aim was to reduce the ship's circulation time and increase the port's efficiency. Also in this model, import and export containers are considered in the same way. (For complex examples, a two-step optimization approach can be used.)

Yue et al. (2021) disclosed that meeting individual needs increases competition between container terminals [209]. To this end, they examined the issue of integrated scheduling of existing equipment and divalent AGVs. They formulated the problem with a two-stage mixed correct planning model to maximize customer satisfaction and minimize service latency. Then they used a sorting genetic algorithm to solve the problem. Numerical results showed the effectiveness of the proposed model and algorithm.

Table 11.1 shows a summary of the literature review of integrated handling equipment scheduling in automated container terminals.

Table 11.1 Summary of the Review Around Integrated Handling Equipment Scheduling. See [106].

Authors (Year)	Handling Equipment	Objective	Constraints	Model	Solution Method
Steenken et al. (2001)	QC, IT, and YC	Avoid waiting times at the QCs	Coordinated between vehicles and cranes	Just-in-time scheduling model	"what if" simulation
Homayouni et al. (2011)	QC, IT, and YC	Minimize delay	Coordinated between vehicles and cranes	Mixed Linear Programming	Genetic algorithm (GA)
Chen et al. (2013)	QC, IT, and YC	Minimize makespan	ITs are shared among different ships	Mixed Linear Programming	A three-stage algorithm consisting of heuristic and disjunctive graph
Tang et al. (2014)	QC, IT, and YC	Minimize makespan	QC and IT Minimize makespan Inequalities and lower bounds MILP	Mixed Linear Programming	CPLEX and particle swarm optimization (PSO)
He et al. (2015)	QC, IT, and YC	Minimize delay and energy consumption	Time-saving and energy-saving	Mixed Linear Programming	GA and PSO
Yang et al. (2018)	QC, AGV, and YC	Minimize makespan prevention	Conflictive and congestion	Bi-level programming model	Bi-level GA

(Continued)

Table 11.1 **Summary of the Review Around Integrated Handling Equipment Scheduling. See [106].** *(Continued)*

Authors (Year)	Handling Equipment	Objective	Constraints	Model	Solution Method
Roy and de Koster (2018)	QC and ALV	Improve seaside processes	Vehicle queuing network	Integrated stochastic models	Markov chain analysis and traffic simulation
Zhao et al. (2019)	QC and AGV	Minimize energy consumption	Transfer platform capacity	Mixed Linear Programming	A two-stage taboo search algorithm
Vahdani et al. (2019)	QC and IT	Minimize costs and minimize the maximum workload	Distribution and sharing of trucks	Bi-objective optimization model	NSGA-II and multi-objective particle swarm optimization
Zhong et al. (2020)	QC, AGV, and YC	Minimize makespan	Coordination of main trolley and portal trolley of QC	Mixed Linear Programming	Hybrid GAPSO algorithm with adaptive
Castilla et al. (2020)	QC and IT	Minimization cost	System uncertainty	Mixed Linear Programming	Simulation
Kizilay et al. (2020)	QC, AGV, and YC	Minimizing the turnover times of the vessels	Coordinated between vehicles and cranes	Constraint programming	Two-step optimization approach
Yue et al. (2021)	QC and AGV	Maximize customer satisfaction, minimize delay of QCs and idle time of AGV	Customer satisfaction, buffer capacity of blocks and AGV endurance	Two-stage and bi-objective Mixed Linear Programming	GUROBI and NSGA-III

11.4 Problem Description and Modeling

In this chapter, the problem of equipment management of a container terminal is investigated with the aim of reducing the duration of the ship at the berth and increasing the speed of the service process. A scenario is considered to examine the problem. In this scenario, a ship anchors at zero time for loading and unloading a number of containers at the berth. During anchoring, it is known how many QCs and which QCs are operating on the ship. It also specifies how many containers should be unloaded from the ship and how many containers should be loaded on the ship. The source and destination of each container job are also specified at the time of ship anchoring. A number of automated guided vehicles are responsible for transporting these container jobs. The problem, here, is to find the shortest possible time to transfer containers from the quay-side to the yard-side or vice versa. The problem was formulated and expressed in terms of complexity in the following.

11.4.1 Complexity of the Problem

The proposed problem has a very large search space and is one of the NP-Hard problems. Given N as the number of container jobs to be carried and C_V as the number of container jobs to be carried by the vehicle v, we can calculate the size of search space to find the optimal solution. For example, if all N container jobs must be carried by only one automated guided vehicle, the number of containers jobs to be carried by this vehicle is the C_1. Hence, we have the equation (11.1) and the size of the search space, in this case, is equal to the number of permutations in the transportation of N container jobs, it will be$(N)!$.

$$C_1 = N. \tag{11.1}$$

In addition, if we have M automated guided vehicles and only one container job to be carried, the size of the search space will be equal to the number of non-negative correct answers of the equation (11.2), i.e.,M.

$$C_1 + C_2 + \ldots + C_M = 1. \tag{11.2}$$

Therefore, if the problem has M automated guided vehicles and N containers, the problem search space will be equal to all permutations of the non-negative correct answers of the equation (11.3). Therefore, in general, the size of the search space is equal to the value of the equation (11.4).

$$C_1 + C_2 + \ldots + C_M = N \tag{11.3}$$

$$(C_1)!+(C_2)!+...+(C_M)! = \begin{pmatrix} N+M-1 \\ M-1 \end{pmatrix} = \frac{(N+M-1)!}{(N)!(M-1)!}s \quad (11.4)$$

The problem can be compared with the Minimum Cost Flow (MCF) model, formulated in Chapter 5. To do this, we assume a directional graph GAGV = (NAGV, EAGV), with four types of nodes as follows:

a. **AGVN$_m$:** a supply node corresponding to AGV m with one unit supply (AGVN stands for the AGV Node). There are M AGVs in the problem. Hence, there are M supply nodes in the GAGV. We define the following set for these supply nodes:
SAGVN: a set of M supply nodes as denoted by SAGVN = {AGVN$_m$ | m=1,2,...,M}.

b. **JPUN$_i$:** It is a node in which an AGV pick-up job i. It stands for the Job-Pick-Up Node. There is neither supply nor demand in this node, i.e., it is a transshipment node. We define the following set for these transshipment nodes:
SJPUN: It is a set of N Job-Pick-Up nodes in the GAGV, denoted by SJPUN = {**JPUN$_i$** | i=1,2,...,N}.

c. **JDPN$_i$:** a node in which an AGV delivers the job i. It stands for the Job-Delivery-Point Node. Like the previous nodes, there is neither supply nor demand in this node. We define the following set for these transshipment nodes:
SJDPN: It is a set of N Job-Delivery-Point nodes in the GAGV, denoted by **SJDPN** = {**JDPN$_i$** | i=1,2,...,N}.

d. **SINK:** It stands for a Sink node or a demand node in the NAGV with M units demand.

Therefore, if we have the number of *M* AGV and the number of *N* container jobs in the problem, the total number of nodes in the MCF model will be equal to $M + 2 \times N + 1$. The set of nodes in GAGV is according to the equation (11.5):

$$NAGV = SAGVN \cup SJPUN \cup SJDPN \cup SINK \quad (11.5)$$

We have four types of edges in the GAGV as follows:

a. **Inward Arcs:** There is a directed arc from every AGV node, to the Job-Pick-Up node of job i. We define the following notation for these arcs as below:
ARC$_{inward}$: a set of arcs from SAGVN to SJSN, denoted by ARC$_{inward}$ = {(m, j)| ∀m ∈ SAGVN, ∀j ∈ SJPUN}

The number of these arcs in the GAGV is M×N. Each arc has the lower bound zero, and the upper bound one, i.e., only one AGV goes through each of these arcs. As we mentioned before (see Assumption 5-10), our objectives are to minimize waiting and traveling times of the AGVs and the lateness times of jobs. The cost between node m and node j is calculated as described in Chapter 5.

b. **Intermediate Arcs:** There is a directed arc from every Job-Delivery-Point node i to other Job- Pick-Up node j. We define the following notation for these arcs:

$ARC_{intermediate}$: It is a set of arcs from SJPUN to SJDPN, denoted by $ARC_{intermediate} = \{(i,j) | \; \forall i \in SJPUN, \forall j \in SJDPN, j \neq JPUN \; i\}$. The number of these arcs in the GAGV is N×(N-1). Each arc has the lower bound zero, and the upper bound one, i.e., only one AGV goes through from one job to another. The cost between node i and node j in the GAGV is calculated as what described in Chapter 5.

c. **Outward Arcs:** There is a directed arc from every Job-Delivery-Point node i and AGV node m to SINK. We define the following notation for these arcs as follows:

$ARC_{outward}$: It is a set of arcs from SJPUN and SJDPN to SINK, denoted by $ARC_{outward} = \{(i,j) | \; \forall i \in SAGVN \; U \; SJPUN, j=SINK\}$. These arcs show that an AGV can remain idle after serving any number of jobs or without serving any job. Therefore, a cost of zero is assigned to these arcs.

d. **Auxiliary Arcs:** There is a directed arc from every JPUN i to its JDPN. We define the following notation for these arcs as follows:

$ARC_{auxiliary}$: a set of arcs from SJPUN to SJDPN, denoted by $ARC_{auxiliary} = \{(i,j) | \; \forall i \in SJPUN, j=$a unique Job-Delivery-Point node in SJDPN, correspond to the JPUN i$\}$. These arcs have unit lower and upper bounds. The transition cost across these arcs is the distance time between the source and destination of container jobs. These auxiliary arcs guarantee that every JPUN and JDPN is visited once only so that each job is served.

Therefore, the set of arcs in GAGV is according to the equation (11.6) and the number of arcs is M×N+N×(N−1)+M+2×N.

$$EAGV = ARC_{inward} \; U \; ARC_{intermediate} \; U \; ARC_{outward} \; U \; ARC_{auxiliary} \qquad (11.6)$$

In this model, the problem search space is equal to finding the number of M paths, starting from each node in the *SAGVN* and ending at the **SINK**. In these routes, all nodes at the beginning and end of each container job must be covered. Figure 11.3 shows the graph for 2 AGV and 4 container jobs. Suppose that for some values of arc costs, the solution paths are $1 \rightarrow 3 \rightarrow 4 \rightarrow 9 \rightarrow 10 \rightarrow 11$ and $2 \rightarrow 5 \rightarrow 6 \rightarrow 7$

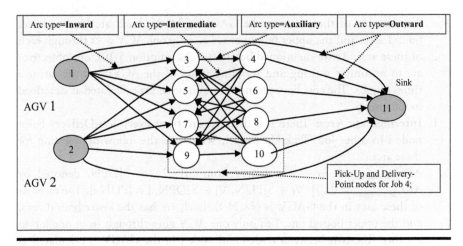

Figure 11.3 An example of the model for 2 AGVs and 4 container jobs.

→ 8 → 11. This states that AGV 1 is assigned to serve container jobs 1 and 4, and AGV 2 is assigned to serve container jobs 2 and 3, respectively.

Since the cost of arcs in the minimum cost flow model is an integer value, it enables us to model the problem as integer linear program. The known parameters before decision making and decision variables are shown in Tables 11.2 and 11.3, respectively.

Table 11.2 Known Parameters before Decision Making

Equation No.	Mathematical Equation	Description
(11.7)	$V = \{1.2.3.....v\}$	The Set of Automated Guided Vehicles
(11.8)	$B = \{1.2.3.....b_j\}$	The Set of total storage blocks in the terminal.
(11.9)	$Q = \{1.2.3....q\}$	The Set of total QCs in the terminal.
(11.10)	$Q_{Active} \subset Q$	The Set of active QC on the ship.
(11.11)	$C_{Inbound} = \{1.2.3.....i\}$	The Set of inbound containers.
(11.12)	$C_{Outbound} = \{1.2.3.....j\}$	The Set of outbound containers.

(Continued)

Table 11.2　Known Parameters before Decision Making *(Continued)*

Equation No.	Mathematical Equation	Description
(11.13)	$C_{Total} = C_{Inbound} \cup C_{Outbound}$	The Set of total containers.
(11.14)	$C_v \subset C_{Total} \ . \ \forall v \in V$	The number of container jobs to be carried by the vehicle v
(11.15)	$\bigcup_{v=1}^{M} C_v = C_{Total} \ ; \bigcap_{v=1}^{M} C_v = \varnothing$	The Set of container jobs that each AGV must carry.
(11.16)	$S = Q_{Active} \cup B$	The Set of pick-up nodes of containers.
(11.17)	$D = Q_{Active} \cup B$	The Set of delivery-point nodes of containers.
(11.18)	CN	The Set of cross nodes in path.
(11.19)	$N^* = Q \cup B \cup CN$	The Set of total nodes in the path.
(11.20)	$L = \{l_1, l_1, ..., l_v\} . \ l_v \in N^*$	The Set of first location of AGV.
(11.21)	$W_{s_i.d_i}$	The distance-time from the location s_i to the location d_i.
(11.22)	$s_i \in Q_{Active} \cup B$	The pick-up node of container job i.
(11.23)	$d_i \in Q_{Active} \cup B$	The delivery-point node of container job i.
(11.24)	If $i = 1 \Rightarrow AT_{v1} = \begin{cases} 0 \ if \ l_v = s_1 \\ W_{l_v.s_1} \ else \ l_v \neq s_1 \end{cases}$ Otherwise $AT_{vi} = \begin{cases} 0 \ if \ d_{i-1} = s_i \\ W_{d_{i-1}.s_i} \ else \ d_{i-1} \neq s_i \end{cases}$	The arrival time of the AGV v to the starting point of the container i.
(11.25)	$TT_{vi} = W_{s_i.d_i}$	Duration of movement of container job i from the source node to the destination by the AGV v.

Table 11.3 Decision Variables

Row	Variables	Description
(11.26)	$Y_{imn} = \{0 \text{ or } 1\}$	If container job i is sent from its source location by the crane m (quay-side or yard-side) to its destination location by the crane n (quay-side or yard-side), then $Y_{imn}=1$, otherwise it is zero.
(11.27)	$X_{vi} = \{0 \text{ or } 1\}$	If the AGV v carries container i, $X_{vi}=1$ otherwise it is zero.

11.4.2 Problem Formulation

The objective function of the model is to minimize the total time to handle all container jobs by the set of vehicles in the container terminal, according to the following function:

$$\min \left\{ \max_{\forall v \in V. \ \forall i \, \in \, C_{Total}} (AT_{vi} + TT_{vi}) \right\} \tag{11.28}$$

The constraints are as follows:

$$\sum_{q \in Q_{Active}} \sum_{b \in B} Y_{iqb} = 1; \forall i \in C_{Inbound} \tag{11.29}$$

$$\sum_{b \in B} \sum_{q \in Q_{Active}} Y_{ibq} = 1; \forall i \in C_{Outbound} \tag{11.30}$$

$$\sum_{v \in V} X_{vi} = 1; \forall i \in C_{Total} \tag{11.31}$$

The constraints in the equation set (11.29) ensure that each inbound container is sent from the quay-side to the yard-side. The constraints in the equation set (11.30) ensure that each outbound container is sent from the yard-side to the quay-side. The constraints in the equation set (11.31) ensure that each container job is handled by only one automated guided vehicle.

11.5 The Proposed Method

As mentioned before in Section 11.4, at the start of the ship processes, parameters such as the number of the containers to be serviced, the number of QCs has to work on the ship, the number of AGVs that must transfer the containers, and the number of storage blocks must be specified. To simplify the problem, the problem is divided into two sub-problems. The first part is assigning the equipment to the container job in the terminal. In this step, it should be specified which container job should be serviced with which QC and which automated guided vehicle. The first part of the problem uses a greedy algorithm to assign source and destination to each container job.

An automated container terminal is provided to examine the proposed method. In this scenario, there is a container terminal with eight QCs, eight blocks, and eight automated guided vehicles. There are five QCs with numbers 4 to 8 operating on the ship. Ten container jobs must be loaded from the ship and sent to the blocks for storage. Six container jobs should be loaded on the ship and sent to the dock crane for delivery. All container jobs are equal to the sum of inbound and outbound container jobs. Figure 11.4 shows the source and destination for ten inbound container jobs and six outbound container jobs. For example, container 1 delivered into storage block 3, and container 11 should be delivered to QC 7.

The second part of the problem is finding the order of servicing container jobs for each automated guided vehicle and routing to transport container jobs from the source to the destination. In each container terminal, there is a specific path for the AGV to transport the container from the quay-side to the yard-side or vice versa. Since finding the number of containers and the optimal order for servicing container jobs and navigating automated guided vehicles is a NP-Hard problem, in this study, a sorting genetic algorithm is used to find the optimal local solution. The flowchart of the sorting genetic algorithm presented in Figure 11.5 is shown.

The layout of a docked ship and the location of the QC and blocks are shown in Figure 11.6. In this picture, the container terminal includes eight QCs and eight storage blocks. In order to prevent congestion and accidents, the movement path AGV was considered clockwise and the speed of all AGV was considered 5 meters per second.

QC-4	QC-5	QC-8	QC-7	QC-7	QC-7	QC-5	QC-7	QC-4	QC-7	B-1	B-3	B-1	B-1	B-7	B-6
B-3	B-8	B-1	B-1	B-4	B-7	B-7	B-2	B-4	B-4	QC-7	QC-7	QC-7	QC-8	QC-7	QC-7
1	2	3	4	5	6	7	8	9	10	11	12	13	14	15	16

Figure 11.4 The source and destination of sixteen containers.

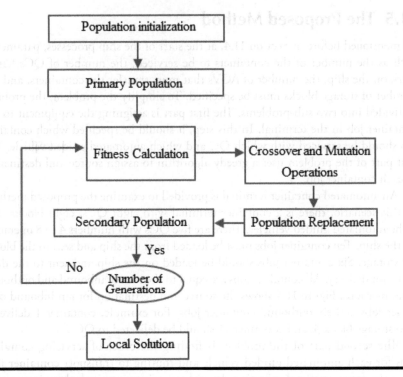

Figure 11.5 Flowchart of the presented sorting genetic algorithm.

11.5.1 Chromosome

The proposed sorting genetic algorithm uses a three-level chromosome. Because in the first part of the problem, the source and destination of each container are specified, the node number of the Job-Pick-Up and Job-Delivery-Point of each container job is identified. In the first level of chromosome, the starting node number is placed, in the level of the node number, the end of the container job is placed, and in the third level, the number of container jobs to be serviced is placed. In Figure 11.7 a three-level chromosome for sixteen container jobs with ten inbound jobs and six outbound jobs has been shown.

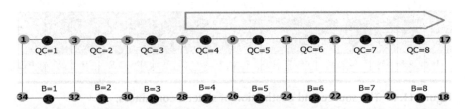

Figure 11.6 A docked ship with five QCs worked on.

8	16	16	14	14	14	10	14	8	14	33	29	33	33	21	23	Source
29	19	33	27	27	21	21	31	27	27	14	14	14	10	14	14	Destination
1	2	3	4	5	6	7	8	9	10	11	12	13	14	15	16	Container

Figure 11.7 A three-level chromosome for sixteen container jobs with ten inbound jobs and six outbound jobs.

Each chromosome represents the order of service of existing container jobs. The amount of fit function for each chromosome is equal to the total time from the previous location node to the Job-Pick-Up node plus the time of carrying the container job from the Job-Pick-Up node to the Job-Delivery-Point node for all container jobs. To solve the problem of the second part, the number of AGVs for servicing container jobs is considered as one. In this case, the problem can be solved by a genetic sorting algorithm.

11.5.2 Crossover Operator

In order to apply the crossover operation, at first, a number of parents must be selected from the existing population based on the specified rate. Depending on the fitness function, each parent is likely to be selected to perform crossover operations. Each chromosome that has a better fitness function, small is better, is more likely to be selected. The crossover operation is performed in four stages. In the first stage, the desired points for the intersection are determined and in the second stage, the existing container jobs are changed between the two intersection points. In the third stage, non-duplicate container jobs, and in the fourth stage, duplicate container jobs are inserted in the chromosomes. Each step has been described in more detail as follows.

A two-point intersection operator has been used to perform the intersection operation. After selecting two chromosomes as parent 1 and parent 2, in this operation, two random numbers with uniform distribution are selected as the intersection points in the parent chromosome. For example, in Figure 11.8 the two selected parents with intersection points 6 and 10 are shown.

In the next step, the genes are exchanged between the two intersection points. The value zero is replaced in the rest of the jobs because the number of container jobs cannot be duplicated. In Figure 11.9 the stage of gene exchanging between intersection points has been shown.

After exchanging genes between the intersection points, the number of non-duplicate container jobs must be added to the children. For example, in child 1, the container job 1 is inserted to the desired location because it is not duplicate, but in child 2, the container job 7 is not allowed to be inserted in the desired location due to duplication. The step of adding non-repetitive container jobs is shown in Figure 11.10.

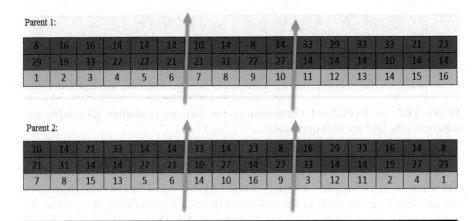

Figure 11.8 Selected parents with intersection points 6 and 10.

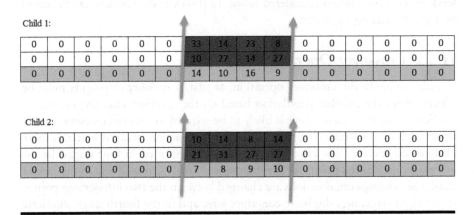

Figure 11.9 Genes exchanging between intersection points.

Child 1:

8	16	16	14	14	14	33	14	23	8	33	29	33	0	21	0
29	19	33	27	27	21	10	27	14	27	14	14	14	0	14	0
1	2	3	4	5	6	14	10	16	9	11	12	13	0	15	0

Child 2:

0	0	21	33	14	14	10	14	8	14	16	29	33	16	14	8
0	0	14	14	27	21	21	31	27	27	33	14	14	19	27	29
0	0	15	13	5	6	7	8	9	10	3	12	11	2	4	1

Figure 11.10 Adding non-repetitive containers to children.

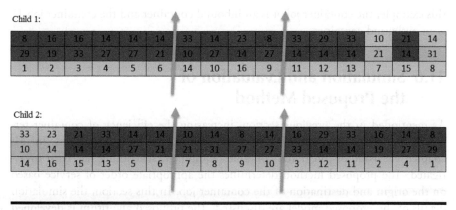

Figure 11.11 Adding non-repetitive containers to children.

After the step of inserting container jobs with non-duplicate numbers, the number of container jobs in chromosomes is checked to determine which container jobs are not inserted in chromosomes. Once the unlisted container jobs are specified, the chromosomes are inserted in ascending order. Figure 11.11 shows the step of adding duplicate container jobs.

11.5.3 Mutation Operator

In the proposed solution, a swap mutation operator had been used. At first, a number of parents are selected based on the Mutation rate. Then, two random numbers are generated using a uniform distribution. The numbers generated indicate the container job places that need to be swapped. For example, in Figure 11.12 swap mutation operation to the displacement of container jobs 4 and 11 are shown. In

Parent:

8	16	16	14	14	14	10	14	8	14	33	29	33	33	21	23
29	19	33	27	27	21	21	31	27	27	14	14	14	10	14	14
1	2	3	4	5	6	7	8	9	10	11	12	13	14	15	16

Child:

8	16	16	33	14	14	10	14	8	14	14	29	33	33	21	23
29	19	33	14	27	21	21	31	27	27	27	14	14	10	14	14
1	2	3	11	5	6	7	8	9	10	4	12	13	14	15	16

Figure 11.12 Swap mutation operation.

this example, the container job 4 is an inbound container and the container job 11 is an outbound container.

11.6 Simulation and Evaluation of the Proposed Method

As mentioned in the previous section, increasing the efficiency of container terminals is directly related to the speed and service life of anchored ships. In this chapter, the issue of integrated container equipment scheduling has been investigated. The proposed method determines the appropriate order of service based on the origin and destination of the container job. In this section, the simulation details of the proposed model are discussed. The proposed algorithm is developed using a structured programming method. The proposed method was implemented using MATLAB programming language and the algorithm parameters were calculated using Taguchi method. Finally, the proposed algorithm was compared with the Particle Swarm Optimization (PSO) algorithm and combinations of the PSO algorithm and Genetic Algorithm. Due to the random method of solving, each problem was solved 10 times. In the end, the execution time and the objective function values were reported for a number of problems. All tests were performed on a computer with a 2.4 GHz processor and 2 GB of RAM.

11.6.1 Parameters

The proposed method has four main factors: number of generations, population number, crossover rate, and mutation rate. For each factor, four different levels have been examined. The values checked are reported in Table 11.4. The parameters of the proposed method were examined using Minitab software and Taguchi method. To investigate 256 problems were designed and due to the random nature of the algorithm, each problem was performed ten times and the mean of the objective function values for each problem was reported. Then the values obtained for each problem were standardized by Robust parameter design (RPD (method and analyzed by Taguchi method.

Table 11.4   The Factors Names and Values

Factor Name	Values			
Number of Generations	100	200	300	400
Number of Populations	30	40	50	60
Crossover Ratio	0.5	0.6	0.7	0.8
Mutation Ratio	0.02	0.04	0.07	0.1

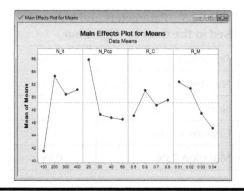

Figure 11.13   Main effects plot for means.

Figures 11.13 and 11.14 show the Main Effects Plot for Means and SN ratio, respectively, for determining the importance of factors in the solution method.

From these figures, we can observe that:

■ **Observation 11-1**: Figure 11-13 identifies which factor has had the greatest impact on the solution. Because they have a wide range, it shows that they are more important. Generally, the larger value indicates greater sensitivity to change the solution. This observation shows that values between 100 and 200 for the number of generation (iterations) have the most changes in the solution.

■ **Observation 11-2**: Figure 11-14 shows the importance of factors in the solution method and identifies which factor has most sensitive to changes the solution. In general, in this figure, the larger value shows greater sensitivity to change the solution. This observation indicates that a value between 100 and

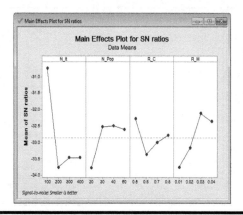

Figure 11.14   Main effects plot for SN ratios.

Table 11.5 Parameters and Values Used in the Genetic Algorithm

Parameters	Values
Number of Generations	100
Number of Populations	40
Crossover Rate	0.5
Mutation Rate	0.03

200 for the number of generations (iterations) have the most changes in the solutions. According to the analysis of the graphs obtained from the Taguchi method, as shown in Figures 11.13 and 11.14, the number of production iterations is 100, the population is 40, the crossover rate is 0.5, and the jump rate is 0.3. The parameters used in the genetic algorithm are shown in Table 11.5.

11.6.2 Numerical Experiments

In order to evaluate the efficiency and effectiveness of the proposed method, several problems were designed and its methods and combinations were examined with the proposed method. Figure 11.15 shows the objective function for the number of iterations of 100 generations and the population size of 50 when the number of

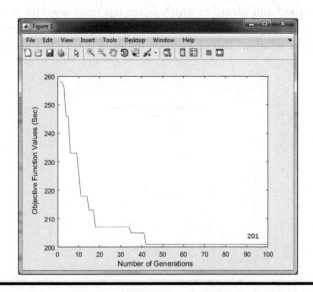

Figure 11.15 Convergence of GA with 100 generations for solving the problems.

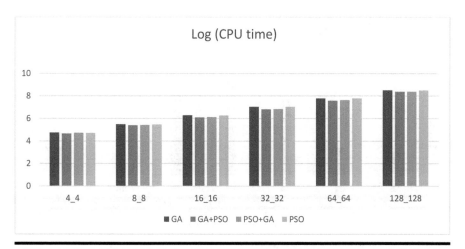

Figure 11.16   A comparison of log(CPU-Time spent by GA, PSO, GA+PSO, and PSO+GA algorithms).

tasks in container 16 (8 inbound containers—8 outbound containers). From this figure, we can observe that:

- **Observation 11-3:** the convergent genetic algorithm finds the optimal local solution for the expressed scenario. In this experiment, the value of the objective function is equal to 201.

Figures 11.16 and 11.17 show a comparison of CPU time and the values objective function when the problems are solved by GA, PSO, GA+PSO, and PSO+GA algorithms, respectively. From these figures, we can observe that:

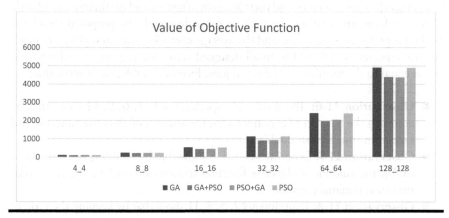

Figure 11.17   A comparison of objective function values for GA, PSO, GA+PSO, and PSO+GA algorithms.

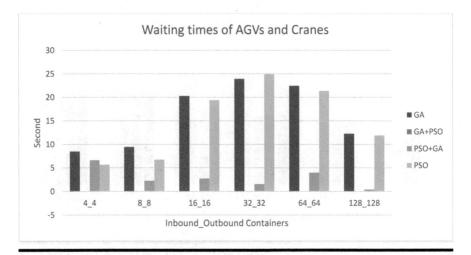

Figure 11.18   The waiting times of AGVs and cranes.

- **Observation 11-4**: The genetic algorithm has less execution time than the other three algorithms. Accordingly, Figure 11.17 shows the genetic algorithm has a better value for the objective function than the other three algorithms.

To compare the efficiency of the proposed method with the three other algorithms, we calculated the waiting time of the AGVs and Cranes. The result of this calculation is shown in Figure 11.18. From this figure, we observe that:

- **Observation 11-5:** The waiting time of the vehicles and cranes in solving the problems by GA is slightly more than the three other algorithms.

Given that the container jobs and their location of source and destination, randomly with a uniform distribution, for each scenario designed, the proposed simulated method is performed ten times, and the average execution time and objective function are reported in Table 11.6. In all designed scenarios, the number of inbound jobs is equal to the number of outbound jobs. From this table, we observe that:

- **Observation 11-6:** The results of experiments 1, 3, 6, 9, 12 show that by doubling the number of container jobs, the amount of objective function and execution time almost doubles.
- **Observation 11-7:** Experiments 3, 4, 5 show that by doubling the number of AGVs, the amount of objective function remains almost half and the execution time remains constant.
- **Observation 11-8:** Experiments 2, 5, 8, 11 show that by keeping the ratio of container job to AGVs constant (half), the objective function is almost constant (slightly increased) but the execution time is increased.

Table 11.6   The Experimental Results of Solving Sixteen Problems

Experiment	Inbound-Outbound Containers	Automated Guided Vehicles	Active QC	Objective Function Values	CPU Time (Sec)
1	4–4	1	5	106	11.396
2	4–4	2	5	52	46.883
3	8–8	1	5	199	16.059
4	8–8	2	5	107	17.233
5	8–8	4	5	61	17.480
6	16–16	1	5	430	24.693
7	16–16	2	5	226	26.764
8	16–16	8	5	70	27.379
9	32–32	1	5	945	44.777
10	32–32	2	5	493	46.360
11	32–32	16	5	75	47.001
12	64–64	1	5	2073	83.540
13	64–64	2	5	1076	90.074
14	128–128	1	2	4253	180.231
15	128–128	1	5	4452	165.477
16	128–128	1	8	4766	163.392

11.7 Summary and Conclusions

In this chapter, the problem of integrated management of equipment in automated container terminals with the aim of reducing the service time of berthed ships. The literature on the problem, including decisions, solutions, formulation, and implementation, was reviewed. The complexity of the proposed problem was investigated and then the problem was formulated as a linear integer-programming model. A solution based on a combination of the greedy algorithm and the genetic algorithm was proposed. This solution was named Sorting Genetic Algorithm (SGA). The parameters of the proposed method were investigated using Minitab software and Taguchi method to determine the appropriate values. To show the efficiency and effectiveness of the proposed method, the results were compared with the PSO algorithm and its combinations with the proposed method. Finally, execution time and objective function values of the comparison were reported.

The results show that not only the sorting genetic algorithm increased the efficiency and productivity of container terminals by adjusting the order of container operations but also can be used for measurement and prediction of the time required to docked the ship at the berth to load and unload containers. Additionally, the proposed method showed a reduction in execution time and finding a better local solution.

Chapter 12

Conclusions and
Future Research

This book was devoted to studying the decisions and solutions for automation in container terminals. There were two main objectives in this book. The first objective was to study optimization problems in container terminals. The second objective was dedicated to developing advanced algorithms for the scheduling problem of AGVs in ports.

To address the first objective, we did a survey on the research done for the decisions in container terminal and then formulated them as Constraint Satisfaction Optimization Problems (CSOPs). The five decisions are formulated separately so that they can be studied independently.

To address the second objective, this book presents effective and efficient solution methods for the Static and Dynamic Scheduling problem of Automated Guided Vehicles (SDSAGV) in the container terminals. A special case of the Minimum Cost Flow (MCF) model was defined and presented for the problem. Then, we studied the effectiveness and efficiency of the Network Simplex Algorithm (NSA) in the literature. We proposed three new versions of the algorithm: Network Simplex plus Algorithm (NSA+), Dynamic Network Simplex Algorithm (DNSA), and Dynamic Network Simplex plus Algorithm (DNSA+). NSA, NSA+, DNSA, and DNSA+ are complete algorithms. They were designed to find optimal solutions. To complement the solutions, Greedy Vehicle Search (GVS) method was designed and implemented. GVS is an incomplete algorithm which can be used for reactive scheduling or when the problem is too big for the complete algorithms. After that, we studied Multi-Load and heterogeneous AGVs scheduling problems. A couple of solutions for the problem are proposed. Moreover, we studied the problem of integrated management of equipment in

DOI: 10.1201/9781003308386-14 **239**

automated container terminals with the aim of reducing the service time of berthed ships.

In this final chapter, we summarize the research conducted on NSA, NSA+, DNSA, DNSA+, and GVS and also discuss the prospects of future research on the subject.

12.1 Summary of This Research Done

The research reported in this book started with the study of problems in container terminals. We classified these problems into five scheduling decisions (Chapter 2). Then we systematically and thoroughly surveyed the literature over these decisions and formulated them as CSOPs (Chapter 3). The survey showed that vehicles are important equipment in the ports and their scheduling is one of the most challenging problems.

In Chapter 4, we addressed three main challenges associated with providing practical software for decision-making. Firstly, we discussed the challenge related to the simulation of the operations in container terminals and then argued the design architecture toward implementation issues. After that, we classified the scheduling techniques and suggested several frameworks. Then, we did a survey on the solution methods to scheduling problems, in general, as well as scheduling and routing vehicles, in particular. Afterwards, we suggested two approaches for simulating container terminals and proposed several frameworks for implementation. Finally, several indices were provided for evaluation and monitoring any solutions for each of the decisions.

We then focused on the scheduling problem of Automated Guided Vehicles (AGVs) in container terminals. Another reason for choosing this problem is that the efficiency of a container terminal is directly related to using the AGVs with full efficiency. The problem was carrying many container jobs by several AGVs in their appointment times. We formulated the problem as a MCF model, a directed graph with particular assumptions. The main motivation to formulate the problem as an MCF model is that MCF has a rich history and arises in almost all industries, including agriculture, communications, defense, education, energy, health care, manufacturing, medicine, retailing, and transportation. The MCF problem is sending flow from a set of supply nodes, through the arcs of the network, to a set of demand nodes at the minimum total cost, without violating the lower and upper bounds on flows through the arcs. We defined and presented a special case of MCF model for the Scheduling problem of AGVs (Chapter 5). The MCF-AGV is an established name for our model. The cost of each arc in the MCF-AGV model was the waiting and traveling time of vehicles as well as the lateness times to serve the container jobs.

The main objectives of this book were to solve the Scheduling problem of AGVs efficiently and effectively. The MCF-AGV model, formulated in Chapter 5, had a huge search space and its solution had to provide the optimal paths for each vehicle. Additionally, the problem was dynamic. From time to time a few new jobs arrived and the distance between the source and destination of the jobs could be changed.

We first tackled the Static problems (defined in Chapter 5). In order to do that, we used NSA, which is one of the solution methods for the MCF model. In Chapter 6, we applied the standard version of the algorithm to the problem. We reviewed the literature over NSA and different schemes to select the next basic solution. Then, implementation of the algorithm and finding the optimal solution in static problems were considered. Many random data were generated and fed to the MCF-AGV model for fifty vehicles. Our software, implemented in Borland C++, by running on a 2.4 GHz Pentium PC, could find the global optimal solution for three thousand jobs and ten million arcs in the MCF-AGV model within two minutes. It has been found that, in practice, the NSA runs in polynomial time to solve the problems.

Another goal of the research reported in this book was to extend NSA in the dynamic aspect. In Chapter 8, DNSA and DNSA+ were presented. The objectives of these algorithms were to solve the new problem faster, to use some parts of the previous solution for the next problem, and to respond to change in the situation. In order to confirm the validity of DNSA+, again we used the Dynamic Scheduling problem of AGVs (the problem defined in Chapter 5). The same problems have been solved by NSA+ and DNSA+. Our experiment showed that the number of iterations is decreased if we repair the current solution for the next problem when any changes happen, compared with starting from scratch by NSA+.

NSA and its extensions are complete algorithms. Although they are efficient, they can only work on problems with certain limits in size. To complement the algorithms, the GVS method was designed and implemented (Chapter 9). GVS is useful for problems where sizes go beyond the limits, or in dynamic scheduling where reactive responses are called for, or when the time available to tackle the problem is too short.

To evaluate the relative strength and weakness of GVS and NSA+ in the Dynamic Scheduling problem (the problem defined in Chapter 5), we used randomly generated problems. The objective function of the problem had three terms, waiting times of the AGVs, traveling times of AGVs, and the lateness time to serve the jobs. We did a simulation for six hours. By the end of the simulation, we show that:

a. NSA+ is efficient and effective in both the waiting and traveling times of the vehicles.

b. GVS is efficient in the average lateness serving the container jobs.

If the capacity of the AGVs increases, the problem is an NP-hard problem. This problem has a huge search space and was tackled by the Simulated Annealing

Method (SAM). Three approaches for its initial solution and a neighborhood function to the search method were implemented. A hybrid of SAM and NSA also was used. This hybrid was applied to the heterogeneous AGVs scheduling problem in container terminals. Several of the same random problems were generated, solved by SAM with the proposed approaches, and the simulation results were compared. The experimental results showed that NSA provides a good initial solution for SAM when the capacity of AGVs is heterogeneous.

In recent years, automation of solutions for decision-making at container terminals has become more necessary and has attracted more attention. To do this, we studied the problem of integrated management of equipment in automated container terminals with the aim of reducing the service time of berthed ships was investigated. The complexity of the proposed problem was investigated and then the problem was formulated as a linear integer-programming model. A solution based on a combination of the greedy algorithm and the genetic algorithm was proposed. This solution was named Sorting Genetic Algorithm (SGA). The parameters of the proposed method were investigated using Minitab software and Taguchi method to determine the appropriate values. To show the efficiency and effectiveness of the proposed method, the results were compared with the Particle Search Optimization (PSO) algorithm and its combinations with the proposed method.

Table 12.1 makes a summary of the solution methods for the scheduling problems of AGVs in container terminals. The main features, complexity, performance, and effectiveness of the algorithms have been compared in the table. Additionally, we specified which algorithms were designed and convenient for the static/dynamic problem. As we can see in the table, NSA and its extensions are complete algorithms, i.e., they find the optimal solution for the problem. GVS, Simulated Annealing, and Genetic Algorithm are incomplete algorithms, i.e., they find a local optimum for the problem.

12.2 Observations and Conclusions

Based on the experimental results by the algorithms, studied in this book for the problem defined in Chapter 5, we summarize the conclusions as follows:

- NSA, NSA+, DNSA, and DNSA+ are complete algorithms whereas GVS is incomplete. The solutions of the complete algorithms are optimal while GVS provides a local optimum solution for the problem.
- NSA, NSA+, DNSA, and DNSA+ solve the whole problem and assign every job to the vehicles. In GVS, each job is assigned to just one vehicle with minimum cost. In the normal situation the number of vehicles is less than the number of jobs in the port. In this case, if the problem is solved by GVS, then the number of remaining jobs after the first run is not zero. This shows the

Table 12.1 A Summary of the Algorithms Studied in This Book for AGV Scheduling

Algorithms (Reference)	Main Feature	Complete/ Incomplete Algorithm	Static/Dynamic Problem	Performance	Complexity (Reference)	Effectiveness (Reference)
NSA (Chapter 6)	A graph algorithm to solve the MCF model	Complete; produce optimal solution	Designed for static problems; when applied to dynamic problems, the changed problems are tackled from scratch	Faster than a linear program of equivalent size. It has a lower complexity than the original simplex method	$O(N^6)$; N is the number of jobs in the problem (Sections 7.5 and 8.7) We assumed the number of jobs is greater than the number of vehicles	Effective in minimizing both traveling and waiting times of the vehicles (Section 9.5)
NSA+ (Chapter 7)	A graph algorithm with enhanced features to solve the MCF model			Faster than NSA in both static and dynamic problems		
DNSA (Chapter 8)	A dynamic version of NSA to solve the MCF model		Designed for dynamic problems; graph structure is changed incrementally	Faster than NSA and NSA+ in dynamic problems		
DNSA+ (Chapter 8)	A dynamic version of NSA+ to solve the MCF model			Faster than DNSA in dynamic problems		

(Continued)

Table 12.1   A Summary of the Algorithms Studied in This Book for AGV Scheduling *(Continued)*

Algorithms (Reference)	Main Feature	Complete/ Incomplete Algorithm	Static/Dynamic Problem	Performance	Complexity (Reference)	Effectiveness (Reference)
GVS (Chapter 9)	Greedy Vehicle Search to solve the MCF model in a special case	Incomplete; produce a local optimum	Designed for both static and dynamic problems, preferred when size of the problem is beyond the limits of NSA, NSA+, DNSA, and DNSA+ or when the time available to tackle the problem is too short	Faster than NSA and its extensions (NSA+, DNSA, and DNSA+)	Given N jobs and M vehicles is: (a) $O(M{\times}N^2)$ for static problems (Section 9.7.1); (b) $O\,(M{\times}N)$ for dynamic problems (Section 9.7.2)	Effective in minimizing the lateness time to serve the jobs (Section 9.5)
Simulated Annealing and Its Hybrid with NSA (Chapter 10)	A meta-heuristic to solve huge problems	Incomplete; produce a local optimum	Designed for Multi-Load and Heterogeneous Vehicles in Static problems	The hybrid of SAM and NSA provide a better solution than SAM	Difficult to compute	Effective in the Objective functions (Section 10.4)
Genetic Algorithm and Its Hybrid with PSO (Chapter 11)	A meta-heuristic to solve huge problems	Incomplete; produce a local optimum	Designed for integrated management of equipment in static problems	The hybrid of GA and PSO provide a better solution than GA	Difficult to compute	Effective in the Objective functions (Section 11.6)

search is continued and the rate of execution to find out a job for the vehicles is significant (when the number of jobs is high) compared with other algorithms.

■ NSA, NSA+, DNSA, and DNSA+ are efficient and effective in both traveling and waiting times of the vehicles. GVS is more effective and efficient in the lateness time to serve the jobs.

■ GVS is useful for both static and dynamic problems when the problem is too big. GVS has lower complexity than the complete algorithms. It can be used when the size of problem is beyond the limit of the complete algorithms or when the time available to solve the problem is too short.

■ The performance of NSA+ is better than NSA in both static and dynamic problems.

■ In the dynamic aspect when there are changes in the problem, DNSA and DNSA+ have a better performance than NSA and NSA+, respectively. We, therefore, suggest DNSA and DNSA+ for dynamic problems and NSA and NSA+ for a static one. If the percentage of changes is more than sixty percent, NSA+ is preferred in our experience.

■ Given the results, we claim that NSA, NSA+, DNSA, and DNSA+ as well as GVS are practical algorithms for Automatic Single-Load Vehicle Scheduling.

■ If the capacity of the AGVs increases, heuristic and meta-heuristic methods must be used. One of the efficient heuristic approaches in our experience is the SAM. A hybrid of SAM and NSA also was used. The experimental results showed that NSA provides a good initial solution for SAM when the capacity of AGVs is heterogeneous.

■ When the problem is an integrated equipment management in automated container terminals, it is better to divide the problem into two subproblems: Allocating resources to containers and arranging the containers serviced by AGVs. This creates a simpler problem to be solved. Most of the problems in container terminals fall into NP-Hard problems.

12.3 Research Contributions

The main contributions of the research reported in this book are as follows:

■ We formulated the five scheduling decisions, defined in Chapter 2, as CSOP (Chapter 3).

■ We presented a definition for the special Graph of the MCF model and a formal definition for the MCF model itself. We formulated the Scheduling problem of AGVs in container terminals and modeled it under the MCF. We established a name for the model, the MCF-AGV (Section 4.5 in Chapter 5). The objective function of the MCF-AGV model is to minimize the traveling and waiting times of vehicles as well as the lateness time to serve container jobs, as a single objective optimization problem.

- We have applied the standard version of NSA to the static problem (Defined in Chapter 5). Our software can find the global optimal solution for three thousand jobs and ten million arcs in the MCF-AGV model within two minutes by running on a 2.4 GHz Pentium PC (Chapter 6).
- We have developed a novel version of the NSA, NSA+. We have demonstrated that NSA+ is faster than NSA (Chapter 7).
- We have extended the NSA to dynamic problems. In this aspect two algorithms, DNSA and DNSA+, were presented. The objectives of these algorithms are to respond to change in the problem and to use some parts of the previous solution for the next problem. In dynamic aspect, DNSA and DNSA+ are faster than NSA and NSA+, respectively (Chapter 8).
- We have developed the GVS algorithm for Scheduling AGVs in the container terminals. It can be applied to both static and dynamic problems. GVS is an incomplete algorithm and is useful when the problem is too big for the complete algorithms or when the time available to tackle the problem is too short (Chapter 9).
- We have produced a set of benchmark problems for AGVs in the container terminals. These are published in our benchmark web pages, which enable other researchers to compare other algorithms to the one proposed in this book. Now there are four sizes of the problem (Small, Medium, Large, and Very Large) with their solutions.
- We have created a hybrid of SAM and NSA for the Multi-Load and heterogeneous scheduling problem in container terminals. This hybrid is based on the concept that NSA provides a good initial solution for SAM when the capacity of AGVs is heterogeneous.
- We studied the problem of integrated management of equipment in automated container terminals with the aim of reducing the service time of berthed ships was investigated. Then we formulated the problem as a linear integer-programming model. A solution based on a combination of the greedy algorithm and the genetic algorithm was proposed. This solution was named Sorting Genetic Algorithm (SGA). To show the efficiency and effectiveness of the proposed method, the results were compared with the PSO algorithm and its combinations with the proposed method. The results show that not only the sorting genetic algorithm increased the efficiency and productivity of container terminals by adjusting the order of container operations but also can be used for measurement and prediction of the time required to docked the ship at the berth to load and unload containers (Chapter 11).

12.4 Future Research

The research reported in this book (discussed in Chapters 4–9) focused on a certain topic of Scheduling problem of AGVs in the container terminals. In this section, several topics for further research are presented.

12.4.1 *Scheduling and Routing of the Vehicles*

The first interesting extension to the research reported in this book is to combine scheduling and routing of the vehicles together. In Chapter 5, this book assumed that there are no traffic problems such as breakdown, congestion, collision, livelock, and deadlock for the vehicles while they are carrying and handling the jobs. Therefore, a possible extension is to relax this assumption and develop a new algorithm for routing of vehicles according to different port layout with respect to those traffic problems.

A few different topologies for container terminal including linear path, single-circle, and mesh-like path [153] may be considered. In linear path topology the scheme is to schedule and route a batch of AGVs concurrently. In the second topology, circle, including single-circles and multi-circles, few vehicles are running in the same direction within the circle. In the last topology, mesh-like path, the storage areas are usually arranged into rectangular blocks, which lead to a mesh-like path topology for the vehicles.

In an automated container terminal, the traffic problems are critical. An AGV malfunction or breakdowns lead to an interruption in container handling. Collision occurs when more than one AGV attempt to occupy the same segment of the path at the same time. Congestion arises at a location where there is insufficient resource so that for a period of time the number of arrivals is greater than that of serviced requests. A livelock may arise at a junction where the horizontal stream of traffic is given higher priority to obtaining the left-of-way such that the vertical one may keep waiting indefinitely. A deadlock will arise when multiple AGVs mutually wait for the release (which will never occur) of the resource held by the others. The problem, here, will be to find a suitable route for the AGVs from origin to destination based on current traffic situations, according to the port topology.

It should be clear that AGV systems are, intrinsically, parallel and distributed systems that require a high degree of concurrency. Our feeling is that the routing and scheduling of these systems are a fertile area where engineers and computer scientists can make significant contributions.

12.4.2 *Economic and Optimization Model*

Investments in container terminals are very substantial and scheduling of their equipment are very challenging problem. In order to obtain maximum benefits, it is necessary to develop an economic model and combine it with an optimization model. It should be pointed out that in the literature there is no significant model with links between economic indicators and the optimization model. Further research on this topic is needed.

As we mentioned, the main functions of container terminals are delivering containers to consignees and receiving containers from shippers, loading containers onto and unloading containers from vessels and storing containers temporarily. A complete economic plan has to identify and represent the fundamental components in a container terminal and transportation system. These components are demand, supply, cost, performance measures, and decision criteria. Their interactions may be considered. Developing a demand function to receiving containers from shippers, developing a supply model to delivering containers to consignees, estimating a cost function for the vehicles, Quay Cranes, Yard Cranes, and even container terminal are in the list for the future. The research may estimate the weights of traveling and waiting times of the vehicles, the weights of holding cost of jobs on the quayside or in the yardside with particular assumptions. A performance function based on some economic indicators may be maximized. Constraints of the function are the spatial allocation of containers in the terminal yard, the allocation of resources and the scheduling of operations.

Therefore development of an integrated system for both aspects, economic and optimization, is suggested for future research. Automatic adaptation and estimation methods in real-time are necessary.

12.4.3 Automated Container Terminal

AGVs in the container terminals, as the most flexible equipment, affect other decisions in the port. Therefore, another possible extension is to integrate the scheduling of AGVs with other decisions. Allocation of berth to arriving vessels, Quay Cranes to docked vessels, storing the incoming containers in the yard and deployment of the Yard Cranes may be in the candidate lists for this integration. These decisions have been formulated in Chapter 3 of this book.

Firstly, the allocation problem of berth and Quay Cranes to arriving vessels may be integrated with the Scheduling of AGVs. An objective function of the integrated decision is to minimize the sum of the handling costs of containers. A set of assumptions and constraints according to the berth, Quay Cranes, and vehicles should be considered. New solution methods may need to be developed.

Secondly, storing incoming containers in the yard has an important role in global productivity of the terminal. It can be combined with Scheduling of AGVs. An objective function of this decision is to minimize distribution of the total number of containers among blocks in the yard and the sum of container transportation costs. A set of assumptions and constraints according to layout of the yard and movement of the vehicles should be considered in the model. New solutions may be needed to be developed.

Thirdly, deployment of Yard Cranes is also highly interrelated to the movement and Scheduling of AGVs. These two decisions can be combined together. The objective function of this decision is to minimize the remaining workload at each block, traveling and waiting times of the vehicles, as well as traveling times of the RTGCs among blocks during the planning horizon. Developing new algorithms and new deployment policy for RTGC are recommended.

12.4.4 *The Next Generation of Container Terminal*

Zaerpour et al. (2019) suggested a next generation container terminal consisting of container storage towers [210]. Instead of horizontal expansion through land reclamation, this research proposed an alternative vertical expansion solution: a "container warehouse." Leading world container ports have studied and developed several types of rectangular container warehouses which have been introduced in this research. This study proposed a cylindrical container tower system which solves the land shortage problem, allows individual access to containers without the need for reshuffling, and is sturdier against strong winds compared to rectangular systems. To investigate the performance and financial feasibility of the container tower, this research compared it with an existing container block of similar storage capacity. According to the analysis, container towers can increase the storage capacity in a given footprint. In addition, such a container tower can increase the annual throughput of a terminal by 120 percent compared to a container block. This analysis also showed that if the investment in material handling technology for a container tower per storage location is increased up to a certain level compared to the conventional container terminal, the container tower can still remain cheaper.

In order to accommodate both hardware and software technologies in the port, the infrastructure of the existing port must be fundamentally changed with many new equipment. It is vital to do many research and feability studies with simulation. Results of simulation and numerical analysis can help terminal managers with selecting the appropriate system configuration to achieve the desired throughput and also to ensure the financial feasibility of new projects.

Appendix: Information on Web

This book is a scientific report of a very solid piece of research. The research is mainly focused on Scheduling of Automated Guided Vehicles (AGV) (http://www. bracil.net/CSP/autoport/Book.html) in container ports. The problem is to schedule several AGVs in a port to carry many containers from the quayside to yardside or vice versa. This problem is formulated as a Minimum Cost Flow problem and then solved by Network Simplex Algorithm (NSA), Network Simplex plus Algorithm (NSA+), Dynamic Network Simplex Algorithm (DNSA), and Dynamic Network simplex Plus Algorithm (DNSA+). The research contributions are NSA+, DNSA, and DNSA+. NSA+ is faster than NSA. DNSA and DNSA+ repair the previous solution when any changes happen.

To test the model and performance of the algorithms in our implementation, many jobs have been generated. Their sources, destinations, and the distance between every two points in the port have been chosen randomly. As it can be seen in Figure Appendix.1, our software, which has been implemented by C++,

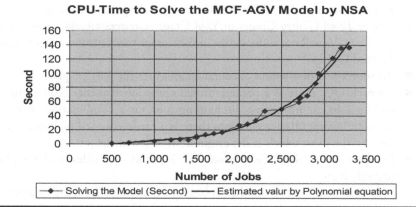

Figure Appendix.1   CPU-Time required solving the graph model.

running on a WinTel PC, can find the global optimal solution for three thousand jobs within two minutes.

Overview of This Research

This research concerns itself with the scheduling of AGVs in a port. Port components that are relevant to our problem include berths, Quay Cranes (QC), container storage areas, and a road network. A transportation requirement in a port is described by a set of jobs. Each job is described by:

    a. The source location of a container.
    b. The target location, where the container is to be delivered to.
    c. The time at which it is available for pickup or dropoff on the quayside.

Any delay will incur heavy penalties. Given the number of AGVs and their availability, the task is to schedule the AGVs to meet the transportation requirements.

Assumptions

- The layout of a port container terminal is given. Also, it is assumed the vehicles move at an average speed so that there are no **Collisions**, **Congestion**, **Livelock**, or **Deadlock** problems.
- The travel time between every combination of pickup/dropoff points is provided according to our layout.
- Every AGV can transport only one container. Also, it is assumed that the start location of each AGV at the beginning of the process is given.
- Rubber Tyred Gantry Cranes or Yard Crane resources are always available, i.e., the AGVs will not suffer delays in the storage yard location or waiting for the Yard Cranes.
- The source and destination of container jobs over the port are given.
- For each QC, there is a predetermined crane job sequence, consisting of loading jobs, or unloading/discharging jobs, or a combination of both. For each loading/discharging job, there is a predetermined pickup/dropoff point in the yard, which is the origin/destination of the job.
- The appointment time of every container job at its source/destination on the quayside is given.
- For the dynamic aspect of the problem, it is assumed that the number of vehicles is fixed, but the number of jobs and the distance between every two points in the port may be changed.

Development

Our software consists of the optimization, scheduling, and a simulation program. The software can find the global optimal solution for three thousand jobs and ten million arcs in the graph model within two minutes by a WinTel PC. Figure Appendix.2 shows the main form of the software.

Some important features of our program are described briefly in the following sections:

- The user can define a few ports, the number of blocks in the yard, the number of working positions or crane and the number of AGVs in each port.
- A facility to generate the distance between different points in the yard or in the berth has been considered. At the first step, this distance is generated randomly, but it is modifiable by the user.
- For static and dynamic fashion, a few container jobs might be generated, which have to be transported from their sources to their destinations. Either the source or the destination of them is the quayside, which is chosen randomly by the Job-Generator. There are three options for Quay Cranes: single crane and multiple cranes randomly and circular. In the

Figure Appendix.2   The main form of the software.

first option, crane number 1 is selected to handle the job whereas in the second option one crane, among several cranes in the berth, is determined to handle the job. In the latter option, choosing the crane number is circular; the first job for the first crane, the second job for the second crane, and so on. After the next job is assigned to the last crane, the turn goes to the first crane.

■ At the start of the process, the start location of each vehicle may be any point in the port. The user can define or change the ready time of the vehicles at the start location and the location as well. But at the first stage, we generate them randomly.

■ The initial time for the operation, the time window of the cranes and vehicles should be defined by the user. The first parameter plays a role as the ship-arrival time; the second one means how long it takes for every job to be picked up or dropped off by the crane. The last one is the time for the vehicle to pickup/dropoff a job from/to the crane. We assume some default values for these parameters.

■ The user can monitor some indices to measure the efficiency of the terminal. The waiting or delay time for every job, the number of jobs and the traveling and waiting times for every vehicle are calculated in the static and dynamic fashion.

Some Interfaces of Our Software

Figure Appendix.3 shows an output of running the software in Static fashion. As we can see, there are several tabs in the user interface, including "Static," "Model," "Dynamic," Result, "Graph," "Algorithm," and "Performance." In the "Static" Tab, there are several parts, "Container Jobs" on top left, "Port Names" in the middle top, "AGVs" on the top right of this figure. On the bottom left, there are some information around "Processing," showing a problem of 1000 container jobs and 50 AGVs can be solved in 5 seconds.

Figure Appendix.4 shows an user interface of the software when the user runs it for solving problems in dynamic aspect. As we can see, there are several parts in the tab "Result," "Port and Container Jobs (Result)" on top left, "Solution" on the top right, "Container Jobs assigned to AGV-11" on the bottom right. The information shown on the left bottom are some indicators of quay cranes as well as traveling and waiting times of vehicles, while several container jobs are arriving from time to time and those that are being serviced.

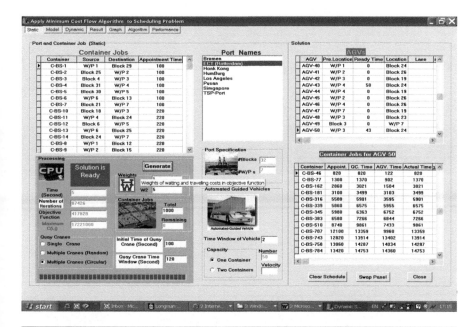

Figure Appendix.3   An output of running the software in static aspect.

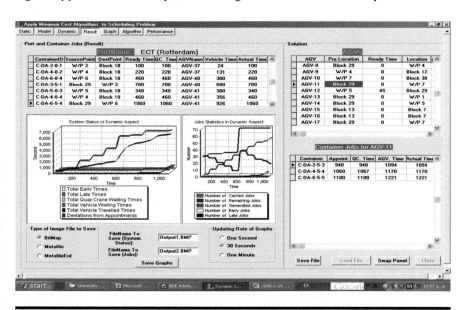

Figure Appendix.4   An output of running the software in dynamic aspect, showing the information of quay cranes, container jobs and vehicles.

References

1. Afshari R.A., Taghizadeh K.P.S.P.H., "Maximum Dynamic Network Flow Interdiction Problem: New Formulation and Solution Procedures Original Research Article," Computers & Industrial Engineering, Vol. 65(4), pp. 4, pp. 531–536, 2013.
2. Aggarwal C.C., Kaplan H., Tarjan R.E., "A Faster Primal Network Simplex Algorithm," Massachusetts Institute of Technology, Operations Research Centre, Working Paper, OR, 315–96, 1996.
3. Ahuja R.K., Orlin T.L. J. B., Network Flows: Theory, Algorithms and Applications, Prentice Hall, 1993.
4. Ahuja R.K., Orlin J.B., Sharma P., Sokkalingam P.T., "A Network Simplex Algorithm with O(N) Consecutive Degenerate Pivots," Operations Research Letters, Vol. 30(3), pp. 141–148, 2002.
5. Akturk M.S., Yilmaz M., "Scheduling of Automated Guided Vehicles in a Decision Making Hierarchy," International Journal of Production Research, Vol. 34, pp. 577–591, 1996.
6. Ambrosino D., Marina M.E., Sciomachen A., "Decision Rules for the Yard Storage Management," University of Genova, Technical Report, Italy, 2002
7. Andrew V.G., "An Efficient Implementation of a Scaling Minimum-Cost Flow Algorithm," *Journal of Algorithms*, Vol. 22(1), pp. 1–29, January 1997.
8. Aronson J., "A Survey of Dynamic Network Flows," Annals of Operation Research, 20, pp. 1–66, 1989.
9. Asperen E.V., Borgman B., Dekker R., "Evaluating Impact of Truck Announcements on Container Stacking Efficiency," Flexible Services and Manufacturing Journal, DOI 10.1007/s10696-011-9108-1, pp. 1–14, 2011.
10. Aykagan A., "Berth and Quay Crane Scheduling: Problems, Models And Solution Methods," PhD Thesis, School of Industrial and Systems Engineering, Georgia Institute of Technology, 2008.
11. Błażewicz J., Machowiak M., Edwin C.P.S.P.T.C., Qğuz C., "On a Certain Berth Scheduling Problem," Proceedings of the 2nd Multidisciplinary International Conference on Scheduling, Theory and Applications (MISTA), Vol. 2, pp. 694–697, 2005.
12. Bohács G., Kulcsár B., Gáspár D., "Container Terminal Modelling in Simul8 Environment," Acta Technica Jaurinensis, Vol. 6(4), pp. 1–8, 2013.
13. Bontempi G., Gambardella M., Rizzoli A.E., "Simulation and Optimization for Management of Intermodal Terminals," European Simulation Multiconference, Instanbul, 1997.

14. Böse J., Reiners T., Steenken D., Voß S., "Vehicle Dispatching at Seaport Container Terminals Using Evolutionary Algorithms," Proceedings of the 33rd Annual Hawaii International Conference on System Sciences, IEEE, Piscataway, pp 1–10, 2000.

15. Burke E., Hart E., Kendall G., Newall J., Ross P., Schulenburg S. "Hyper-Heuristics: An Emerging Direction in Modern Search Technology," Handbook of Meta-Heuristics, pp. 457–474, 2003.

16. Burke E.K., Kendall G., Soubeiga E., "A Tabu-Search Hyper-Heuristic for Timetabling and Rostering," Journal of Heuristics, Vol. 9(6), pp. 451–470, 2003.

17. Cai B., Huang S., Liu D., Yuan S., Dissanayake G., Lau H., Pagac D., "Multi-Objective Optimisation for Autonomous Straddle Carrier Scheduling at Automated Container Terminals," IEEE Transactions on Automation Science and Engineering, 2012.

18. Carrascosa C., Rebollo V., Julian M., Botti V., "A MAS Approach for Port Container Terminal Management," World Multi-Conference on Systemics, Cybernetics and Informatics, pp. 1–5, 2001.

19. Carre B., "Graphs and Networks," Oxford University Press, Oxford, UK, 1979.

20. Carteni A., de Luca S., "Tactical and Strategic Planning for a Container Terminal: Modelling Issues within a Discrete Event Simulation Approach," Simulation Modelling Practice and Theory, Vol. 21(1), pp. 123–145, 2012.

21. Castilla Rodríguez I., Exposito-Izquierdo C., Melian-Batista B., Simulation-Optimization for the Management of the Transshipment Operations at Maritime Container Terminals. Expert System Application, 139, 112852, 2020, https://doi.org/10.1016/j.eswa.2019.112852.

22. Cave A., Nahavandi S., Kouzani A., "Simulation Optimization for Process Scheduling Through Simulated Annealing," Proceedings of the 2002 Winter Simulation Conference, pp. 1909–1913, 2002.

23. Chan S.H., "Dynamic AGV-Container Job Deployment," Master of Science, University of Singapore, 2001.

24. Langevin L., Lu A., Z., "Integrated Scheduling of Crane Handling and Truck Transportation in a Maritime Container Terminal," European Journal of Operational Research, Vol. 225(1), 142e152. 2013, https://doi.org/10.1016/j.ejor.2012.09.019.

25. Cheng Y., Sen H., Natarajan K., Teo C., Tan K., "Dispatching Automated Guided Vehicles in a Container Terminal," Technical Report, National University of Singapore, 2003.

26. Chiang W.C., Russell R.A., "Simulated Annealing Metaheuristics for the Vehicle Routing Problem with Time Windows," Annals of Operations Research, Vol. 63, pp. 3–27, 1996.

27. Chowdhury M.S., Chein S.I., "Dynamic Vehicle Dispatching at Inter-Modal Transfer Station," Transportation Research Board, 80th Annual Meeting, Washington, 2001.

28. Christiansen M., Fagerholt K., Ronen D., "Ship Routing and Scheduling - Status and Trends," Norwegian University of Science and Technology, Trondheim, Norway, University of Missouri, USA, accepted for publication in Transportation Science, 2003.

29. Chuanyu C., "Simulation and Optimization of Container Yard Operation: A Survey," Technical Report, Nanyang Technological University, Singapore, 2003.

30. Ciurea E., Parpalea M., "Minimum Flow in Monotone Parametric Bipartite Networks," NAUN International Journal of Computers, Vol. 4(4), pp. 124–135, 2010.

31. Corréa A.I., Langevin A., Rousseau M., "Scheduling and Routing of Automated Guided Vehicles: A Hybrid Approach," Computers & Operations Research Vol. 34, pp. 1688–1707, 2007.
32. Cowling P., Ouelhadj D., Petrovic S., "Dynamic Scheduling of Steel Casting and Milling Using Multi-Agents," Production Planning and Control, Vol. 15, pp. 1–11, 2004
33. Cowling P.I., Ouelhadj D., Petrovic S., "A Multi-Agent Architecture for Dynamic Scheduling of Steel Hot Rolling," Journal of Intelligent Manufacturing, Vol. 14(5), pp. 457–470, 2003.
34. Czech Z.J., Czarnas P., "Parallel Simulated Annealing for the Vehicle Routing Problem with Time Windows," 10Th Euromicro Workshop on Parallel, Distributed and Network-Based Processing, Canary Islands - Spain, pp. 376–383, 2002.
35. Dondo R., Mndez C.A., Cerd J., "An Optimal Approach to the Multiple-Depot Heterogeneous Vehicle Routing Problem with Time Window and Capacity Constraints," Latin American Applied Research, Vol. 33, pp. 129–134, 2003.
36. Duinkerken M.B., Ottjes J.A., "A Simulation Model for Automated Container Terminals." Proceedings of the Business and Industry Simulation Symposium (ASTC2000), April 2000.
37. El-Sherbenym N.A., "A New Class of a Minimum Cost Flow Problem on a Time Varying and Time Window," Scientific Research and Impact, Vol. 1(3), pp. 18–28, 2012.
38. Eppstein D., "Clustering for Faster Network Simplex Pivots," Proceeding of 5th ACM-SIAM Symposium, Discrete Algorithms, pp. 160–166, 1994.
39. Eppstein D., Galil Z., Italiano G.F., "Dynamic Graph Algorithms," CRC Handbook of Algorithms and Theory, chapter 22, CRC Press, 1997.
40. Fazlollahtabar H., Eshaghzadeh A., Hajmohammadi H., Taheri–Ahangar A., "A Monte Carlo Simulation to Estimate TAGV Production Time in a Stochastic Flexible Automated Manufacturing System: A Case Study," International Journal of Industrial and Systems Engineering, Vol. 12(3), pp. 243–258, 2012.
41. Fazlollahtabar H., Saidi-Mehrabad M., "Methodologies to Optimize Automated Guided Vehicle Scheduling and Routing Problems: A Review Study," Journal of Intelligent & Robotic, Springer, 2013.
42. Fink A., Voß S., "HOTFRAME: A Heuristic Optimisation Framework," Optimisation Software Class Libraries, Kluwer, Boston, pp. 81–154, 2002.
43. Fonoberova M., "Algorithms for Finding Optimal Flows in Dynamic Networks," In: Rebennack, S., Pardalos, P.M., Pereira, M.V.F., Iliadis, N.A. (eds) Handbook of Power Systems II, Energy Systems, pp. 31–54. Springer, Berlin, 2010.
44. Fonoberova M., Lozovanu D., "Optimal Dynamic Flows in Networks and Applications," The International Symposium, The Issues of Calculation Optimization, Communications, Crimea, Ukraine, pp. 292–293, 2007.
45. Froyland G., Koch T., Megow N., Duane E., Wren W., "Optimizing the Landside Operation of a Container Terminal," OR Spectrum, Vol. 30, pp. 53–75, 2008.
46. Galati M., Geng H., Wu T., "A Heuristic Approach for the Vehicle Routing Problem Using Simulated Annealing," Lehigh University, Technical Report IE316, 1998.
47. Gambardella M., Rizzoli A.E., Zaffalon M., "Simulation," Simulation, Vol. 71(2), pp. 107–116, 1998.
48. Gebraeel N.Z., Lawley M.A., "Deadlock Detection, Prevention, and Avoidance for Automated Tool Sharing Systems," IEEE Transactions on Robotics and Automation, Vol. 17(3), pp. 342–356, 2001.

49. Geranis G., "Dynamic Trees in Exterior-Point Simplex-Type Algorithms for Network Flow Problems," Electronic Notes in Discrete Mathematics, pp. 41, pp. 93–100, 2013.

50. Geranis G., Paparrizos K., Sifaleras A., "On a Dual Network Exterior Point Simplex Type Algorithm and Its Computational Behavior," Operations Research, 46, pp. 211–234, 2012.

51. Goldberg A.V., Kennedy R., "An Efficient Cost Scaling Algorithm for the Assignment Problem," Technical Report, Stanford University, 1993.

52. Gribkovskaia I., Halskau O., Bugge M., Kim N., "Models for Pick-Up and Deliveries from Depots with Lasso Solutions," Working Paper, Molde University College, Norway, 2002.

53. Grunow M., Günther H.O., Lehmann M., "Dispatching Multi-Load AGVs in Highly Automated Seaport Container Terminals," OR Spectrum, Vol. 26(2), pp. 211–235, 2004.

54. Gudelj A., Kezić D., Vidačić S., "Planning and Optimization of AGV Jobs by petri Net and Genetic Algorithm," Journal of Information and Organizational Sciences, Vol. 36(2), pp. 99–122, 2012.

55. Guerrero D., Rodrigue J.P., "The Waves of Containerization: Shifts in Global Maritime Transportation," Journal of Transportation Geography, Vol. 34, pp. 151–164, 2014.

56. Gunadi W.N., Rose A.A., Shamsuddin S.M., Mohd N.M., "Vehicle Routing Problem for Public Transport: A Case Study," Proceedings of International Technical Conference on Circuits/Systems, Computers and Communications, Vol. 2, pp. 1180–1183, 2002.

57. Guo P., Cheng W., Liang J., "Particle Swarm Optimization for Gantry Crane Scheduling with Interference Constraints," Research Journal of Applied Sciences, Engineering and Technology, Vol. 4, pp. 1117–1123, 2012.

58. Guo P., Chenga W., Wang Y., "A Modified Generalized Extremal Optimization Algorithm for the Quay Crane Scheduling Problem with Interference Constraints," Engineering Optimization, Vol. 46(10), pp. 1411–1429, 2014.

59. Guo X., Huang S.Y., Hsu W.J., Hean M.Y., "Yard Crane Dispatching Based on Real Time Data Driven Simulation for Container Terminals," Proceedings of the 40th Conference on Winter Simulation, ISBN:978-1-4244-2708-6, pp. 2648–2655, 2008.

60. Guo X., Huang S.Y., Hsu W.J., Hean M.Y., "Yard Crane Dispatching Based on Real Time Data Driven Simulation for Container Terminals," Proceedings of the 40th Conference on Winter Simulation, ISBN:978-1-4244-2708-6, pp. 2648–2655, 2008.

61. Güvena C., Türsel E.D., "Trip Allocation and Stacking Policies at a Container Terminal," Transportation Research Procedia, Vol. 3, pp. 565–573, 2014.

62. Hansen P., Oguz C., "A Note on Formulation of the Static and Dynamic Berth Allocation Problems," Technical Report, Department of Management, Hong Kong Polytechnic University, 2003.

63. Hartmann S., "Generating Scenarios for Simulation and Optimisation of Container Terminal Logistics," Working Paper, 564, University of Kiel, Germany, 2002.

64. Hasama T., Kokubugata H., Kawashima H., "A Heuristic Approach Based on the String Model to Solve Vehicle Routing Problem with Backhauls," Proceeding of the 5th World Congress on Intelligent Transport Systems (ITS), Seoul, 1998.

65. He J., Huang Y., Yan W., Integrated Internal Truck, Yard Crane and Quay Crane Scheduling in a Container Terminal Considering Energy Consumption. Expert Syst. Appl. 42 (5), 2464e–2487, 2015, https://doi.org/10.1016/j.eswa.2014.11.016.

66. He J., "Berth Allocation and Quay Crane Assignment in a Container Terminal for the Trade-off between Time-Saving and Energy-Saving," Advanced Engineering Informatics, Vol. 30(2016), pp. 390–405, 2016.

67. Héctor J.C., Iris F.A., Kees J.R., "Transport Operations in Container Terminals: Literature Overview, Trends, Research Directions and Classification Scheme," European Journal of Operational Research, Vol. 236(1), pp. 1–13, 2014.

68. Helgason R., Kennington J., "Primal Simplex Algorithms for Minimum Cost Network Flows," Handbook on Operations Research and Management Science, Vol. 7, Amsterdam, pp. 85–133, 1995.

69. Wernstedt L., Davidsson F. P, "Market-Driven Control in Container Terminal Management," 2nd International Conference on Computer Applications and Information Technology in the Maritime Industries, 2003.

70. Ying Y.K.L., Chuanyou Z. P, "Integrated Scheduling of Different Types of Handling Equipment at Automated Container Terminals," Proceedings of the 2nd Multidisciplinary International Conference on Scheduling, Theory and Applications (MISTA), Abstract paper, Vol. 2, pp. 536–537, 2005.

71. Holguin-Veras J., Jara-Diaz S., "Optimal Pricing for Priority Service and Space Allocation in Container Ports," Transportation Research (B),Vol. 33, pp. 81–106, 1999.

72. Hollingworth J., Gustavson P., Swart B., Cashman M., "Borland C++ Builder 6 Developer's Guide," Sams Publishing, 2003.

73. Homayouni S.M., Tang S.H., Ismail N., Ariffin M.K.A., "Using Simulated Annealing Algorithm for Optimization of Quay Cranes and Automated Guided Vehicles Scheduling," International Journal of the Physical Sciences, Vol. 6(27), pp. 6286–6294, 2011.

74. Hoppe B., "Efficient Dynamic Network Flow Algorithms," PhD Thesis, Cornell University, 1995.

75. Hu X., Liang C., Chang D., Zhang Y., "Container Storage Space Assignment Problem in Two Terminals with the Consideration of Yard Sharing," Advanced Engineering Informatics, Vol. 47(2021), p. 101224, 2021.

76. Huang S.Y., Li Y., A Bounded Two-Level Dynamic Programming Algorithm for Quay Crane Scheduling in Container Terminals, Computers and Industrial Engineering, 123, pp. 303–313, 2018.

77. Hussein S.A., "An Introduction to Dynamic Generative Networks: Minimum Cost Flow," Applied Mathematical Modelling, Vol. 35(10), pp. 5017–5025, 2010.

78. ILOG optimisation suite- White papers, available via https://www.ibm.com/products/ilog-cplex-optimization-studio (address last checked 6th Sep 2021).

79. Indra-Payoong N., Kwan R.S.K., Proll G.. "Constraint-Based Local Search for Rail Container Service Planning," Proceedings of the MISTA Conference, Nottingham, August 2003.

80. Ioannou P., Chassiakos A., Unglaub H. R, "Dynamic Optimization of Cargo Movement by Trucks in Metropolitan Areas with Adjacent Ports," Metrans Technical Report, Center for Advanced Transportation Technologies, University of Southern California, June 2002.

81. Ioannou P.A., Jula H., Liu C.I., Vukadinovic K., Pourmohammadi H., "Advanced Material Handling: Automated Guided Vehicles in Agile Ports," CCDoTT Technical Report, Center for Advanced Transportation Technologies, University of Southern California, January 2001.

82. Ioannou P.A., Kosmatopoulos E.B., Vukadinovic K., Liu C.I., Pourmohammadi H., Dougherty E., "Real Time Testing and Verification of Loading and Unloading Algorithms Using Grid Rail (GR)," Center for Advanced Transportation Technologies, University of Southern California, Los Angeles, Technical Report, October 2000.
83. Iris F.A. Vis, available at http://www.irisvis.nl/container (address last checked 6 September 2021).
84. Islam S., Olsen T.L.., "Operations Research (OR) at ports: An update," 22nd National Conference of the Australian Society for Operations Research, Australia, 2013.
85. István M., "A General Pricing Scheme for the Simplex Method," Department of Computing, Imperial College, Technical Report, London, 2001-03.
86. Jianyang Z., Wen-Jing H., Yee V.V., "An AGV," Centre for Advanced Information Systems, School of Computer Engineering, Nanyang Technological University, Singapore, Technical Report, Singapore, 2003.
87. Junliang H., Caimao T., Yuting Z., Yard Crane Scheduling Problem in a Container Terminal Considering Risk Caused by Uncertainty, Advanced Engineering Informatics, Vol. 39(2019), 14–24, 2019.
88. Kee, Neagu C., Nicita A., "Is Protectionism on the Rise? Assessing National Trade Policies During the Crisis of 2008," Review of Economics and Statistics, Vol. 95(1), pp. 342–346, 2013.
89. Kelly D.J., O'Neill G.M., "The Minimum Cost Flow Problem and the Network Simplex Solution Method," Master Degree Dissertation, University College, Dublin, 1993.
90. Kendall G., Mohd Hussin N., "An Investigation of a Tabu-Search-Based Hyper-Heuristic for Examination Timetabling, Multidisciplinary Scheduling; Theory and Applications," Springer, pp. 309–328, 2005.
91. Kilby P., Prosser P., Shaw P., "Guided Local Search for the Vehicle Routing Problem," Proceedings of 2nd International Conference on Mataheuristics - MIC97, Sophia-Antipolis, France, July 1997.
92. Kim K.H., Won S.H., Lim J.K., Takahashi T., "A Simulation-Based Test-Bed for a Control Software in Automated Container Terminals," Department of Industrial Engineering, Pusan National University, Technical report, Pusan, 2000.
93. Kim J., Choe R., Ryu K.R., Multi-objective optimization of dispatching strategies for situation-adaptive AGV operation in an automated container terminal. In Proceedings of the 2013 Research in Adaptive and Convergent Systems (pp. 1–6), 2013.
94. Kim J., Hong E.J., Yang Y., Ryu K.R. Noisy Optimization of Dispatching Policy for the Cranes at the Storage Yard in an Automated Container Terminal. *Applied Sciences.* 2021, *11*, 6922. https://doi.org/10.3390/app11156922
95. Kizilay D., Van Hentenryck P., Eliiyi D.T., "Constraint Programming Models for Integrated Container Terminal Operations," European Journal of Operational Research, Vol. 286(3), pp. 945–962, 2020.
96. Klima V., Kavika A., "Agent-based simulation model design," in Proceedings of European Simulation Multiconference, Istanbul, pp. 254–258, 1996.
97. Kocifaj M., "Modelling of container terminals using two-layer agent architecture," IEEE 12th International Symposium on Applied Machine Intelligence and Informatics (SAMI), 2014.
98. Koshy R., Scheduling in distributed system: a survey and future perspective. International Journal of Advanced Technol Engineering Science, 2014.

99. Kozan E., Wong A., "An Optimisation Model for Export and Import Container Process in Seaport Terminals," 25th Australasian Transport Research Forum, Canberra, CD-ROM, 2002.

100. Kumar K., Optimization of Minimum Cost Network Flows with Heuristic Algorithms, International Journal of Information and Education Technology, Vol. 2, No. 1, February 2012.

101. *Lau H.C., Liang Z.*, "Pickup and Delivery with Time Windows: Algorithms and Test Case Generation," 13th IEEE International Conference on Tools with Artificial Intelligence, *ICTAI-2001, Dallas, USA, pp.* 333–340, 2001.

102. Tsang T.L. E.P.K, "Guided Genetic Algorithm and Its Application to Radio Link Frequency Assignment Problems," Constraints, Vol. 6, pp. 373–398, 2001.

103. Lau H.Y., Zhao Y., "Integrated Scheduling of Handling Equipment at Automated Container Terminals," International Journal of Production Economics, Vol. 112(2), pp. 665–682, 2008.

104. Leong C.Y., "Simulation Study of Dynamic AGV-Container Job Deployment Scheme," Master of Science, National University of Singapore, 2001.

105. Li J., Xu B., Yang Y., Wu H. (2018). Quantum Ant-Colony Optimization Algorithm for AGVs Path Planning Based on Bloch Coordinates of Pheromones. Natural Computing, 1–10.

106. Lijun Y., Houming F., Mengzhi M., "Optimizing Configuration and Scheduling of Double 40 Ft Dual-Trolley Quay Cranes and AGVs for Improving Container Terminal Services," Journal of Cleaner Production, Vol. 292(2021), p. 126019, 2021.

107. Lim A., Rodrigues B., Zhu Y., "Crane Scheduling Using Squeaky Wheel Optimization with Local Search." Proceedings of the 4th Asia-Pacific Conference on Simulated Evolution and Learning, Singapore, 2002.

108. Lin W., "On Dynamic Crane Deployment in Container Terminals," Master of Philosophy in Industrial Engineering and Engineering Management, University of Science & Technology, Hong Kong, January 2001.

109. Liu C.I., Jula H., Ioannou P.A., "Design, Simulation, and Evaluation of Automated Container Terminals," IEEE Transaction on Intelligent Transportation Systems, Vol. 3(1), pp. 12–26, 2002.

110. Löbel A., "MCF: A Network Simplex Implementation," Konrad-Zuse-Zentrum für Informationstechnik Berlin (ZIB), Technical Report, 2000.

111. Luca S., Pace R.D., Cartenì A., "Simulating Container Terminal Performances: Microscopic vs. Macroscopic Modelling Approaches," 2013 8th EUROSIM Congress on Modelling and Simulation, pp. 478–483, 2013, doi: 10.1109/EUROSIM.2013.86.

112. Lutz W., Sanderson W., Scherbov S., "The Coming Acceleration of Global Population Ageing," Nature, Vol. 451(7179), pp. 716–719, 2008.

113. Lutz W., Sanderson W., Scherbov S., "The End of World Population Growth," Nature, Vol. 412(6846), pp. 543–545, 2001.

114. Ma, Felix T.S., Chung S.H., "A Fast Approach for the Integrated Berth Allocation and Quay Crane Assignment Problem," Proceedings of the Institution of Mechanical Engineers, Part B: Journal of Engineering Manufacture, August 14, 2014.

115. Chen L., Hu H., Zhu K. Y., "Hierarchical Artificial Bee Colony Algorithm for RFID Network Planning Optimization," Scientific World Journal, Vol. 2014, 2014.

116. Macal C.M., North M.J., Tutorial on Agent-Based Modeling and Simulation. Journal of Simulation, Vol. 4, pp. 151–162, 2010.

117. Macal C.M., North M.J., "Introductory Tutorial: Agent-Based Modeling and Simulation," Winter Simulation Conference, Vol. 2013(1), pp. 362–376, 2013.
118. Mai H.P., Kim K.H., "Collaborative Truck Scheduling and Appointments for Trucking Companies and Container Terminals," Transportation Research Part B, Vol. 86(2016), pp. 37–50, 2016.
119. Malekahmadi A., Alinaghiana M., Hejazia S.R., Saidipourb M.A., "Integrated Continuous Berth Allocation and Quay Crane Assignment and Scheduling Problem with Time-Dependent Physical Constraints in Container Terminals," Computers & Industrial Engineering, Vol. 147(2020), p. 106672, 2020.
120. Marco U., "Combinatorial Simple Pickup and Delivery Paths," Central European Journal of Operations Research, 2003.
121. Meersmans P.J.M., Dekker R., "Operations Research Supports Container Handling," Technical Report EI 2001-22, Erasmus University of Rotterdam, Econometric Institute, 2003.
122. Meersmans P.J.M., Wagelmans A.P.M., "Dynamic Scheduling of Handling Equipment at Automated Container Terminals," Technical Report EI 2001-33, Erasmus University of Rotterdam, Econometric Institute, 2001.
123. Meersmans P.J.M., Wagelmans A.P.M., "Effective Algorithms for Integrated Scheduling of Handling Equipment at Automated Container Terminals," Technical Report ERS-2001-36-LIS, Erasmus University of Rotterdam, Econometric Institute, 2001.
124. Mitrovic-Minic S., "Pickup and Delivery Problem with Time Window: A Survey," Technical Report 1998-12, School of Computing Science, Simon Fraser University, Burnaby, BC, Canada, May 1998.
125. Moin N.H., "Hybrid Genetic Algorithms for Vehicle Routing Problems with Time Windows," submitted to Computers & Operations Research, 2002.
126. Moon K.C., "A Mathematical Model and a Heuristic Algorithm for Berth Planning," Industrial Engineering/Pusan National University, Telecommunication Grooming, Vol. 2 (3), May/June 2001.
127. Hock-Guan R.L., Wig-Cheong W., Chung-Piaw N. T, "Cyclic Deadlock Prediction and Avoidance for Zone Controlled AGV System," International Journal of Production Economics, Vol. 83, pp. 309–324, 2003.
128. Murakami K., Time-Space Network Model and MILP Formulation of the Conflict-Free Routing Problem of a Capacitated AGV System, Computers & Industrial Engineering 141, 106270, 2020.
129. Muramatsu M., "On Network Simplex Method Using Primal-Dual Symmetric Pivoting Rule," Journal of Operations Research of Japan, Vol. 43, pp. 149–161, 2000.
130. Murty K.G., "Yard Crane Pools and Optimum Layouts for Storage Yards of Container Terminals," Journal of Industrial and Systems Engineering, Vol. 1(3), pp. 190–199, 2007.
131. Murty K.G., Liu J., Wan Y.W., Linn R.J., "A Decision Support System for Operations in a Container Terminal," Decision Support System, Vol. 39, pp. 309–332, 2005.
132. Nannan Y., Zhenhong L. X, "A Multi-Agent System for Container Terminal Management," WCICA 2008, 7th World Congress on Intelligent Control and Automation, pp. 6247–6252, 2008.
133. Narasimhan A., Palekar U.S., "Analysis and Algorithms for the Transtainer Routing Problem in Container Port Operations," Transportation Science, Vol. 36(1), pp. 63–78, 2002.

134. Nasrabadi E., Hashemi S.M., "Minimum Cost Time-Varying Network Flow Problems," Optimization Methods and Software, Vol. 25(3), pp. 429–447, 2010.

135. Nguyen V.D., Kim K.H., "A Dispatching Method for Automated Lifting Vehicles in Automated Port Container Terminals," Computers & Industrial Engineering, Vol. 56, pp. 1002–1020, 2009.

136. Nuhut Ö, "Scheduling of Automated Guided Vehicles," Technical Report, Department of Industrial Engineering, Bilkent University, 1999.

137. Orlin J.B., "A Polynomial Time Primal Network Simplex Algorithm for Minimum Cost Flows (An Extended Abstract)," Mathematical Programming 78 Series B, pp. 109–129, 1996.

138. Ouelhadj D., Cowling P., Petrovic S., "Contract Net Protocol for Cooperative Optimisation and Dynamic Scheduling of Steel Production," Published in the Book of Intelligent Systems Design and Applications, Springer-Verlag, pp. 457–470, 2003.

139. Ouelhadj D., Petrovic S., Cowling P., Meisels A., "Inter-Agent Cooperation and Communication for Agent-Based Robust Dynamic Scheduling in Steel Production," Advanced Engineering and Informatics, Vol. 18(3), pp. 161–172, 2005.

140. Paparrizos K., Samaras N., Sifaleras A., "An Exterior Simplex Type Algorithm for the Minimum Cost Network Flow Problem," Computers and Operations Research, Vol. 36, pp. 1176–1190, 2009.

141. Park Y.M., Kim K.H., "A Scheduling Method for Berth and Quay Cranes," OR Spectrum, Vol. 25, pp. 1–23, 2003.

142. Parpalea M., "A Parametric Approach to the Bi-Criteria Minimum Cost Dynamic Flow Problem," Open Journal of Discrete Mathematics, Vol. 1(3), pp. 116–126, 2011.

143. Parpalea M., Ciurea E., "The Quickest Maximum Dynamic Flow of Minimum Cost," Journal of Applied Mathematics and Informatics, Vol. 5(3), pp. 266–274, 2011.

144. Parpalea M., Ciurea E., "Maximum Flow of Minimum Bi-Criteria Cost in Dynamic Networks," Recent Researches in Computer Science; pp. 118–123, 2011.

145. Petrovic S., Fayad C., "A Fuzzy Shifting Bottleneck Hybridised with Genetic Algorithm for Real-world Job Shop Scheduling," Proceedings of Mini-EURO Conference, Managing Uncertainty in Decision Support Models, Coimbra, Portugal, pp. 1–6, 2004.

146. Petrovic S., Fayad C., Petrovic D., "Job Shop Scheduling with Lot-Sizing and Batching in an Uncertain Real-Wold Environment," The 2nd Multidisciplinary Conference on Scheduling: Theory and Applications, pp. 363–379, 2005.

147. Powell W., Jaillet P., Odoni A., "Stochastic and Dynamic Networks and Routing," Handbooks in Operations Research and Management Science, Vol. 8, North-Holland, Amsterdam, The Netherlands, Chapter 3, pp. 141–295,1995.

148. Hsu L., "A Bi-Directional Path Layout for Conflict-Free Routing Of AGVs," International Journal of Production Research, Vol. 39(10), pp. 2177–2195, 2001.2001.

149. Hsu L. W.J, "Algorithms for Routing AGVs on a Mesh Topology," Proceedings of the 6th European Conference on Parallel Computing (Euro-par 2000), pp. 595–599, Munich, Germany, 2000.

150. Hsu L. W.J, "Conflict-Free AGV Routing in a Bi-Directional Path Layout," Proceedings of the 5th International Conference on Computer Integrated Manufacturing, Vol. 1, pp. 392–403, Singapore, 2000.

151 -. Hsu L. W.J, "Routing AGVs by Sorting," Proceedings of International Conference on Parallel and Distributed Processing Techniques and Applications (PDPTA 2000), Vol. 3, pp. 1465–1470, Las Vegas, Nevada, USA, 2000.

152. Hsu L. W.J, "Scheduling of AGVs in a Mesh-Like Path Topology," Technical Report CAIS-TR-01-34, Centre for Advanced Information Systems, School of Computer Engineering, Nanyang Technological University, Singapore, July 2001.

153. Hsu L., Huang W.J., Wang S.Y., "Scheduling and Routing Algorithms for AGVs: a Survey," International Journal of Production Research, Taylor & Francis Ltd, Vol. 40(3), pp. 745–760, 2002.2002.

154. Rashidi H., "Discrete Simulation Software: a Survey on Taxonomies," Journal of Simulation, Vol. 11(2), pp. 174–184, 2017.

155. Rashidi H., Tsang E.P.K., "Applying the Extended Network Simplex Algorithm and a Greedy Search Method to Automated Guided Vehicle Scheduling," Proceedings, 2nd Multidisciplinary International Conference on Scheduling: Theory & Applications (MISTA), Vol. (2), pp. 677–692, 2005.

156. Rashidi H., "A Dynamic Version for the Network Simplex Algorithm," Applied Soft Computing, Vol. 24, pp. 414–422, 2014.

157. Rashidi H., "Scheduling Single-Load and Multi-Load AGVs in Container Terminals," AmirKabir Journal of Science and Technology, Vol. 42(2), pp. 1–10, 2010.

158. Rashidi H., Tsang E.P., "A Complete and an Incomplete Algorithm for Automated Guided Vehicle Scheduling in Container Terminals," Computers & Mathematics with Applications, Vol. 61(3), pp. 630–641, 2011.

159. Rauch M., "Fully Dynamic Graph Algorithms and Their Data Structures," PhD Thesis, Department of Computer Science, Princeton University, 1992.

160. Ravindra K.A., Thomas M., James B.O., Giovanni M.S., Zuddas P., "Algorithms for the Simple Equal Flow Problem," Management Science, Vol. 45(10), pp. 1440–1455, 1999.

161. Rebollo M., Julián V., Carrascosa C., Botti V., "A Multi-Agent System for the Automation of a Port Container Terminal," Workshop in Agents in Industry, Barcelona, 2000.

162. Rizaldi A., Wasesa M., Rahman M.N., Yard Cranes Coordination Schemes for Automated Container Terminals: an Agent-Based Approach, Procedia Manufacturing, 4 (2015) 124 –132, 2015.

163. Rizzoli A.E., Gambardella M., Zaffalon M., Mastrolilli M., "Simulation for the evaluation of optimised operations policies in a Container Terminal," HMS99, Maritime & Industrial Logistics Modelling and Simulation, Genoa, Italy, 16-18th September, 1999.

164. Roy D., de Koster R., Stochastic Modeling of Unloading and Loading Operations at a Container Terminal Using Automated Lifting Vehicles, European Journal of Operational Research,. 266 (3), 895e–910, 2018, https://doi.org/10.1016/j.ejor.2017.10.031.

165. Saanen Y., Van Meel J., Verbraeck A., "The Next Generation Automated Container Terminals," Technical Report, TBA Nederland/Delft University of Technology, 2003.

166. Saanen Y.A., "Examining the Potential for Adapting Simulation Software to Enable Short-Term Tactical Decision Making for Operational Optimisation," Technical Report, TBA Nederland/Delft University of Technology, 2000.

167. Salehi F.H., Khodayifar S., Raayatpanah M.A., "Minimum Flow Problem on Network Flows with Time-Varying Bounds", Applied Mathematical Modeling, Vol. 36(9), pp. 4414–4421, 2012.

168. Schwientek A.K., Lange A.K., Jahn C., "Effects of Terminal Size, Yard Block Assignment, and Dispatching Methods on Container Terminal Performance," 2020 Winter Simulation Conference (WSC), 2020, pp. 1408–1419, doi: 10.1109/WSC48552.2020.9384062.

169. Seifert R.W., Kay M.G., Wilson J.R., "Evaluation of AGV Routing Strategies Using Hierarchical Simulation," International Journal of Production Research, Vol. 36(7), pp. 1961–1976, 1998.

170. Sha M., Zhang T., Lan Y., Zhou X., Qin T., Yu D., Chen K., "Scheduling Optimization of Yard Cranes with Minimal Energy Consumption at Container Terminals," Computers & Industrial Engineering, Vol. 113(2017), pp. 704–713, 2017.

171. Shen W., Nie Y., Zhang H.M., "A Dynamic Network Simplex Method for Designing Emergency Evacuation Plans," Transportation Research Record, 2022, pp. 83–93, 2007.

172. Shih H., Chang H.C., "A Routing and Scheduling System for Infectious Waste Collection," Environmental Modelling & Assessment, Vol. 6, pp. 261–69, 2001.

173. Siebers P.O., Macal C.M., Garnett J., Buxton D., Pidd M., "Discrete-Event Simulation Is Dead, Long Live Agent-Based Simulation," Journal of Simulation, Vol. 4(3), pp. 204–210, 2010.

174. Skutella M., "An Introduction to Network Flows Over Time," Research Trends in Combinatorial Optimization, pp. 451–482, Springer, 2009.

175. Steenken D., Vob S., Stahlbock R., "Container Terminal Operation and Operations Research- a Classification and Literature Review," OR Spectrum, Vol. 26, pp. 3–49, 2004.

176. Steenken D., Winter T., Zimmermann U.T., "Stowage and Transport Optimisation in Ship Planning," Springer, Berlin, pp. 731–745, 2001.

177. Stojaković M., Twrdy E., Determining the Optimal Number of Yard Trucks in Smaller Container Terminals, European Transport Research Review 13(1),22, 2021.

178. Taguchi G. (1986), Introduction to Quality Engineering. New York: Quality Resources.

179. Tan K.C., Lee H., Ou Q.L. K, "Heuristic Methods for Vehicle Routing Problem With Time Windows," Artificial Intelligent in Engineering, pp. 281–295, 2000.

180. Tan C., Yan W., Yue J., "Quay Crane Scheduling in Automated Container Terminal for the Trade-off between Operation Efficiency and Energy Consumption," Advanced Engineering Informatics, Vol. 48(2021), p. 101285, 2021.

181. Zhao L., Liu J., J., Modeling and Solution of the Joint Quay Crane and Truck Scheduling Problem. European Journal of Operation Research, 236 (3), 978e990, 2014, https://doi.org/10.1016/j.ejor.2013.08.050

182. Thurston T., Hu H., "Distributed Agent Architecture for Port Automation," Proceedings of the 26th Annual International Computer Software and Applications Conference, Oxford, England, August 2002.

183. Toth P., "The Vehicle Routing Problem Discrete Math," SIAM (Society for Industrial and Applied Mathematics) Press, 2003.

184. Tsang E.P.K., "Spatio-Temporal Conflict Detection and Resolution," Constraints, Vol. 3(4), pp. 343–361, 1998.

185. Tsang E.P.K., "Foundations of Constraint Satisfaction," Academic Press, London, 1993.

186. Tsang E.P.K., "Scheduling Techniques — A Comparative Study," British Telecom Technology Journal, Vol. 13(1), pp. 16–28, Martlesham Heath, Ipswich, UK, 1995.

187. Tsang E.P.K., Wang C., Davenport A., Voudouris C., Lau T., "A Family of Stochastic Methods for Constraint Satisfaction and Optimisation," Proceedings of the First International Conference on the Practical Application of Constraint Technologies and Logic Programming (PACLP'99), London, pp. 359–383, April 1999.

188. Türkogullar Y.B., Taskin Z.C., Aras N., Altinel I.K., Optimal Berth Allocation, Time-Variant Quay Crane Assignment and Scheduling With Crane Setups in Container Terminals, European Journal of Operational Research, 254 (2016), 985–1001, 2016.

189. Tyagi R., Gupta S.K., A Survey on Scheduling Algorithms for Parallel and Distributed Systems. In: Mishra A., Basu A., Tyagi V. (eds) Silicon Photonics & High Performance Computing. Advances in Intelligent Systems and Computing, Vol 718. Springer, 2018, https://doi-org.ezp2.semantak.com/10.1007/978-981-10-7656-5_7

190. Umar U.A., Ariffin M.K.A., Ismail N., Tang S.H., "Hybrid Multi Objective Genetic Algorithms for Integrated Dynamic Scheduling and Routing of Jobs and Automated-Guided Vehicle (AGV) in Flexible Manufacturing Systems (FMS) Environment," The International Journal of Advanced Manufacturing Technology, Vol. 81(9), pp. 2123–2141, 2015.

191. Vacca I., Bierlaire M., Salani M., "Optimization at Container Terminals: Status, Trends and Perspectives," 7th Swiss Transport Research Conference, Monte Verità/Ascona, 2007.

192. Vahdani B., Mansour F., Soltani M., Bi-Objective Optimization for Integrating Quay Crane and Internal Truck Assignment With Challenges of Trucks Sharing. Knowl. Base Syst. 163, 675e–692, 2019, https://doi.org/10.1016/j.knosys.2018.09.025.

193. Verny J., "The Importance of Decoupling between Freight Transport and Economic Growth," European Journal of Transport and Infrastructure Research EJTIR, 7, pp. 113–128, 2007.

194. Voudouris C., Tsang E.P.K., "Guided Local Search and Its Application to the Travelling Salesman Problem," European Journal of Operational Research, Vol. 113(2), pp. 469–499, 1999.

195. Voudouris C., Tsang E.P.K., "Guided Local Search Joins the Elite in Discrete Optimisation," Proceedings of DIMACS Workshop on Constraint Programming and Large Scale Discrete Optimisation, Rutgers, New Jersey, USA, September 1998.

196. Voß S., "Meta–Heuristic: The State of the Art," Local Search for Planning and Scheduling: ECAI 2000 Workshop, Berlin, Germany, August 2000.

197. VRP Web, http://www.bernabe.dorronsoro.es/vrp/ (address last checked 6th Sep 2021).

198. Wang Z.X., Felix T.S., Chung S.H., Niu B., "A Decision Support Method for Internal Truck Employment," Industrial Management and Data Systems, Vol. 114(9), pp. 1378–1395, 2014.

199. Wayne K.D., "A Polynomial Combinatorial Algorithm for Generalized Minimum Cost Flow," Proceedings of the 31st Annual ACM Symposium on Theory of Computing, pp. 11–18, 1999.

200. Weber R., "Mathematics for Operational Research," Lecture Notes, Department of Pure Mathematics and Mathematical Statistics, University of Cambridge, 2003.

201. Westbrook J., "Algorithms and Data Structures for Dynamic Graph Problems," PhD Thesis, Princeton University, 1989.

202. Winter T., "Online and Real-Time Dispatching Problems," GCA-Verlag, Herdecke, PhD Thesis, 2000.

203. Wook B.J., Hwan K.K., "A Pooled Dispatching Strategy for Automated Guided Vehicles in Port Container Terminals," International Journal of Management Science, Vol. 6(2), pp. 47–67, 2000.

204. Worldshipping 2012, <http://www.worldshipping.org/about-the-industry/global-trade/top-50-world-container-ports> (Accessed 20.07.2014).

205. Yang Y., Zhong M., Dessouky Y., Postolache O., An Integrated Scheduling Method for AGV Routing in Automated Container Terminals. Computers & Industrial Engineering, 126, 482–493, 2018.

206. Yokoo M., Durfee E.H., Ishida T., Kuwabara K., "The Distributed Constraint Satisfaction Problem: Formalization and Algorithms," IEEE Transaction on Knowledge and Data Engineering, Vol. 10(5), pp. 673–685, 1998.

207. Yokoo M., Hirayama K., "Algorithms for Distributed Constraint Satisfaction: A Survey," Autonomous Agents and Multi-Agent Systems, Vol. 3(2), pp. 198–212, 2000.

208. Yu H., Ning J., Wang Y., He J., Tan C., Flexible Yard Management in Container Terminals for Uncertain Retrieving Sequence, Ocean and Coastal Management, 212,105794, 2021.

209. Fan L., Ma H., M., Optimizing Configuration and Scheduling of Double 40 Ft Dual-Trolley Quay Cranes and AGVs for Improving Container Terminal Services. Journal of Cleaner Production, 292, 126019,2021.

210. Zaerpour N., Gharehgozli A., Koster R., Vertical Expansion: A Solution for Future Container Terminals, College of Business Administration, California State University San Marcos, San Marcos, CA, USA, 2019.

211. Zaghdoud R., Mesghouni K., Dutilleul S.C., Zidi K., Ghedira K., "A Hybrid Method for Assigning Containers to AGVs in Container Terminal," IFAC-PapersOnLine, Vol. 49(3), pp. 96–103, 2016.

212. Zeng Q., Yang Z., "Integrating Simulation and Optimization to Schedule Loading Operations in Container Terminals," Computers and Operations Research, Vol. 36, pp. 1935–1944, 2009.

213. Zeng Q., Yang Z., "Integrating Simulation and Optimization to Schedule Loading Operations in Container Terminals," Computers & Operations Research, Vol. 36(6), pp. 1935–1944, 2009.

214. Zhang C., Liu J., Wan Y.W., Murty K.G., Linn R.J., "Storage Space Allocation in Container Terminals," Transportation Research B 37, 2001.

215. Zhang C., Wan Y., Liu J., Linn R.J., "Dynamic Crane Deployment in Container Storage Yard," Transportation Research B 36, 2002.

216. Zhang H., Collart S., Khaled M., "Parameters Optimization of Resources in a Container Terminal," 13th IFAC Symposium on Large Scale Complex Systems: Theory and Applications, pp. 395–400, 2013.

217. Zhang W., Ye R., Huang S.Y., Hsu W.J., "Two Equivalent Integer Programming Models for Dispatching Vehicles at a Container Terminal," School of Computer Engineering, Nan Yang Technological University, Technical Report, Singapore, 2002.

218. Zhang X., Wang S., Xue L., Yang H., Xiong S., "An integrated ant-colony optimization algorithm to solve job allocating and tool scheduling problem", Proceedings of the Institution of Mechanical Engineers, Vol. 232(1), pp. 172–182, 2018.2018.

219. Zhao Q., Ji S., Guo D., Research on Cooperative Scheduling of Automated Quayside Cranes and Automatic Guided Vehicles in Automated Container Terminal. Math. Probl Eng. 1e–15 https://doi.org/10.1155/2019/6574582,2019.

220. Zheng H., Chiu Y., "A Network Flow Algorithm for the Cell-Based Single-Destination System Optimal Dynamic Traffic Assignment Problem," Transportation Science, Vol. 45(1), pp. 121–137, 2011.
221. Zhicheng B., Weijian M., Xiaoming Y., Ning Z., Chao M., "Modified Hungarian Algorithm for Real-Time ALV Dispatching Problem in Huge Container Terminals," Journal of Networks, Vol. 9(1), pp. 123–130, 2014.
222. Zhong M., Yang Y., Dessouky Y., Postolache O., Multi-AGV Scheduling for Conflict-Free Path Planning in Automated Container Terminals. Computers & Industrial Engineering, 142, 106371, 2020.

Index

For the latest Society, Congress and Exhibition information please contact our
European sponsors: OPSR ... recommends dem Taylor & Francis
Verlag GmbH, Kaufingerstr... 24, 80331 München, Germany.